TRAINING
THE GERMAN SHEPHERD DOG

JOHN CREE

D1375227

The Crowood Press

First published as *Training the Alsatian* in 1977 by Pelham Books

Fully revised and reset in 1996 by
The Crowood Press Ltd
Ramsbury, Marlborough
Wiltshire SN8 2HR

www.crowood.com

Paperback edition 2003

This impression 2011

British Library Cataloguing-in-Publication Data
A catalogue record for this book is available from the British Library.

ISBN 978 1 86126 559 3

Dedication
To Irene, my wife. She has looked after our two daughters, our dogs and me. She has encouraged, sympathized and criticized. She has typed and retyped the manuscript. Without her help there could not have been a book.

All photographs principally by John Cree and Steve Noy
Line-drawings by Annette Findlay

Typeset by Phoenix Typesetting, Burley-in-Wharfedale, West Yorkshire
Printed and bound in Spain by GraphyCems

Contents

Acknowledgements

The writing of a book can never be the complete work of one person. In this instance, I may well have put pen to paper, but the knowledge expressed is an accumulation from many sources. The foundation received during my earliest days as a member of the Dundee branch of the Associated Sheep, Police and Army Dog Society (A.S.P.A.D.S.) has been a corner-stone to the development of my thinking. My involvement with the breed and my association with various German Shepherd clubs have helped to maintain my enthusiasm for, and commitment to, the breed and have given me some thirty-seven years of pleasure and enjoyment to date.

Visits to foreign lands where I have judged, instructed or just been involved in discussion with like-minded people — Zimbabwe, South Africa, Canada and U.S.A., as well as islands nearer to home -- have broadened my mind and given me an appreciation of attitudes and methods which all contribute to the application of sound training practices.

I must thank the people at Elmwood College in Cupar, Scotland, for their co-operation and participation in the photography for this publication, particularly Steve Noy, the college photographer, for his many shots and the cover photograph, also for his time and hard work in developing and printing such a large selection of photographs. Friends and family must also receive acknowledgement for their part in demonstrating the various situations with their dogs which capture the circumstances being displayed. In short, my appreciation goes to all who helped to make this book possible.

Finally, my thanks go to Irene, my wife, for her efforts and help. This book is justly dedicated to her.

Abbreviations

C.C.	Chief Constable
C.D.	Companion Dog
Ch.	Champion
Ex.	Excellent
F.C.I.	Federation Cynologique Internationale
G.S.D.	German Shepherd Dog
Int.	International
Ob.	Obedience
P.D.	Patrol Dog
Sch.HI,III,III	Schutzhund (Guard or Defence Dog)
T.D.	Tracker Dog
U.D.	Utility Dog
Unr.	Unregistered
v.d.	von der
W.D.	Working Dog
W.T.	Working Trials

Introduction

This book is written primarily for the German Shepherd owner, whether he is responsible for one dog or is a breeder with a large kennel. Anyone owning a German Shepherd should know how to educate himself and his dog to ensure the fullness of their companionship. He should also know something of his dog's potential and the training which can be carried out to change that companionship into a partnership. The capabilities of this breed are commonly known from its police, security and mountain rescue work, and from its contribution as guide dogs, but those are all specialized jobs calling for specialized conditions of work. Most German Shepherds settle into private homes, with the main outlet for the development of their intelligence and character restricted to training for working trials, obedience and agility shows. However, with a basic knowledge, many pet owners would welcome the chance of developing this intelligence and character to achieve greater satisfaction and companionship.

Control problems can be a worry to many pet dog owners. A dog which will not obey simple requests, will not come when called or will not mix with his owner's friends certainly needs some help. This help can be at hand for an owner ready to learn and apply the basic principles of dog training, and I have tried throughout this book to show one approach to training which has been very successful and should assist pet owners and training enthusiasts alike.

As my own experience is through competing, stewarding and judging at working trials and obedience shows plus the counselling of owners with problems, I have been able to watch the development of characters through the various stages of competitive or behaviour training. I have also competed, stewarded and judged in the breed show ring and have kept a particularly close interest in the breed. I am not sure whether my greatest pleasure is taking a dog with working titles into the show ring or going after these working titles with a show winner. It does not really matter, because I believe that the two are interdependent, and the more breeders and working dog owners understand each other's requirements, the better the breed will fare.

As for the companion dog owner, what better than to understand the needs of this intelligent breed and do what he can to develop the character of his companion? After all, dogs that work are, first and foremost, companions who, through their working ability, become full partners. The highest reward any owner can have is to feel that his dog has become a full partner through a working relationship.

Our breed is full of character. Let us develop this to the full potential of its inheritance. By training his active mind we shall have a friend who will be grateful for the opportunity to show his value and loyalty.

All German Shepherd owners can benefit from dog training. In fact, it is important for the companion dog owner to understand the intelligence of his animal if for no other reason than that he wants to prevent trouble. We all know the name that bad, ignorant or inconsiderate owners have given the breed in the past. The companion dog owner should at least know the basic principles of training and practise them. Preventive training is always much more successful and satisfying than corrective training.

Breeders are not fully equipped for sell-ing puppies unless they understand the problems their stock can create by going into a home which does not appreciate the intelligence that will develop in those little eight-week-old bundles of fur that leave their kennels. I hope the breeders who read this book feel it has been worth their time and that they will encourage new owners to give their new charge an opportunity to develop into an obedient companion or working partner.

Throughout this book I have used the male pronoun for both owners and dogs in general. This has been done solely for reasons of clarity, and no bias, either canine or human, is intended.

CHAPTER 1

What Value in Training?

Why Train?

Any German Shepherd owner will find that thoughtful training will develop the character and loyalty of his dog. The wider the breadth of training, the greater the bond between dog and owner. Even the companion dog owner, who just wants an obedient dog, may well find it difficult to resist going a little further and finally deciding to train for competitions. After all, at least ninety-five per cent of today's competitors started with a companion dog and just wanted a well-behaved canine friend. It may also be surprising to find how many of today's 'big names' attended their first training class because they thought they had a problem dog, ONLY TO FIND THAT THE DOG HAD A PROBLEM OWNER.

Although my own start was not with a problem dog, it was through a friend who suggested that I would enjoy the local training classes. My first dog was a Labrador puppy and, although we lost him when he was still a puppy, the few months we attended those outdoor classes were sufficient for me to realize that a whole new field of enjoyment had opened up. As you might have guessed, my new puppy was a German Shepherd, a grand all-rounder who became W.T.Ch. Quest of Ardfern C.D.Ex., U.D.Ex., P.D.Ex., T.D.Ex.

However, the individual or breeder who has no intention of competing in working trials or obedience shows will find that training for the fun of it will be greatly appreciated by his canine friend.

The Companion Dog

Your puppy may well have been brought in to your life as a companion for yourself, your wife or the children. The real joy of this companionship can only become a reality if he behaves and 'does as he is told'. Every day we can see examples of various breeds, including our own, that just do as they please and give dog owners a name for being inconsiderate.

Bringing a puppy up to maturity can be the same as bringing up a child: the mistakes of early life can be difficult to eradicate because when it is discovered that we have lost control he will have probably have developed a mind of his own. Any dog will find our weaknesses long before we find his, and it takes a lot of thinking on our part to reverse this situation. I often wonder if we are ever completely successful.

To make our companion a fully acceptable member of the community he has to be controllable in the same way as a well-behaved child. We should not have to shout at him or keep pulling on his lead. We are fortunate that our breed accepts discipline; if he becomes a nuisance it is because we have not applied the correct measure of control.

As a companion he requires exercise in both body and mind. It is one thing to give him physical exercise but quite another to keep his mind active in the right direction. The training details that will follow are geared mainly towards the competitive dog, but the companion dog owner will find that the basic approach is the same. The basic training approach is all-important, with the foundation obedience exercises just as valuable to your companion as are the precision exercises to the competitive dog.

The Obedience Partner

The obedience dog is just a companion dog evolved into a sharper thinking and reacting canine friend. Obedience training for competition work adds greatly to the character so long as an overbearing and demanding approach is not applied. One of the dangers of competition obedience training is the obsession with winning at all costs. Unfortunately there are handlers who seem to have forgotten that their dogs are supposed to be companions. These handlers are few and far between but obedience shows could well do without them. With the correct mental approach to training, both handler and dog will enjoy competing and they will also have their share of winning.

Obedience competitions start with the Beginners class and work through a total of five grades to the top Class C. As would be expected the work becomes progressively more demanding through each stage. The basic grounding, however, can briefly be given as four main exercises:

1 Heel work (on and off lead).
2 Recall to handler.
3 Retrieve an article.
4 Stay while handler moves a distance from the dog.

Any owner who achieves a good mark in each of these exercises with all the distractions of a show will be proud and ready to advance through the more demanding stages of work.

The Working Trials Partner

The trials dog is called upon to display by far the greatest sense of independence whilst working. There are times when he becomes the 'senior' partner in the company, where your training has taught him to become the 'packleader'. At the same time he must be prepared to accept responsible authority when it is required. He should be able to 'read' your next move and be ready to act in response to your requests.

Very briefly, working trials require the basic teachings for obedience work plus the ability to search and track. Agility tests are also essential, and 'criminal' work can be considered as optional if one wishes to develop in the police dog field of work.

There are four different stages in working trials, from the C.D. (Companion Dog) stake where obedience, agility and an elementary search cover the work requirements, to the top T.D. (Tracker Dog) or P.D. (Patrol Dog) stake where a very high degree of nosework or criminal work ability is required.

Scotland's four W.T. Champions in the 1960s.

The Fully Competitive Partner

I have often heard it said that you cannot mix working trials with obedience shows or obedience with breed showing. The correct approach to training with the right dog can give you success in each form of competition. It takes a lot of hard work and time to compete in two of these fields and real dedication to be successful in all three.

There has never to date been a triple champion, although there have been a few (very few) champions in breed and obedience or trials and obedience. Only once have we had a breed/trials champion, and this goes back to 1932 when Ch. Benign of Picardy P.D.Ex., U.D.Ex., C.D.Ex. became a working trials champion.

Many people think that the training for obedience adversely affects a working trials dog and vice versa. From my own experience this only happens if the handler is not capable of differentiating between the approaches for both forms of competition. It certainly requires harder work and more thought on the part of the handler, but it can be successfully achieved, and with a happy dog.

The main concern seems to be the mixing of scent discrimination in obedience shows and searching in working trials. I can only say that within a space of three consecutive Saturdays I worked at two obedience shows and a championship working trial with the following results:

Championship Trial:
    P.D. stake: First (which included a half-mile track and search for judge's articles with steward's scent)

Championship Obedience:
    Class A: Third (scent discrimination of owner's article)
    (No Class B at this show)
    Class C: Third (scent discrimination of judge's scent)

Open Obedience:
    Class A: First (scent discrimination of owner's article)
    Class B: First (scent discrimination of judge's article, owner's scent)
    Class C: Third (scent discrimination of judge's scent)

A W.T. test from the past. Quest retrieving over the Scale Jump.

A fully competitive partner, W.T. Ch. Quest of Ardfern C.D.Ex., U.D.Ex., P.D.Ex., T.D.Ex.

*Tanfield Atholl of Ardfern C.D.Ex., U.D.Ex., W.D.Ex., T.D.Ex., a
working Shepherd rated 'V' (Excellent) in Breed.*

It can be seen that every nosework exercise was carried out successfully in that short period of time by one dog, my own Quest of Ardfern.

The Agility Dog

Agility competitions are relatively new in the world of dog training, with the first such competition being carried out in the form of a demonstration at Crufts in 1978. It has now become an extremely popular national sport.

Agility tests involve training dogs to go over, through, under and round various obstacles on the course, and this course may vary from one competition to another. There are jumping hurdles, an 'A' frame ramp, a cat walk (or is it a dog walk?) some four and a half feet from the ground. A see-saw, a hoop, poles to weave through and a tunnel are included in the variety of probable obstacles.

The objective is to complete the round with the minimum of failures at the obstacles in the shortest possible time. It is a very enjoyable sport which requires a fit dog and a quickthinking handler. German Shepherds enjoy this activity.

Although control training is not a feature of agility training there is no question that the dogs must be very responsive to a handler's requirements, and dogs with obedience or working trials training have a distinct advantage.

Training for agility tests is an extensive subject in itself and, although it is not specifically catered for in this publication, the control and agility training detailed for other purposes have their value. However, *The Agility Dog* by Peter Lewis

Coming down off the 'Dog Walk'.

Hurdling at the end of an 'Agility' round.

Negotiating the 'A' Frame.

and published by Canine Publications gives full details of the competition requirements and training procedures.

Where to Train

Although this book is prepared in a manner that should give you most of the information you require to achieve a good obedience friend or a working partner, there is no doubt that properly organized training classes are invaluable. You can learn from other people's mistakes, get direct advice on immediate problems and have your dog accustomed to distractions and other dogs. There is also the social pleasure of meeting and talking with other people, all of whom share a common interest.

Although classes can be invaluable,

most of the training must be carried out elsewhere, in the house, in the garden or a nice quiet piece of ground, and eventually in a park where there are greater distractions. Beginners' training should only take about ten to fifteen minutes most days; a day missed now and again does not really matter but a regular daily stint can never be replaced by a hard two-hour session at the weekend.

Some dog owners attend training classes purely to improve their own approach to training, but most take their dogs along because they have a specific problem. A number of these problems can only be solved in the environment in which they occur, but the basic principles and training can be given at organized training sessions. All dog owners wishing to start at these sessions should, however, inform the trainer of any special problems or peculiarities, so that the trainer can take them into consideration during the training session and also give advice on correcting them at home.

There are training clubs in most areas, the majority of them catering for all breeds – there are not many that confine their activities to German Shepherds. Most clubs cater for the pet owner and dogs can graduate from basic training for normal home requirements to the competitive obedience field of work. Help in training for working trials can be obtained through the various working trials societies. Although training sessions are organized for trials work, the handler has to do much more on his own or with individual trials enthusiasts. A number of people do, however, combine both obedience classes and trials training: they attend regular obedience training classes to obtain the advantages of a weekly training session and also train on their own, or perhaps with a few friends, to achieve a good working trials standard. Details of the nearest training club or working trials society can be obtained on request from the Kennel Club.

The elementary work at a training club usually covers the exercises required for the Kennel Club beginners' routine.

When attending training sessions and listening to all the advice being given by trainers and other handlers, care must be taken to analyse all that has been said. There are many different ways of training a dog and there are many different dogs with different strengths of character. Your approach must be tailor-made to suit your dog. The principles that follow in this book, and also the approaches to the different exercises, may well need to be modified or moulded to suit your dog. It may also be essential for you to look deeply into your own personality to make it compatible with your present dog.

Competitions

Most obedience clubs do run progess tests and small competitions within their organisations, although this varies quite a bit from club to club. However, there are open and championship shows throughout the country during most of the year. These shows are held on a Saturday or Sunday but midweek shows can be found during the summer months. The number of shows available to you throughout the year depends largely on where you live, also on the time you have available and the cash you are prepared to allocate to this form of pastime.

Working trials societies generally run tracking rallies as well as open and championship trials. Open working trials are normally two or three-day events, although you can usually carry out all your work in one day. Championship trials normally run for three to five days, although I have judged at a six-day event. At some trials you may be expected to complete all your work in one day, but at other trials you will be tracking and searching on one of the days with the remainder of the work being carried out on the final day. The one exception is the C.D. (Companion Dog) stake, where competitors normally do all their work on the final day, but a large entry can take judging to a second day.

Brief details of the Kennel Club requirements for obedience competitions and working trials are given later in this book. If you are interested in competing it will be well worth while obtaining a full copy of the Regulations.

CHAPTER 2

The German Shepherd Dog at Home

You, The Owner

Before thinking of buying a German Shepherd puppy a prospective owner should take a close look at himself, be honest and ask if he is temperamentally suited to look after an animal who is going to be so dependent on him. If you have not owned a dog before you may wonder if you have the knowledge, ability and patience to educate a German Shepherd. This knowledge can be gained by reading, asking and observing, but ability depends on the value you place on the knowledge obtained and also the use you make of it. Patience may have to be worked on, but the key to patience is understanding a situation. Educating a dog means gaining control of him through your own self-control.

We normally find that beginners come along to the training club without any knowledge of dog training and usually very unsure of themselves. It is surprising, however, what hidden talents come to the fore: within six to eight weeks most of these owners have achieved a fair measure of confidence because they can see the progress their dogs have made. Many also find that they possess a greater degree of patience and adaptability than they expected. It is usually the brash 'know-it-all' type who comes unstuck and

will drift out because he is not prepared to learn and modify his approach to suit the dog's requirements.

The owner must be prepared to look continually at his own approach – if the dog fails to understand what seems to be a simple request then he should not be too readily blamed. In most cases it is the owner's fault and not the dog's, and insufficient grounding, lack of consistency or an unusual situation can be causes of a dog's failure to understand.

I would like to take a simple example of a dog who will not come back when called and look at the possible causes:

Insufficient grounding – if, in the past, the dog has been permitted to come back when he wanted to, the ground work has not been prepared for an instant response;

Lack of consistency – if the same approach or phraseology is not maintained in calling the dog back, he may not understand his owner's requirements;

An unusual situation – there may be a distraction too great for the measure of control being applied. The distraction of another dog in the vicinity may be beyond the control an owner has over his dog.

It is usually the dog who gets the blame for failing to come when called but, to an expert watching, the result may have been a foregone conclusion.

There were two particular instances I remember when I was a very new handler and was training my first dog, Quest, for working trials. The first was a 'seek back' exercise, which entailed walking through a field with the dog at your side, dropping an article without the dog noticing and walking on for about a hundred yards, then sending the dog back to find the article. My instruction to go back for the article was in the form of an excited question: 'Where is it?' and Quest knew exactly what was wanted. For no apparent reason Quest now seemed to lose the understanding of my requirements, until I realized that I had changed my approach from a question to a command: 'Fetch it'. The dog failed to understand the change and it would have been easy to blame him. This failure on my part indicated how much of a novice I was, but at the same time I was learning through self analysis.

The other example was during the same period, when we were coming up to a U.D. standard track (tracks half an hour old). Instead of taking the dog on the track in the same direction as the tracklayer, I sometimes approached the track at a right angle so that he would have to sort out the correct direction. On some occasions he would start to backtrack, which was very puzzling until I realized he only did this when I laid the track. It was then obvious that, at this stage, he thought he should backtrack on my scent, as my scent was used for the 'seek back'. After that I never put him on my tracks at more than a slight angle but varied the approach when someone else laid the track. Quest never backtracked in competition. This only indicates the care that must be taken be-

fore blaming the dog for any error or lack of understanding.

Whether it is the owner with a pet dog out on the street or a competitive dog doing his best for a handler, it is continually found that dogs are being blamed for some mistake, inattention or downright disobedience when it is apparent that the owner or handler is at fault. We generally find in competition that handlers lose far more marks than the dog, either by their own handling or by their lack of correct training and preparation prior to the show.

The greatest problem with canine education is that of educating the owner (handler). As many are starting with their first German Shepherd, and probably their first dog, they learn the hard way with a young puppy who has had no form of behaviour education or an older dog with bad habits. There is no real alternative for the first-time owner but to learn with his dog. Others may help and guide, certainly, but the person or family living with the dog are the only people on the spot to carry out the educational process of teaching a German Shepherd to become a social asset and not a liability.

Your Dog

You may be planning to buy a puppy, you may have just taken a young puppy into your home, or you may have taken in a dog who is past the puppy stage. However you acquired him, you must assess the mental and physical suitabilities of the dog in your home, and again assess them honestly. Most German Shepherds are ideal material for training, and in general they are a breed which is willing to please the owner. Temperament, however, does vary considerably and an early assessment can help to determine the approach to be adopted during the early educational process and also the final result. Physical limitations are probably less obvious but equally important, especially if you wish to develop in the competitive field of working trials.

Character and temperament change as a dog becomes educated, and the quiet, timid dog will improve if brought out in the correct manner, which means being introduced to kindly and understanding strangers, mixing with other dogs and, most important, getting something to think about. The aggressive dog is probably the result of an incorrect upbringing and may well require some firm handling to make him accept a civilized way of life. Creating an active mind and a real keenness to work can help to put 'nerves' into the background. Although this is not always the case, there is generally a right home for the right dog. If your home is not suited to your dog then I believe your first responsibility is to modify your way of life and help change your dog's approach to his life so that you become compatible. It is your responsibility, as the owner, to make every effort possible to let your dog enjoy fully the normal existence of a German Shepherd.

If a German Shepherd is worth keeping, he is worth training. Even an education in social behaviour helps him become a well-behaved companion. Most German Shepherds are worthy and capable of being trained for obedience shows, agility and working trials, with one exception – police work. This calls for the highest qualities in character and temperament. A shy dog is useless and an uncontrollably aggressive dog worse than useless – a German Shepherd should be safe and re-liable. Some people seem to think that hyperactive dogs are good prospects for training. This may be the case in the hands of an expert but a hyperactive dog can be difficult to live with and the lifetime of such a dog does not enhance canine ownership. Bitches suitable for police work are much more difficult to find than dogs because, with their motherly instincts, they can become too protective and unreliable once they have been introduced to this work. We very rarely see a good, reliable German Shepherd bitch doing patrol work at working trials. Bitches can, however, excel at tracking and are often unbeatable in the right hands at obedience work. Unfortunately many handlers do not appreciate that bitches can go through a 'broody' period after their season – when this happens it usually becomes noticeable about two or three weeks after the end of the season and normally finishes at the time they would have whelped had they been mated. This condition is not generally noticed in a bitch unless she is being trained for obedience or working trials.

My own bitch, Jeza, was a prime example of this condition. She was about five weeks out of season when she went for a U.D. championship qualification. About two or three weeks before this I could see the broodiness coming on but I carried on and worked her, and was ashamed of our performance. She had great difficulty in tracking out the first leg. We then tried the search, and if anything this was worse; she had no interest, and no amount of encouragement or help would induce her to work. I apologized to the judge for taking up his time and drove the 350 miles home. Just nine weeks after she would have been mated we had the A.S.P.A.D.S. Scottish Championship Trials. Jeza was entered to give support to the event and, because we saw a change in her outlook on life, I decided to have a try. She worked a most beautiful fifteen-leg, complicated track and then worked her heart out in the search. She did not get enough search articles to qualify but I went home the happiest of failures that day.

This broodiness may not be evident in the companion dog and is often unnoticed in the obedience dog, but where a great deal of concentration is required in working trials the problem can become very evident.

There is no such problem with the male species of our breed but the working of a kennel stud dog can have problems. They may tend to be a little bit jealous when bitches are around and although I have not had any problems I have been concerned that a fight could develop at the stay exercises with dogs and bitches mixed. As this is not a major issue at trials and I have never witnessed a fight of this nature it may well indicate that stud dogs will contain their instincts, if properly trained, while their handlers leave them in line at the sit or down/stay exercises.

Physical fitness is very important in working trials. Training for the agility tests will soon highlight a dog who is not fit, and hip dysplasia is of major concern to triallists. Although perfect hips are not essential, a fair degree of fault in this area will certainly show up at some stage during a working life. Many people believe that the Scale Jump is the first to highlight a hip weakness, but in fact the Long Jump is more demanding on the hip joints and a dog will usually fail or show reluctance to try the Long Jump before the failure to Scale becomes apparent.

Educating Your German Shepherd Dog

With a dog of any age the first day in his new home is the time to start the educational partnership. The owner will study and learn the mannerisms of his dog and the dog will learn to become socially acceptable. Education commences by avoiding situations where the dog is likely to disobey your requirements. Remember, it takes time for him to understand what you want. This approach will, of course, continue throughout the rest of his life. If you expect disobedience do not try to exert authority. This may sound negative, but the secret of willing and faithful compliance with your wishes is to ensure that your dog understands and enjoys obeying your requests. Your approach must always be tempered to suit your dog's mental maturity.

A new owner can find himself with a puppy straight from the nest, or an older pup, say eight to twelve months, acquired from the breeding kennel, or even a junior coming to his second home. These differing circumstances create different settling-in problems.

Young puppies take time to develop their minds and only a very simple, progressive form of training along with social education should be given up to an age of five or six months. However, a great deal of conditioning can be carried out during these early months in preparing for an actively controlled future as an adult. During this early stage of his puppy life he should appreciate the security of your company and you should build up his loyalty for the future. Your puppy should realize the need for immediate response to your call and should also recognize that those destructive little ventures of chewing at will are just 'not on'. Education in the early stages is mainly the prevention of bad habits.

The New Puppy

What better than planning the acquisition of a little eight-week-old puppy, especially when you have looked around and decided that the parents of your new charge are satisfactory – of good temperament and sound construction? Dog or bitch puppy, it is your choice.

The decision on his name may not seem to be particularly important, but I feel that it is nice to be reasonably original, and I find that the choice of name can make a difference to his reaction when called. At least one strong-sounding syllable, and used strongly, can gain immediate attention. I think the strong Scottish voice can have an advantage over some of the more mellow English accents. My first German Shepherd was Quest, and because the strong Dundee accent cultivated to overcome the noise of jute weaving looms could produce a very penetrating 'E', Quest had no excuse for not hearing his name.

Bringing the puppy home from the kennels also requires some thought and planning. First, there is every possibility that it will be his first journey in a car, bus or train, and you can expect him to be sick, so go well prepared with newspapers and towels. This problem can possibly be avoided by visiting your veterinary surgeon for a suitably mild tranquillizer to sedate your puppy before you start that long journey home. Although Sunday afternoon may seem to be a convenient time to collect a new puppy, it does not give the man of the house much opportunity to get to know his pup during the first vital days. If the pup is to become Mum's dog and she is at home all week with it then time of collection does not matter so much.

Each dog I have owned has been trained for working trials, and the arrival of each one to our household was arranged to give me at least a few days at home before settling back to the usual routine of going to work in the morning and returning in the evening. There was, however, one exception, Tanya. Owing to circumstances beyond our control, my wife had to go to the airport to collect Tanya on a Friday afternoon, bring her home in the train, spend the weekend and then the whole of the following week looking after this puppy before I had a real opportunity to get to know her. This was the one dog who continued to show first preference to my wife during the whole of her life. For all the time I spent training her, Tanya continued to give my wife her first loyalty.

If a puppy is to be fully trained by a particular member of the family then that person should be 'number one' in the eyes of the puppy from the first day in his new home.

During the first few weeks a puppy can do no wrong. He may well do things that do not suit you, like chewing slippers, socks and all the other sweet-smelling bits and pieces left lying around by us humans in our careless manner, or he may soil the carpet because his toilet requirements were not anticipated. This, therefore, brings us to the first stage of social education.

Prevention and understanding are much more effective than attempts at correction after the event. If we consider a puppy's toilet requirements, the critical times are immediately after eating and

A German Shepherd puppy looking for attention.

after sleeping, so these are the times when a puppy should be taken out to the garden to perform.

This is where the first association of place and performance becomes effective. Every 'accident' in the house indicates a lack of the correct association. The more often you fail to take the puppy to the toilet area in time, the less chance there is of building up the required association, and 'accidents' will continue to happen. An extension of this toilet area association will be achieved by giving him the opportunity to perform in his own time. Any attempt to hurry him along may create inhibitions and delay the final outcome. It is better to wait for him to perform before

giving the encouraging 'Clean boy, hurry up' and eventually this phrase can be used as an inducement to perform.

If there is any thought of punishment for 'accidents' by smacking or nose rubbing in the soiled area this could be reserved for the owner and not the puppy. After all it was the owner's fault for not anticipating the situation.

Correct and timely associations should be the main form of education for a young puppy. Whilst a puppy is in the act of sitting ask him to sit. When he is in the act of lying down ask him to go down. If he is going to bed of his own accord then ask him to go to bed. The most important association of all is to call your puppy when he is coming to you. If you see that it is his purpose to come to you then call him in. Future training will be much easier with the back-up of these planned, early associations.

Young puppies require plenty of rest and they themselves know when to sleep and for how long. A puppy's sleeping habits should be recognized and respected. A puppy who is continually woken up and fussed over may well turn into an edgy dog. Just consider how bad-tempered humans can be when woken up. Puppies, like young babies, should be given the opportunity to sleep to suit their own requirements.

Travel sickness can sometimes be quite a problem with a young puppy but the sooner a youngster gets used to car travelling, the easier it is to overcome the problem. Although a puppy should not be taken out in public until he is clear of inoculations, he can be taken for short runs in the car to get him used to travelling. In fact a quiet seat in a stationary car can get him used to his surroundings and may well help to make him a better traveller.

It will now be appreciated that the first few weeks in his new home are possibly the most important of his life. This is the time when a relationship is going to be moulded. It may help if it can be remembered that during this period the objective is to prevent problems from arising and not to spend your time scolding him for 'misbehaviour'. It is understandable that a puppy will get bored and will look around for his own forms of enjoyment. His enjoyment may be a good chew at a favourite slipper or suchlike. Rather than scold him it is much more sensible to distract him from the object in question and attract his attention to one of his own toys. The first thing I have ready for a new

puppy coming into my home is a knitted jersey or cardigan, minus buttons or zips. This is his tug-of-war article and comforter; it always goes to bed with him and every time I catch him doing something I do not want I get the jersey, call him from the scene of the 'crime', and then we have fun with it. I think my Callum was on his fifth jersey when he was two and a half years old and qualified P.D.Ex. If I said to him 'Where's your jersey?' he would stop, think, then disappear. He would return with the jersey looking for some fun.

Taking Home a Junior

This may be a young dog past the small puppy stage, say from five months onwards to a full junior having lived more than a year of his life before joining your family, and during this period he may have had the opportunity to pick up many undesirable habits. His earlier life may have been totally within the breeding kennel or he may have come from another home.

In either case he should be given time to settle and develop some sense of security with his new owner. The initial few days are very important, with the first week being used to gain his confidence. The older puppy straight from a breeding kennel can create his share of problems. With a maturing mind he will take time to settle in, perhaps three months to settle fully into his changed environment. In all probability he has not known the fun that more constant companionship can give, nor will he have experienced the effects of living in the so-called civilized community. He may also have picked up bad habits during kennel life. Kennel staff do not always have the time or the patience to put up with troublesome little puppies who do not wish to go back to their kennels, or will not be caught to be shut away last thing at night, especially when the kennel maid has a boyfriend waiting. These are factors one never hears or knows about, and they can have a great deal of effect on the approach to educating your new charge.

With the older pup or junior, coming into his second home, I consider this as the second change in the youngster's life, remembering that he probably went from a breeding kennel into his first home. Temperament and character can play a big part in his ability to settle in and, again, patience is probably required to help him through his period of uncertainty. It is not uncommon for a youngster to take three to four months to settle in fully and great care should be taken with his education and training during this period.

We hear many stories about why owners wish to part with a young dog, but unfortunately the truth is seldom told. There is generally something wrong with the dog, or should I say that he has probably acquired faults through his previous owner's lack of knowledge or consideration. The new owner must learn to recognize the problems associated with his youngster and patiently set about correcting them as part of the dog's education.

In general the new owner is competing against a mature and experienced mind, one that already knows most of the little dodges so easily acquired by a dog not suitably disciplined. The owner's objective is to be one move ahead of the dog and be ready to prevent or counter any unsatisfactory habit.

Making Your Dog Socially Acceptable

To be socially acceptable a dog must be controlled, but it should also be evident that he enjoys life to the full. There is no pleasure in owning a dog who does not know how to enjoy himself, but he must be prepared to accept you, his owner, as 'number one'. If you are the true 'pack leader' you will have his loyalty and respect and will also find that he enjoys his controlled form of freedom. On the other hand if he becomes the 'pack leader' your life can be one of misery. He will not lead a better life and will certainly be considered socially unacceptable by others.

I think there are three main conditions to consider as targets when achieving a socially acceptable dog.

1 That he is easy to live with.
2 That his manners are admired and he is accepted by neighbours.
3 That he is controlled in a manner that will minimize the possibility of injury or death by accident.

Many of the problems I am asked about by troubled owners can be difficult to cure, especially those occurring when the owner is not present or is caught unprepared. Some of the cures require expert handling and timing. It is easy for the expert to advise but it is often too much to ask the average owner to apply these cures. However, many problems can be prevented, and a little thought or anticipation can overcome most of the bad habits already acquired by a dog.

At home my own bitch, Jeza, was one of the greatest kitchen pedal-bin rakers of all time, especially when she was on a diet. To stop this would probably have required a set-up that would automatically have frightened her from the bin every time she went to lift up the lid with her nose. As she only misbehaved in this manner when we were out of the house for a lengthy period it was much simpler to put the bin out of her reach. In this case prevention was easier than correction. If I forgot to put the bin out of reach and returned home to find eggshell, potato peelings etc. all over the kitchen floor I only had myself to blame.

If your dog is a car chaser, why let him out on the street? Anyway, he should not be out on the street without a lead. If he is a fence jumper, why let him out in the garden without a suitable means of control? If the problem has become a habit then prevent the opportunity, and if it is serious enough take measures to correct the fault. Anticipate the problem, take preventive measures or corrective action.

One problem I had with Callum as a youngster was his aversion to stray dogs coming into the front garden. Callum normally had the freedom of the back garden and the gate was level with the front of the house. This gate was of open spars and about two and a half feet high. He never made any attempt to jump this gate but would put his front paws on the top when welcoming me home from work, and I did not discourage him. Twice, however, Callum decided to take exception to a stray dog in his front garden, jumped over the gate and gave chase across the road into a field. This could easily have caused a bad accident and could not be permitted to continue. Thereafter he was never allowed to place his paws on the top of the gate. When I came home in the evening, as soon as his paws touched the top of the gate I hit them hard with my hands. This hurt him, and it was rough justice when you consider that I had not discouraged

him previously. He had to be taught very fast and in a positive manner to prevent any recurrence of the previous two chases. The treatment was effective and Callum never jumped the gate again. This was one instance when a forceful solution was used to correct my earlier failing and in this case had to be used to minimize the risk of an accident.

Forceful solutions to problems should not, however, become a habit; nevertheless there are occasions when they are the most effective.

There are occasions when various preventive measures are required to overcome a problem. Take the problem of the canine thief – we are, of course, speaking about the dog who steals food. This is a very common problem and I am sure many stories have been told of Sunday dinners and suchlike which have gone missing.

My daughter's lovable little bitch, Dornie, demolished about two dozen Christmas pies which were thought to be in a safe place. Then there was Rowdy, who disposed of an uncooked chicken which had been taken out of the refrigerator. He was subsequently fed with cotton wool soaked in milk. The cotton wool became wrapped round the chicken bones to assist with an easier and less damaging passage. We also had our Callum, who at eleven months old discovered the butcher had left the garage door open after delivering a frozen ox head. By the time the head was about five pounds short of its normal weight Callum was found with his prize. Callum must have had an iron constitution because this gorging on frozen meat did not seem to cause him any real discomfort.

I remember another German Shepherd called Chuffy, who was only about eight months old when a newly baked cake went missing with only a few crumbs to show that it had ever existed. When confronted with this evidence Chuffy looked at his owner's twins in an attempt to divert the blame, but as the twins were barely at the crawling stage Chuffy had no hope of getting out of that situation.

There are many cases of stolen morsels, and most of these cases are due to human thoughtlessness. Some dogs will steal at every opportunity and others will only do so when they are severely tempted. Only the owner can determine the magnitude of his problem and apply the necessary self-discipline to ensure that opportunities are not available for his dog to thieve.

There are, of course, times when a more forceful attitude must be applied when a dog shows interest in forbidden food. A very short and instantaneous use of the voice will be required and, if this proves to have insufficient effect, a smack on his hindquarters can be used to let him know you mean business. Do not pull him away but call him from the food and make sure that he does not get the opportunity to regain interest in this particular item. To scold a dog after he has helped himself to food is rather late and will probably be of little value. A scolding may relieve your feelings, but at the dog's expense. The dog owner can do a great deal to prevent food stealing, and by anticipation can educate and assist his dog to overcome the temptation.

Food refusal is a completely different problem and, if considered by the owner to be a necessity, should not be confused with the educational requirements to prevent stealing. I have been asked on occasions about training for food refusal and have found it difficult to understand the desire to put a pet dog through this form of train-ing, which is very much against the dog's nature, as there is no inherited instinct to work on. The only justification I can see for the owner of a pet dog wishing to teach his dog to refuse food is the genuine fear of deliberate poisoning.

I have trained only two of my own dogs for food refusal and this was purely for the Patrol Dog stake in working trials. The training was geared to the conditions one would expect when competing, but it meant that friends could not give these dogs titbits.

By its nature, training for food refusal is unpleasant for the dog. We are creating unpleasant associations under particular circumstances and, at any time unpleasant associations are being created, great care must be taken to ensure that the correct associations are forming in the dog's mind. It is too easy to introduce unwanted side-effects. It should be recognized that a pet owner cannot train a dog to refuse food under practical conditions without outside assistance in the shape of an experienced helper, preferably a stranger to the dog. For simplicity and reliability any training should be limited to the circumstances and localities where the poisoned food is liable to be left.

I remember one police dog handler who trained his dog to refuse food from everybody but himself. He was so successful that the day he went into hospital his dog stopped eating and even refused the food offered by the handler's wife. The answer was to bring the dog's meal to the hospital each day and have the handler spend the visiting period squeezing the food through his fingers so that the food contained a high concentration of his scent. This was the only way they could find to get the dog to eat.

Code of Good Manners

Preventing bad habits from taking a firm hold is the responsibility of the dog owner, and most bad habits can be avoided by the recognition of a code of good manners. The application of such a code will go a long way to making our dogs socially acceptable.

The Code

1 Some people love dogs and others hate them. There is no need to try and convert the dog lovers but respect for the views of the others can only help to convert them in the long run.
2 A dog should NEVER be out on the street on his own. The temptation to investigate the outside world and become one of the pack can be very great. The stray dog is 'gun fodder' for the 'dog haters'.
3 Keep your dog on the lead until you reach a suitable exercise area. There is nothing clever about taking a dog for a walk without a lead. Another loose dog may cause a fight, a cat may cause him to dart onto the road. It only requires a passing motor car and the prospect of human and canine tragedy is very real.
4 When your dog is free in an exercise area keep an eye on him, especially if another dog comes into view. The other dog may be a fighter, and experience has taught us that the German Shepherd always gets the blame.
5 Always carry Poop bags to clean up after your dog.
6 A walk on the lead should not be a constant battle between dog and owner, with the dog constantly trying to pull the owner's arm out of the socket.

Although there is no need for obedience-style heel work when out for a walk, the dog should be taught to walk on a 'loose' lead. The attention-getting routine should be very helpful in gaining the correct measure of control.

7 Your dog must respond to the recall when instructed, not as an obedience exercise but as an essential form of control.
8 Your dog should be taught to go down immediately where and when instructed. In an emergency this may be more necessary than the recall.
9 Your dog should always be prepared to accept a reasonable measure of control and when young children or elderly people are around it may be advisable to keep him on a lead. A boisterous dog can so easily knock the very young or elderly down. Children can become frightened of dogs for life and the elderly are very prone to injury.
10 Tough games with a dog can be enjoyable, but can be a dangerous form of amusement if the dog is not under sufficient control to stop when required.
11 Do not let your dog become over-protective, either of yourself or of his food. He should be quite prepared to accept strangers, although he does not have to welcome them. He should never be permitted to show signs of aggression when he is eating.
12 Do not tolerate unnecessary barking. If he is telling you that somebody is approaching, tell him how good he is then distract him from the cause. If the barking continues then forceful action is required.
13 Do not let your dog jump up to welcome people. If you and your friends get down to his level when he comes to

welcome you the habit of jumping up can be avoided.

14 Do not let your dog jump out of the car in an uncontrolled manner. It is preferable to train him to wait until after the door has been opened, then call him out when you are ready. This may well prevent an accident.

15 Always be on the lookout for faults developing. An amusing situation with a puppy can develop into a very serious problem as he matures.

16 Respect the farmer's land and livestock. You may know that your dog will not cause problems but there is no need to worry the farmer.

17 Teach yourself and your dog the elements of control (see Chapters 3 and 4).

CHAPTER 3

Approach to Training

The Basis for Training

Very few German Shepherd puppies are non-starters for a life of obedient companionship or for work in the field of obedience competitions, agility competitions or working trials, although their upbringing and conditioning for adult life can affect their full potential.

A lot of effort, worry and plain hard graft can be prevented by conditioning your puppy for an obedient future. A puppy can enjoy the early part of his life and may well enjoy it more if he is given the opportunity to follow and respect his 'pack leader' – that is, you, the handler. A puppy should experience authority, fairness and also the great excitement of life. All these can be experienced in preparing him for a happy and faithful future.

Initial training of any puppy must be based on two requirements:

1 His respect for you, which can only be based on his happy desire to please you.
2 The prevention of bad habits.

He should give his immediate attention to you, no matter what he is doing, when commanded. He must also be prepared to come to you when called, and he should learn the need for a prompt response to this request.

It should be noted that COMMANDS are used to obtain immediate attention, and REQUESTS are used to achieve something positive and active. I shall be going into the philosophy of this approach and it will be seen that this concept of control and training is based on the command and request. A request does not mean that you accept a refusal or allow time to think about it. It means that your tone of voice is that of a request, with your actions that of urgency and excitement.

An example of this approach to training is getting a puppy to come when called. There should never be a need to teach a puppy to come in the formal sense of the expression. He should be conditioned to want to be with you when he is called, with the sole objective of an immediate response. This can best be achieved if the puppy has a genuine desire to be with you and if there is something to come back for, something much more interesting than the thought taking his attention when called.

I have found the best way to condition a very young puppy initially is just to give him a flick or tap on the hindquarters with a finger when he is going away from me – this, of course, is whilst he is under no control and free to do what he wants. When giving this flick I call his name and he will turn his head to see what is wanted – remember he is only a few feet from me. I then make a great thing of him coming back and let him know he is really wanted.

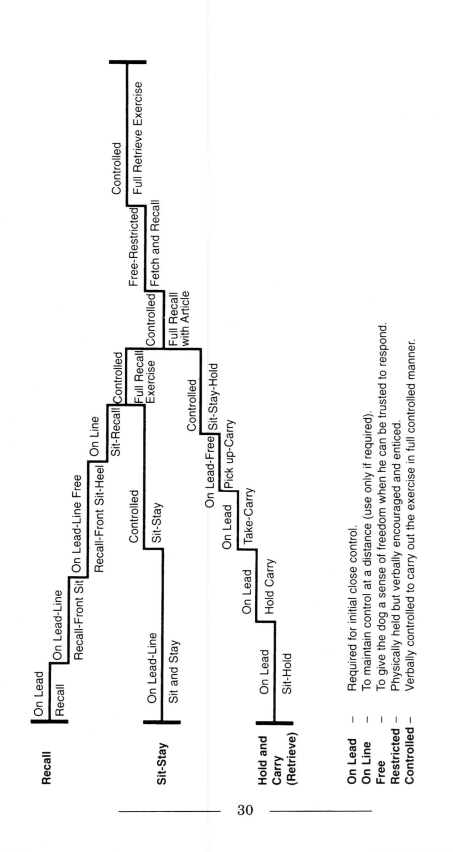

Recall

On Lead

Recall

On Lead-Line

Recall-Front Sit

On Lead-Line Free

Recall-Front Sit-Heel

On Line

Sit-Recall

Controlled

Full Recall Exercise

Controlled

Full Recall with Article

Free-Restricted

Fetch and Recall

Controlled

Full Retrieve Exercise

Sit-Stay

On Lead-Line

Sit and Stay

Controlled

Sit-Stay

Hold and Carry (Retrieve)

On Lead

Sit-Hold

On Lead

Hold Carry

On Lead

Take-Carry

On Lead-Free

Pick up-Carry

Controlled

Sit-Stay-Hold

On Lead – Required for initial close control.

On Line – To maintain control at a distance (use only if required).

Free – To give the dog a sense of freedom when he can be trusted to respond.

Restricted – Physically held but verbally encouraged and enticed.

Controlled – Verbally controlled to carry out the exercise in full controlled manner.

A foundation training schedule.

He must feel that it is good to be with me or that something great is going to happen.

In using this approach you must make your puppy feel that something is going to happen when he comes in to you. Sometimes you give him plenty of love and affection, sometimes you make it fun and games and on other occasions make it a nice juicy titbit. Whatever you do, vary your response to his return, make it worth his while and let him think 'What is it going to be this time?' The secret of initial training is to have him want to come back to you. The request to come is the signal for something pleasant.

This approach can be built on by eventually allowing a little more distance between yourself and your puppy. At this stage do not call him when his attention is on something, do not create a clash of desires until he is fully responsive to your call when little appears to be on his mind. At no time do you move towards your puppy once you have called him; if anything move away and draw him to you with plenty of encouragement.

Commands, and with a stern tone of voice, are used to stop him from doing something and should be of the severity required to achieve the objective. The command may only be to get his attention so that the recall request can be given. The command, however, should not be given until you are in a position to reinforce it, or from past experience are guaranteed an immediate response. The 'in your own time' attitude at this stage is out of the question. In general the 'command' need only be the use of the puppy's name.

Although the correct approach to the conditioning and upbringing of a puppy is most important, it does not mean to say that all is lost if a young or adult dog has not had the benefit of this start in life. It may well mean a lot more hard work on the part of the handler to retrieve the situation. It is much easier to be patient with a young puppy than with a young dog or adult, especially if by then you are correcting your own earlier failings, as there is a strong tendency to blame the dog for the faults that have developed. There can also be the feeling that time has been lost and must be made up in the correction of these faults. Short cuts in training must not be confused with efficient training. Efficient training may appear to be the long way round, but it is built on a solid foundation with sound, long-lasting results, and this approach is usually quicker in the long run. Short cuts lead to all sorts of trouble. They may, if you are good enough, get you through a show or trial, but in most cases we find that the dog is only half-trained. His handler usually says 'That worked' and continues to build on the temporary success only to wonder why failure or poor performance follows later on.

Efficient training is dependent on a sound approach with a capable and understanding handler, and any training method is only as good as the trainer's ability to pass it on and also the handler's ability to apply it.

A dog will learn through habit or conditioning, from encouragement, reward or displeasure; he will also learn through his desire to please you. A German Shepherd will only satisfy that desire if he knows that you are pleased and he will certainly know that something is wrong when he thinks you are displeased. The point is will he know what you are displeased about?

The biggest mistake which many owners make is expecting their dog to think and reason as a human. A dog does not think as a human being, although a highly trained dog may well appear to do so. Dogs learn through habit, they learn from the pleasant and also from the unpleasant.

The best example one can give is that of the dog who will not come back when called and when he eventually does come back is given a telling off, or a hiding, for staying away. In fact, the dog thinks that he is being punished for coming back, because that was the last thing he did. He relates the pleasant and the unpleasant with his last action. Under these circumstances the next time he is called he remembers he got a hiding the last time, and will be reluctant to return. If the handler maintains this approach the dog will become bored and more reluctant to come back when called.

You may well be saying 'What is the answer?' The answer to that particular problem is given in the training for the recall. The main point is, however, that you should remember he will relate your response to his last action. This is the most important principle in dog training.

What does a dog trainer mean by conditioning, habit, encouragement, rewarding and displeasure? This is my interpretation:

CONDITIONING means preparing a dog for the exercise or element, building him up in the manner which will lead to the reaction you require.

HABIT is the repetition of an element of an exercise in such a way that it will become a natural function and in a manner the dog enjoys.

ENCOURAGEMENT is the verbal and physical support given to the dog in assisting him to carry out the element or exercise.

Encouragement can be in many forms.

REWARD is the spontaneous pleasure you show when he responds to your wishes. This may, of course, be reinforced by the use of titbits on completion of the task.

DISPLEASURE should only be 'the sharp edge of your tongue' if you do not receive the instant or correct response to your wishes. This is, of course, when training is sufficiently advanced for him to know that he is doing wrong. There may well be occasions when more drastic action is required when the dog is beside you. There is nothing more effective than taking two handfuls of loose skin at his neck and giving him a three-second blast with your

Titbits for a reward.

most books on training and it is the same – working a dog to commands. So long as we continue to use this word freely we shall think that way and tend to train that way. Many people, however, realize that it is just a figure of speech.

If we consider our life in industry, commerce or with the family at home, how unbearable it would be if all instructions were carried out to commands. We would then find that there would be many a rebellion or we would become immune to this approach. Life is normally much more acceptable because we are usually REQUESTED to carry out our functions, and in the main these requests are just commands dressed up to maintain a pleasant and cooperative atmosphere.

As our dogs are obedient companions or working partners we should not be required to give commands to carry out what should be a pleasant task, but dogs, like children, need to be controlled, instructed and encouraged to obey instructions, and yet enjoy life to the full. It is, therefore, preferable to think of instructions and requests rather than commands. If you keep in mind that you wish to finish with a happy dog, one who is very keen to please you, a dog who knows you appreciate everything that he does for you, the main consideration is to use an approach which creates a real desire to please.

tongue whilst you are looking him straight in the eye (or as I have heard it put 'Having a little word in his ear'). This sort of treatment should not really be necessary but, if used, it should immediately be followed by something exciting that you know will achieve the correct response.

Commands, Instructions and Requests

'Giving commands' in dog training is an expression that is generally used and applied. Everything seems to be based on giving commands for this, and that and the next thing. Go to a training club, read

Before discussing the replacement for the command approach I would like to go into the response we expect from a trained dog, for it is a reflection of our own attitude to training. If we are demanding and lacking in consideration we may have a dog who does as he is told but is probably devoid of character. If we are firm but fair, happy and full of encouragement, constructing our training in such a manner that the dog enjoys these sessions, we should finish with an eager dog full of character.

We want to train in a manner which releases the dog to carry out our requests. If we want him to retrieve we should not find it necessary to give him a command and send him for the article: we want to be in a position to release him so that his great desire takes him out to get this article and bring it quickly back. If we do a 'send away', again we wish to release him to go out in the direction that has been indicated. Every active movement is a release from a controlled situation.

If you think this way, you can train this way.

When you want to obtain a dog's undivided attention or have him remain in a stationary position (i.e. creating a static situation) you instruct him, and there should just be sufficient edge in your voice to achieve the desired effect. When you want to create an active situation you request him to do it. As training develops you may well find your instructions become less frequent and requests will achieve the reaction you are after.

Now we are thinking in terms of instructions and requests. Instructions in varying degrees of firmness may be used to obtain attention or create a closely controlled static situation. Requests are used to release him to carry out a controlled exercise.

When giving instructions or making requests to a dog, it must be recognized that dogs learn from actions. If a dog is being taught to go down when required, it is of no value to tell him to go into the DOWN position until he understands the meaning of the word. He requires to be enticed or physically assisted to go down. Verbal instructions will only be of value to your dog when he responds to meaningful visual or physical movements from yourself. The visual or physical movements are signals and it is his recognition of these signals which can be connected to the verbal instructions or requests.

Training Elements

Everything we teach a dog can be broken down into elements, or even sub-elements. If we take the simplest action of asking a dog to sit, this can be broken into three elements, each one as important as the other. These elements are: obtaining the dog's undivided attention; getting him to sit; and keeping him in the sit position. It will be obvious that getting a dog to sit on request is not practical if his undivided attention cannot be obtained, and it is a waste of time getting him to sit if you cannot get him to stay in the sit position for a short period of time. This is a very elementary exercise for any dog, and it may appear to be very simple. It can be achieved by the overbearing and domineering approach, or the dog can find it to be a pleasing function because it makes his boss happy. The overbearing approach may achieve the result you wish but it is a poor beginning if you wish later to control him at a distance, and even with the companion dog it is essential to obtain control at a distance.

Each element of an exercise or sub-element is STATIC or ACTIVE. The static elements are those which stop a dog from doing something, and involve getting and maintaining his attention in an inactive position. The active elements are those which require the dog to do something. Let us now consider the elements of the sit exercise. They are:

APPROACH TO TRAINING

1 Obtaining the dog's undivided attention: a static element which, until the dog understands, is taken as an instruction. The instruction may only be the use of the dog's name with an urgent tone of voice. The dog's name can be used as an instruction to pay attention.
2 Getting the dog to sit: an active element, requesting, encouraging and helping the dog to go into the sit position.
3 Keeping him in the sit position: another static element. This requires firm instruction with a soothing appreciation for obeying the instruction. In this instance his name is not the dominant word although the instruction to sit/stay is applied with the firmness required to maintain this static situation. To keep a dog inactive for a period of time requires a great deal of concentration from the handler during the initial training stage. The handler should use his voice as a steadying influence and give the dog full assurance that he is doing fine, but he must be ready with a sharp instruction if there is any inclination to move.

Another requirement that can be considered essential for any dog is to come back when called. This again has three elements:

1 Obtaining the dog's undivided attention: a static element, this probably lasts for a split second until you have given the call to come immediately back to you. Without his undivided attention there is not a hope of achieving Element 2.
2 Getting him to come back to you

immediately and smartly: an active element that requires all the encouragement you can muster to create in him the habit of returning when called. This should be applied as an excited request to return. Any attempt to use a firmly voiced instruction will result in a reluctant return or even a complete refusal to come in when called.
3 Staying with you willingly: a calm and reassuring situation follows in keeping the dog quietly inactive until you have had time to tell him how good he is and also to clip on his lead again.

As a handler your own actions and the correct use of your voice will create the static and active situations which the various elements require. This comment is just as important for the companion dog owner as for the working dog owner.

Breaking Down Exercises into Elements

Every exercise can be broken down into a number of elements as indicated above and, with consideration for the static or active functions, most elements can be broken into sub-elements. If we take teaching a dog to sit as part of a full exercise, such as the recall, then this becomes an element of the recall with the previous example showing the three parts as sub-elements.

If we take the recall as an exercise it can be broken down into the following elements:

1 Stay when told until recalled by handler.

Recall

ELEMENT		SUB-ELEMENT	CLASSIFICATION
1	Stay till called.	Obtaining dog's attention.	Static
		Getting dog to sit.	Active
		Keeping him in the sit position whilst you leave him.	Static
2	Recall to handler.	Maintaining attention for the recall.	Static
		Recall and return of dog to handler.	Active
3	Sit in front of handler.	Sit in front.	Active
		Remain sitting.	Static
4	Round to heel.	Maintaining attention for the final step.	Static
		Round to heel on request.	Active
		Sit at handler's side.	Active
		Remain sitting.	Static

2 Come directly to handler when called.

3 Sit squarely in front of the handler.

4 Go smartly round to heel to finish the exercise.

As we have already seen, element (1) can be broken into three sub-elements: (a) pay attention; (b) sit; (c) stay sitting. We can now take the complete exercise and break it down fully to show the various static and active situations (see table above).

It will be seen that even with this simple exercise there are eleven different situations for the dog, requiring six changes by the handler as he controls the dog from static to active or active to static situations. Each change requires a change in the tone of voice, a change in attitude of mind, a change from subdued attention to immediate activity and then back again to subdued attention. A handler must think this way and act this way to obtain the most effective and efficient response from the dog.

Every exercise should be broken down in this manner. Many experienced hand-lers do this without thinking very much about it – the process has become second nature to them. When breaking down an exercise into elements consider which one to teach first and whether various elements should be taught quite separately from each other but in parallel, so that they may be dovetailed together later when being executed to satisfaction. The full process of this form of teaching is given in the chapters for each individual exercise. The companion dog owner should note that the same basic principle applies for any normal domestic control.

Conditioning for an Element

We have already discussed the need to consider and treat each element separately, so we can now go into the preparation for each element or sub-element. Conditioning is really another word for controlled anticipation.

Without anticipation we could not train a dog.

A dog will show us dozens of examples of his anticipation every day, and if we study the causes we can understand how a dog is a trainable creature. For instance, take his feeding dish out of the cupboard at a particular time of day and he knows he is going to be fed – he anticipates the event. Put on your walking shoes last thing at night and he anticipates his final chance of the day for exercise. Close the car tailgate on his ear and see what happens the next time the tailgate is closed: he anticipates trouble. It may take a few uneventful closures of the tailgate before he anticipates that no harm will come to him. Yet if he is a sensitive dog or he has had a really nasty nip he may always anticipate it happening and keep away from the tailgate and never give it the chance to inflict pain again.

Anticipation must be turned to our advantage: if we can have the dog anticipating our every intention we have achieved a tremendous understanding. However, like everything else we use to our advantage, it must be controlled – that is why I have used the phrase 'controlled anticipation'. This anticipation can be used to build up the power behind his desire to carry out the function he knows is coming, and your actions or the way you speak to him will tell him what is coming next. As a result of the correct application of habit and routine he anticipates the next move and enjoys it. If he does not enjoy the next move you will soon know by his reaction, for the way he anticipates it will make it obvious that your method of conditioning has not been pleasant to him.

Training Sequence

If we accept that the foundation training in Chapter 4 is the first essential, and that training for an immediate response for basic control is top priority, we can then think beyond the foundation training exercises and move on to the more advanced stages.

The question then is do we concentrate on a very small number of exercises for a quick return or do we tackle a broader field for a slower, long-term return? Although I feel that there is only one answer, there must be a good, sound reasoning behind it. This comes down to our own mental approach to training rather than the dog's ability to cover a broad field at the one time. If we tackle one or two exercises fully and look for perfection in their execution, we start with the feeling that with a fair amount of concentration it should not take long to get the dog licked into shape. With this approach it is all too easy to become impatient, to have excessive determination and to feel that time is slipping by without the expected response from the dog. There can be a tendency to move on from one element to the next without consolidating the work previously carried out. There can also be a tendency to spend too long within each session on too few elements, thereby creating boredom.

If we now consider the full range of training exercises beyond the foundation group, we should again break them down into elements and decide on the initial training element for each exercise. We should look for those initial training elements that are natural for a dog, so that we may not even need to wait until the foundation training is complete before starting with some of them. It is much easier to pick out the natural elements in training for working trials than for obedience competitions.

Earliest stages of Trials Agility training.

A number of exercises which can be started by early conditioning and have elements which are natural to the dog are:

1 THE AGILITY TESTS. It is quite natural for a dog to jump if he wishes so long as heights are kept to the minimum. Even with a four-month-old puppy we can have great fun conditioning him so that the Scale Jump with one sixinch board becomes so enjoyable that he looks forward to it. Similarly jumping over a single board from the Long Jump lays a good foundation for this exercise later. The Clear Jump can be laid down flat and the puppy have fun charging over it. All this can be done to condition him and prepare for serious training at a later date.
2 SPEAK ON REQUEST. What is more natural than a puppy barking? If we encourage, but control, this barking from the very start we can make life so much easier for ourselves. This should be a 'must' for all house dogs.
3 TRACKING. Another exercise that can be practised at an early age, but the chapter on tracking should be studied and the various pitfalls appreciated before streaming ahead.

Although the above can be considered as 'natural' exercises which can be taught along with the foundation group, almost any exercise can be started from the sound basis of foundation training.

A dog enjoys variety in training. Boredom from repeating the same thing time and time again is his greatest enemy. Many dogs make progress even on a poor foundation and with an impatient handler, but few of them reach the top of

A tracker of the future.

the ladder, and it is generally found that such dogs are working to please their handler through fear.

Basic Requirements for all Training

Before starting with the foundation training exercises described in the following chapter there a few basic requirements that a handler should appreciate before going into the training of any exercise. These are as follows:

1 HANDLER ATTENTION. If you want one hundred per cent attention from your dog you must be prepared to give this to him during training. He is entitled to your full attention – any failure on your part will result in failure on his. This being so, keep the sessions short but intensive whilst they last.

2 VOICE CONTROL. Probably the most important thing for a handler to learn is how to use his or her voice to obtain the right response from the dog. Any sharpness used to get his attention must be short and snappy with an immediate softening of tone afterwards and with the recall in an excited tone to encourage the dog to come in. A sharp tone of voice should only be used to get the dog's attention and at no other time. If this sharpness of tone is not successful on the first call then your training is not soundly based. Continual shouting is of little value in successful dog training.

3 BODY AND HAND CONTROL. It can be of great value to use body and hand movements as signals, but you must be conscious of their useful application. The proper and natural use of signals will help your dog, so long as you know you are using them. You can later minimize these signals or cut them out when no longer needed. Hand and arm signals in particular can be used to reinforce acts of encouragement.

4 TITBITS AND TOYS. Titbits and toys are inducements that become rewards, and thought must be given to their choice and application. Titbits can be very effective and their choice will reflect the enthusiasm expressed for them. A dry dog biscuit will have some effect, but a nice tasty morsel may well be required to obtain the best result.

There are many proprietary types of titbit that can be purchased at little cost, but some dogs will sell their souls for just a piece of cheese. I find that a proprietary brand of liver treat is economical and clean, and dogs love them. They can easily be stored in a small container in your pocket. I am never without them.

Presentation of titbits is as important as the tasty morsels themselves. Your dog should be able to recognize the presence of titbits from a distance, either by sight, or sound, or both. They will be seen and heard in a plastic bag. Certain types of titbit kept in a rigid container may not be seen so easily by the dog but will be recognizable by their rattling sound. The knowledge that titbits are there for the taking can be sufficient to achieve the desired response.

The dog should come in close enough to take the reward rather than the handler stretching out arm and hand to give. Titbits ought to be held close to your body and at dog's nose level when standing or sitting.

Body and hand movements to induce the desired response.

Play toys can be used instead of titbits – fun and games act as a reward for behaving in the desired manner – but it is all too easy to lose control of your dog in the early stages of control training. Play toys can be successfully used if you are selective about them.

Control Equipment

Equipment for control training and everyday use does require some consideration. It is quite easy to say that you only require a collar and lead but the choice and use of such simple equipment can make all the difference between success and failure.

Collars and leads are used to cover such a varied set of circumstances and yet it is expected that dogs will react just as we want them to at any given time. They are an indispensable aid to training, and your application of such equipment affects the future actions and reactions of your dog. They are also used as a form of control when you are not in a position to give full attention to your dog.

Collars

The most common type of collar tightens on the dog's neck and checks his activities, and when correctly used on a trained dog the first indications of tightening should

Correct check chain fitting.

Incorrect check chain fitting.

be sufficient to create the desired reaction. However, greater use is made of this tightening effect in the earlier stages of training, to achieve the attention and reaction which will allow for a more moderate approach as training progresses.

The most common collar of this type in use today is known as the COMBI-COLLAR and can be very effective. It has been designed to have a limited amount of tightening and can also be adjusted to fit neatly on the dog as a permanent form of neck wear.

The CHOKE or CHECK CHAIN has had a long history of use, but has now lost its popularity. However, as it is still used within certain quarters, its existence must be included. Although the CHECK CHAIN is no longer used to choke a dog into submission in these enlightened days, its use

can be a very effective means of control without applying harsh handling techniques. The standard choke chain is made of metal links as the name would indicate, but similar types can be purchased of either leather or rope construction. These are much less likely to tear or cut the hairs round the dog's neck than the chain type. The fitting of the choke collar is very important to ensure that it will automatically slacken on release.

The HALTI, or DOGALTER, and similar types of head harness represent another concept which has been introduced to the techniques of canine control. These head harnesses can be used in conjunction with standard collars and they are most effective with any dog, particularly dogs whose owners find difficulty in handling them. As the HALTI was the first of its kind on the

Combi-collar.

A nice length of lead.

market, that term now seems to be the common name given to all such equipment. Any future reference to this type of equipment will be to a HALTI.

Leads

The lead is the connecting link between dog and handler and consideration must be given to the choice of such equipment. For general training and everyday use the lead should be of a suitable length and comfortable to handle.

A standard four to five feet length of lead is generally satisfactory, although the police type of double lead can be of value. A good, strong lead is essential, and good-quality leather which has been softened with the appropriate dressing is a pleasure to handle. However, a good, soft nylon or cotton webbing lead can be a reasonably priced substitute for leather.

A lead is only as strong as the clip on the end and it is important to ensure that the clip will stand up to the use it will receive during its lifetime.

A five- to seven-foot length of cord can be a useful addition for puppy conditioning or for the more difficult adult dog that has not had the benefit of a controlled upbringing. A long line of some thirty feet is another useful aid in obtaining initial control.

CHAPTER 4

The Foundation Exercises

General

The first aim of every German Shepherd owner must be to achieve complete control with instant response to his wishes. Whether the dog is to remain a companion or be trained with a broader field in mind, every dog should know who is boss and at the same time he should have complete trust in his master. He should obey, but he should also experience fun and enjoyment such as any child can expect from his parents.

The basis of this companionship and the foundation of future training can best be attained through training in the foundation exercises. Precision may well be required for competitive work but instant response should be expected from ALL dogs at ALL times. Any sluggishness in response will only lead to an even more sluggish approach on the next occasion, unless something is done to arrest the trend.

The recall, loose lead walking and sit/stay training is essential for basic control, with the retrieve as an important addition which helps to coordinate the various basic functions. The retrieve is also important for the development of character, and its training creates the opening for your canine friend's intelligence and natural working ability.

Basis for Control

Before we can expect a dog to react positively to our wishes we must be able to obtain the dog's attention. Once we have his attention we must be able to hold it for long enough to make use of it. Attention-getting is, therefore, the first training principle and the foundation of our control; it is applied from the preliminary stages in recall training. It is also the basis of loose lead walking, which can eventually be developed for competitive heel work.

The attention-getting routine, which is now going to be developed, is based on the application of the collar and lead. In the previous chapter we have already discussed the conditioning of puppies to a responsive start to their lives.

Developing from puppies to the more mature dogs, it will be found that as these pups approach adolescence or maturity they may bring a streak of defiance to the fore where a conflict of interests can rear its ugly head. This situation must be recognized immediately to prevent defiance, through independence, from developing into a way of life.

A defiant dog can show this trait in a number of ways and it may well be due to handler failing rather than the dog's natural stubbornness. The dog may ignore his handler's call completely as if he were deaf, he may run away expecting to be chased, he may come running back until he is almost within reach then run away or he may carry on and run right past. Whatever causes the problem, it can become exasperating and will take a less understanding handler beyond the limits of a reasonable reaction.

The secret of a sound, instant response to the handler's call is never to be in a position where the dog is likely to refuse and defy his handler. If you expect a refusal, do not call, deploy yourself into a position where refusal is extremely unlikely or wait for the correct moment. Create success and avoid failures.

To overcome such defiance problems or to prevent them, it is advisable to consolidate on the puppy conditioning approach as described at the beginning of Chapter 3 with the use of a suitable collar and good length of lead, say four to six feet. This brings in the training element which overcomes the conflict of interest situation.

This training element is the basis for an instant response to the call at any time. The preconditioned puppy will respond very quickly but the defiant creature will take a little longer to realize that he must respond immediately every time and much ground work may be required to ensure success.

The principle we shall apply is that of a sharp backward movement to obtain and maintain the dog's attention. Attach the lead to your dog's collar when there is a distraction available which is going to take your dog's attention. During the course of basic training distractions of various kinds can be utilized. A member of the family in the area, another dog, an attractively scented lamppost are examples which are of value. If there are no distractions available, boredom through the lack of activity can be just as effective. He may sniff the ground, decide to sit or lie down; then is the time to act.

Whether through boredom or distraction, as soon as your dog decides to act you should move backwards very smartly and as you call his name give a sharp tug on the lead. Continue your backward movement until his attention has been fully maintained on you for a few seconds. Give your dog praise for cooperating with your requirements as you are moving backwards. Change direction by moving forwards and at the same time draw your dog into line at your left side so that he has the opportunity to walk at heel. Continue forwards, towards a distraction if possible, and any sign of your dog moving ahead of you must be countered immediately by a repeat of the smart backward movement to maintain his attention on you.

This activity should develop into a flowing movement backwards with your dog following you and watching for a sudden change of direction, then a forward movement to pass on your dog's left side so that he can turn and fall into the heel-walking position at your left side. A few repeats of this action during each training session will soon have your dog watching your every movement.

During your backward movements encourage your dog with a bit of chat: 'COME on, son, that's a good boy' should be adequate, and when he is walking at your side during your forward movement: 'HEEL close, son, that's a good boy' should be sufficient.

Your dog is actually learning the meaning of your phrases from your movements. When moving backwards keep your hands low with the lead/collar below your dog's lower jaw. Always keep the lead loose

'Attention-getting' routine – changing from backward to forward movement.

unless there is a need to give a quick but positive jerk to obtain full attention.

Lead Handling

Lead handling can be a very important factor in achieving an attentive and a physically close relationship without a tight lead. The lead may be jerked in a very positive manner to achieve the attention you require but, thereafter, it is verbal and physical inducements which maintain the attention.

The loop end of the lead should be over your right thumb in a manner which allows you to grasp the end and let it go as required. When applying backward movement with your dog following you, the loop of the lead over thumb can allow you to keep both hands open as you use your fingers, hands and arms in an encouraging manner.

As soon as you move forward you can grasp the end of the lead and also gather the lead in your right hand so that the surplus is at your right side. Your left hand is then used as a guide for the lead or to hold it as necessary. With your left hand immediately in front of your left leg there should be the minimum of lead between the left hand and the dog's collar.

When moving forward for those few paces both hands should be resting on and in front of your legs. There should be approximately six inches of lead between your left and right hands and your arms should be in a relaxed position.

The important features of lead control when moving forward are:

1 Loop in right hand.
2 Surplus lead at your right side.
3 Minimum lead between left hand and collar (but not tight).
4 Both hands in front of, facing and against your legs.
5 Approximately six inches of lead between left and right hands.

Gaining and keeping your dog's attention at close range is one thing but obtaining a satisfactory response at a distance is quite another matter. Getting a dog to come back when called is dependent on two controlling and very significant factors; they are:

1 Conflict of interests.
2 Distance between dog and handler.

The conflict of interests can vary tremendously and may well be the greatest cause of a failure to respond to the call to come back to you. A short distance between dog and handler can weaken any reluctance by the belief that he will not get away with it, but a greater distance can strengthen the reluctance along with the dog's realisation that he can run faster than his human companion and he may well enjoy the chase. Any punishment after his capture or belated voluntary return will not be related in the dog's mind to his failure to respond in the first place, but it will be considered a very unpleasant experience at the hands of his master for the latest event in his mind – that of returning. He may have been cornered and will be more cunning the next time; he will not wish to

experience the wrath of his master. If he has finally returned voluntarily and received punishment he will be more apprehensive next time. A succession of such events will finally implant the unpleasantness in the dog's mind to such an extent that he will always be reluctant to return.

If the dog has found an attractive smell his interest may well exceed the handler's control for an immediate response. If he has found a bitch with amorous inclinations a real problem has developed with a great conflict of interests. If two male dogs start squaring up to each other, neither will wish to back down and very effective handler control will be required if a dog is going to show any sign of weakness by turning his back and walking away from his adversary. There are times when the conflict of interests is so great that it can be good policy to go up to the dog and prevent this conflict by putting him on the lead and abandoning the thought of recalling under these particular circumstances.

Each situation should be fully assessed and the dog recalled only when a favourable response is expected. Otherwise the situation should be created where immediate attention and a willing recall is guaranteed.

To overcome problems of defiance, or to prevent them, it is advisable to consolidate on the prompt conditioning approach with the use of a suitable collar and lead, or a cord some five to seven feet in length could be used to bring in the training element which overcomes the conflict-of-interest situations.

This training element is the basis for an instant response to the call at any time. The preconditioned puppy will respond very quickly, but a defiant creature will take some time to realize that he must respond immediately every time and much ground work may be required to ensure success.

Take the dog on the lead and just walk. Do not apply any control and let your dog do just what he wants for a few seconds. If he pulls just let him, or if he stops to sniff just let him. When you are ready, call his name as you give a sharp tug on the lead, move back and away from him calling him to you and with urgency and enthusiasm, create a real desire to be with you. Any harshness in the voice should be only in the use of his name so that you obtain instant attention and this must always be followed immediately by the encouraging call to come.

The preconditioned puppy will become very attentive and will watch the handler's every move after a minimal period. Good timing and a sensible application of the collar and lead will also have a remarkable effect on the more defiant dog, but this will take much longer to consolidate and be sure of the desired response every time.

With this in mind it may be advisable to continue the process of attention-getting with the use of a long line. The more responsive dog should not need to be subjected to this process but guaranteed success is more important than discarding this option. A line of twenty-five to thirty feet in length should be sufficient. (A strong nylon cord should suit the purpose.)

The application of the long line is identical to that of the lead. Again give the dog plenty of freedom to do what he wants, if necessary creating distance between yourself and the dog. Allow him to take an interest in something of his own choice, then call him. Do not accept a negative response. Failure to respond to the first call will necessitate positive and immediate action. A further call should coincide with a sharp tug on the line. Use enthusiasm and urgency in your voice and any movements, to ensure that he comes back to you quickly. If necessary move back at speed to draw him to you more quickly. Never move towards your dog when you call him: this will only slow him down.

The use of titbits or some other form of appreciated reward can be vital at this stage. This reward must initially be seen, heard or smelt by the dog to be appreciated and effective. To hold a titbit in your hand where the dog cannot see it is of no value in the early stages, and if he is a distance away, or with the wind in the wrong direction, he will not smell it. To produce the plastic bag of titbits and rustle it is quite another matter, or to throw a ball in the air and catch it will let him see that coming back can be in his best interest. Apply all the encouragement you wish and make that return worth his effort.

Do not forget to praise him: he must enjoy coming back to you. Do not be too ready to discard the line. Let your dog drag it around for some time and be sure he comes in at every call, no matter where you are or what he is doing. Only ten consecutive successes can give a handler confidence in the result of the eleventh.

The Foundation Exercises and Principal Elements

The foundation exercises can be considered as the basic training requirements for an obedient German Shepherd. They are also essential for development into the various competitive fields of work.

These foundation exercises, with their objectives, are as follows:

1 SIT STAY. Objective: To ensure that your dog will go into the sit position and remain in that position whilst you go out of sight for a specified period of time. Your dog should remain in that position until you return and finish the exercise.

2 RECALL. Objective: To ensure that your dog will stay at a distance away from you but will respond immediately to your requirements to come back to you when called.

3 LOOSE LEAD WALKING. Objective: To have your dog walk close to you and level with your left leg. He should also be prepared to move off from a sitting position and sit immediately you halt.

4 RETRIEVE. Objective: To have your dog go out to pick up, return and deliver to hand any suitable article. The exercise may be carried out in an informal manner as a practical function for domestic enjoyment, or it can be carried out to comply with the competitive requirements of the various fields of activity.

The precision and absolute attention you require from your dog in each of these exercises is dependent on your own requirements and your purpose in training.

As already discussed in Chapter 3, each exercise should be broken down into the various elements, and some of these elements are common to more than one exercise. Selected elements or groups of them should be treated as training exercises in their own right. The breakdown of elements against each of the foundation exercises should be noted.

When we discuss the training for any specific exercise there are elements, or groups, in which training should be given before trying to incorporate them into the routine of the individual exercises. The introduction of some elements into an exercise must be carefully timed to ensure that they do not affect the success of another exercise. For example, to apply the sit/stay at an early stage of recall training may create difficulties in establishing a sound sit/stay exercise. Therefore, a controlled sit and stay should not be introduced to the recall

FOUNDATION EXERCISES

ELEMENTS	Sit/ Stay	Recall	Loose Lead Walking	Retrieve
Sit at your left side (Sit at heel)	x	x	x	x
Stay while you are away	x	x		
Return when called		x		x
Sit in front		x		x
Round to heel and sit		x		x
Walk at heel			x	
Go away from you				x
Pick up an article				x
Give article to hand				x

until a stable stay exercise has been established.

It will be seen that the sit at your left side applies to all exercises and this is the start and finish of each exercise. This element can be taught on its own in various ways or it can be added to other elements, such as the sit in front followed by the round to heel. These three elements can become a training routine in their own right prior to the training of the individual exercises. This routine is also one natural conclusion to the attention-getting procedure which has already been discussed. The other natural conclusion to attention-getting is to finish with your dog walking at heel for a few paces, then to sit at the halt. We shall start with the routine of getting your dog to sit at your left side on the forward movement of the attention-getting routine.

Sit at Your Left Side

With your dog on the lead carry out the attention-getting routine by moving backwards until you have your dog's full attention, then change to the forward movement until you have your dog close in at your left side with his head level with your left leg. Remember to apply the form of lead control already described.

When you are prepared to stop and MAKE your dog sit, grasp the lead/collar attachment in your right hand and at the same time let go of the lead in your left hand. Place your left hand at the left side of your dog's croup. As you press the croup down and in towards your left leg pull a little towards you and upwards on the lead/collar attachment to create a smart, controlled sit. This ensures a straight and quick, attentive sit.

Gently praise your dog but ensure that

he maintains the sit position for about five seconds before releasing with abundant praise.

The verbal instruction to sit can be introduced with the physical action when you feel that he is beginning to anticipate your movements.

Sit in Front

When your dog has been taught to sit at your left side without any physical reinforcement and he knows the meaning of the instruction to sit, you can develop the SIT IN FRONT. Some dogs, however, find this routine quite easy to perform without the training to sit at your left side.

This technique can be applied at any time and the inducement to sit in front of you is a titbit. With your dog on or off the lead move backwards and induce him to follow you by drawing the bag or container of titbits close to your body as he is following and comes close in to you.

Stop and draw the container up to bring his head upwards and encourage him to sit. If he already knows the meaning of the instruction to sit, it will become a simple and pleasant training routine. Always give him his reward as soon as he sits. He may act quicker if you hold a titbit in your hand along with the container.

Your training routine should be varied. On some occasions try the SIT IN FRONT after 'attention-getting', and on others carry out the flowing movement of drawing your dog in to your left side for forward movement to finish the sitting at heel position or to create a finish free.

Round to Heel and Sit

This element completes the finish of the recall and retrieve exercises where the dog

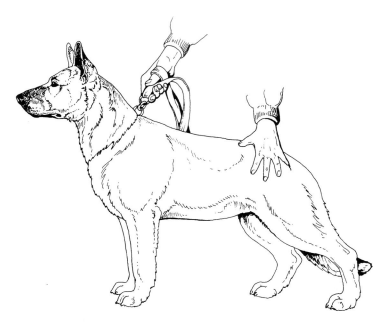

Hand positions for the SIT.

Pulling on right hand with push on left for a quick straight SIT.

sits in front of you, then, when instructed, he moves from the front to your left side. There are two ways in which this manoeuvre can be carried out.

1 By swivelling his rear end round to his right so that he finishes sitting in the heel position.
2 By the dog going round close behind you to finish in the heel position.

Method 1 The backward and forward attention-getting routine has started to prepare the dog for this manoeuvre. He knows how to turn as he passes your left side to fall in to heel.

While he is on the lead have your dog sitting in front of you, or go and stand in front of him while he is sitting. Side-step with your right foot and, as soon as it touches the ground, move your left foot towards it and continue the movement forwards so that your dog is at your left side. Encourage him quickly to heel as you continue walking forwards. Halt and instruct him to sit when he is satisfactorily in position. The training that you have already carried out for SIT AT YOUR LEFT SIDE will now be of value.

Continue with this routine until your dog is by your side before you have taken your second pace forward. At this stage you will be able to start to minimize your own movement. Reduce this movement very gradually until the instruction to HEEL or IN along with a visual indication from your left hand creates the full swivel of his body into the correct position without any movement from yourself.

Method 2 On occasions during the attention-getting routine you can change from backward to forward movement by moving to the right side of your dog. Take the lead round your back as you encourage the dog to go behind you and fall in at heel before getting him to sit.

This routine will help him to accept your eventual requirements. With your dog sitting or standing in front of you on the lead call him to your left side as you pivot round on the spot in a clockwise direction. Use titbits or hold a toy in front of your left leg at dog head height as an inducement to achieve a tight circle. You can make one complete circle or more to ensure that he stays in close and very attentive. When you are ready to stop, smartly put or induce your dog into the sit; he has already been taught to sit at your left side.

When you have achieved the smart, close action you require you can start to minimize your own actions. A reduction in your own body movements is taken gradually. Instead of pivoting right round start the movement clockwise then switch back so that you can encourage the completion of your dog's movements. During this procedure the encouraging verbal instruction 'HEEL' can be used with the visual indication from your right hand at the start of the movement and then the left hand for completion.

With the three basic elements – Sit at your Side (Heel position), Sit in front, Round to Heel and Sit – mastered you can now consider teaching the foundation exercises. All foundation exercises can be taught over the same period by gradually building up experience and rapport. Although heel work can be taught without direct consideration for the development of the other exercises the others are much more directly inter-related. However, the graphic illustration on page 30, showing the training schedule, will help you to co-ordinate the various stages of progress.

Movement from SIT IN FRONT and ROUND TO HEEL with titbit to induce STRAIGHT SIT.

Sit/Stay

The basic elements. Dog to:

1 Sit at your left side;
2 a Stay sitting while you leave him;
   b Remain sitting while you are away from him, in or out of sight;
   c Remain sitting while you return to him;
3 Remain sitting at your left side until released.

The initial element (1) of having your dog sit at your left side has already been described and should be fully accomplished before commencing the STAY exercise. However, during the teaching of the various foundation exercises the sit to verbal instruction without physical assistance will require to be developed.

It is now important that your dog will stay sitting for as long a period as you require. In the competitive field of work dogs are not asked to stay sitting for a period much in excess of two minutes. The conditions may vary from the handler being only five yards away from the dog and facing him to walking quite a distance and going out of sight. There can also, on occasions, be distractions of a severe nature which can cause a dog to break from the stay position.

It is, therefore, essential that you start by creating an attitude within the dog of trust and stability.

Sit your dog and stand straddled over him so that you are facing in the same direction. Avoid touching his body with your legs, but your hands can be positioned so that you can fondle your dog's neck as required to give him reassurance or to ensure that you are in a position to prevent movement at the appropriate times.

When your dog is sitting without physical contact with yourself give him gentle praise with 'That's a good boy' to let him know that you are pleased with him. The use of this praise may induce a change of position. Any change must be anticipated and stopped. If he is allowed to stand up or lie down you have failed to act with urgency or purpose.

Control at this early stage is very important, and the best way of achieving this control is to create situations which are a little beyond his capabilities while you are in a position to PREVENT undesirable movement. The gentle praise can, therefore, be increased gradually to that of great excitement for staying. Any attempt to move must be countered by voice and if necessary by holding him by the scruff of his neck or/and putting your knees

Standing straddled for a SIT/STAY.

Standing straddled over dog in earliest stage of SIT/STAY.

together to prevent him from standing. Praise and prevention are essential at this stage to create the stability which will be required for more advanced training.

When you are confident that your dog will accept excited praise without any thought of moving you can consider walking round him while he sits at the end of the lead. Move round him during this period but verbally instruct your dog with 'Stay, son' in a gentle tone of voice and follow at times with gentle praise: 'That's a good boy'. On other occasions apply more enthusiastic praise but be prepared to verbally stop your dog from moving.

In training for any of the stay exercises it is important to recognize that the dog's name is never used until completion. Your dog's name is an attention-getter and it can cause confusion to use it at the incorrect time. Visual signals have great value and a show of the flat of your hand along with the verbal instruction will induce stability. However, hand signals must be carried out where the dog can see them. Dogs that cannot see signals cannot interpret their meaning.

Maintaining the SIT / STAY while moving round.

Even at this early stage the finish of the exercise is very important and dogs should not be allowed to relax and change position without a positive and meaningful instruction. Always go back and stand at your dog's right side (dog on your left) for a few seconds before giving an excited and positive 'OK, son' as you take a step to your right to release him from the stay.

Distance and time away from your dog requires patience, with a slow build up to give your dog the confidence of knowing that you will go back to him and also to give yourself the confidence of his ability to stay under more exacting conditions. A continuation of praise while he is staying is advisable, the measure of excitement in your voice to be tempered by his ability to accept it without moving.

A build-up of distance to about twenty paces from your dog should be adequate and a build-up of time to two minutes should also be sufficient. Out of sight can now be brought into the routine but again the periods that you go out of his sight should be increased gradually. Until you are fully confident your dog should never be out of your sight although he will be unable to see you.

Recall

The basic elements. Dog to:

1 Sit at your left side;
2 a Stay sitting while you leave him;
  b Remain sitting while you are away from him;
3 Come to you when called;
4 Sit in front of you;
5 a Go round to heel when instructed and sit;
  b Stay sitting at your left side until released.

The training described in this chapter to date has covered a substantial portion of the recall exercise. In fact, all elements have been covered although the recall in itself (3) has only been performed as a means of control rather than part of a complete exercise.

We can start to coordinate the various elements in a manner which would satisfy the requirements of the exercise in full. We do not, at this stage, require to perfect elements (1) and (2) which are the stay parts of the exercise. These can be introduced at a time which will not cause canine confusion. That is to call him from a sit position while you are at the earlier stages of teaching your dog to stay. This is quite often the cause of unstable stay situations.

Initial training can be carried out while the dog is free and off the lead. The call of his name will obtain his attention and the immediate follow up of the call to come back to you is a continuation of the earlier requirements. Give verbal and visual assistance with encouragement and guidance to have your dog come straight in front of you. If necessary move backwards and display the plastic bag of titbits as described to achieve the SIT IN FRONT element. Reward your dog in that sit position then complete the ROUND TO HEEL and follow up with a further reward.

Use titbits as and when required to achieve the desired results but progression with the training routine should ensure compliance with your requirements without the need to make continual use of titbits. However, never be frightened to return to this form of inducement if it is felt that your dog's performance warrants such an action.

Training from the stay position can now be undertaken to complete the programme. By this stage you will have created a good, sound SIT/STAY exercise and now wish to create a controlled break from the stay. It is possible that your dog is so good and solid with his SIT/STAY that it may be difficult to have him break when instructed. This is an excellent situation and easy to overcome, but it must be carried out in a manner which will not create instability on the stay exercise.

Consider that your basic recall distance will be from fifteen to twenty paces. When leaving your dog during the SIT/STAY exercise you have used the flat of your hand in front of the dog's face and the instruction to STAY. When leaving your dog for the recall again use the flat of your hand, but changing the verbal instruction to 'Wait, that's a good boy, wait' will let your dog know whether you will be coming back or calling him to you.

Walk away the twenty paces or so, face your dog and, if you feel it to be advisable in the earlier stages, reinforce your instruction with a gentle 'Wait, son'. Walk towards your dog until you are about five paces from him. Stop, chat to him, then call him to you as you move backwards very smartly. When you are happy that he has moved nicely and is positioned in front of you stop as for the SIT IN FRONT element, then complete the exercise with the ROUND TO HEEL.

Recall by hand signal.

1 Sit at your left side;
2 Walk at heel;
3 Sit at your left side when you halt.

The training for loose lead walking is the foundation of competitive heel work, which will be described at a later stage, but, more importantly, it is a necessity for every day of life with a German Shepherd.

One of the most common problems to be encountered by the various owners with whom I have been involved is that of a dog which does not react satisfactorily to lead control. So many dogs pull their owners at will, either straight in the intended direction or to the nearest gate post that takes their fancy. It is very unusual to find a German Shepherd which lags behind unless it is getting on in years or a strict heelwork training routine has been incorrectly applied.

Basic training for loose lead walking has already been described under the section on BASIS FOR CONTROL. In that section you have been instructed on your movements to obtain and maintain your dog's attention. This is the development and continuation of forward and backward movement with your dog on the lead to keep his attention on you.

The execution of right, left and about turns which are commonly associated with this type of training can be left for the precise heelwork routine which will be described at a later stage. You just wish to have your dog walking nicely by your side on a loose lead.

During training, lead control is very important and the details given on pages 47–48 should be applied. Lead handling with a trained dog can create a much more relaxed approach.

Now to the continuation of the section on BASIS FOR CONTROL where you have

Continue this training but when you move towards your dog increase the distance between yourself and your dog before calling him. Eventually you will walk away the twenty paces or so, about turn, then call your dog. By this time your dog will understand the routine and should be competent in both the SIT/STAY and RECALL exercises.

Loose Lead Walking

The basic elements. Dog to:

developed the flowing backward movement with your dog following you and watching for a sudden change of direction, then the forward movement to pass on your dog's left side so that he can turn and fall in to the heel-walking position at your left side. Initial encouragement to remain at your left side while walking, with 'Heel, son, that's a good boy', should be part of the routine and any indication of distraction or deviation must immediately be countered by the sudden backward movement to regain his attention. When this has been fully attained there can be a return to forward movement.

A continuation of this process will achieve the desired attention to ensure that your dog remains by your side. The sit at your left side is not an essential element for loose lead walking although the added control is of value. Your dog has already been taught to sit at your side quite separately and during the attention-getting training routine. Loose lead walking is just an extension of this routine and the sit when you stop can be applied with the appropriate instruction to sit. Initially, physical assistance as described on page 51 may be required until the routine has been established.

You may now wish to have your dog sit on occasions prior to loose lead walking and, again, verbal instruction with or without physical assistance can be introduced. However, when stepping out from a stationary situation, it is important to get your dog's attention immediately prior to moving off. A smart 'Good boy' (or his name) and as soon as he looks at you step forward with your left foot and use the encouraging but positive 'Heel, son, good boy'.

Lead handling of a trained dog can create a more relaxed attitude and approach. When you are satisfied that your dog can walk nicely at your left side without the need to apply backward movement to maintain attention you may find it more convenient to hold the lead in your left hand. It may also be advisable to minimize the amount of slack lead between yourself and your dog. If there is just sufficient lead in use to create a minimum of slackness for comfort your dog will realize that any excess movement out of line will cause a tightening of the slip collar. This can help to give your dog a greater sense of responsibility.

One convenient and effective method of holding the lead in the left hand is to slip two or three fingers into the loop at the end of the lead, leaving your thumb and index finger free to control your use of the lead. Let the rest of the lead drop, then assess the length you wish to work with. Loop the lead over your hand so that you are holding it between your thumb and index finger. This is the point of control with the desired length of lead between your hand and the dog's collar.

Use of the Halti for Loose Lead Walking

The Halti is a form of head harness which controls the dog's actions via the lead attached to a ring on the harness positioned under the dog's muzzle. Dogs are very sensitive to control and will not pull on the lead when attached to the Halti.

There are many people in the world of dog training who believe that the use of the Halti is an admission of defeat. In other words 'If you cannot train a dog, use a Halti'. To some extent I sympathize with these sentiments. There are very few dogs of any breed which are unmanageable when control is applied with the conventional lead and collar.

However, the use of the Halti does make it much easier with more difficult dogs. I have only met one dog which required a Halti but have advised quite a number of dog owners to use it and have often instructed on its use.

It is not a matter of shame for any dog owner to recognize that a situation has developed where he cannot control his dog by the normally accepted practices. Many dogs are allowed to develop the determination which cannot be countered by their owners and the fate of the dog can be determined by the decision to use, or not to use the Halti. I have seen young mothers with a child in a pram and a pulling dog on the lead. Most of these mothers cannot cope with both and the use of the Halti can turn a very disagreeable situation into a very pleasant family outing. The day may come when the Halti becomes a standard means of control for the domestic pet dog.

However, in the meantime it can be recognized that the use of the Halti is a good interim measure which can be applied whilst out walking your dog when you wish to be free from continual attention to loose lead walking.

With the lead kept short so that the dog must walk by your side the Halti will prevent pulling. During the same period daily training sessions using the conventional collar can be applied when attention-getting is utilized along with the strictly controlled loose lead walking already described in this section.

This temporary use of the Halti will allow you freedom to enjoy casual walks and prevent loss of the effects of the strict training sessions. Your dog can become accustomed to walking by your side much

HALTI fitted and ready.

more quickly with the conventional collar than would otherwise be possible.

The Retrieve – The Principles

If all dogs could have the carrying instinct of the working Labradors, Golden Retrievers and Spaniels, dog training would be so much simpler. They seem to be the most natural dogs for carrying and delivering to hand. No gamekeeper is going to waste his time teaching a dog to bring to hand if he can breed from 'natural' stock.

A natural carrier for retrieving.

To pick up and carry is the most natural action for any dog. How else could he take a treasured bone to bed? In days gone by, a dog would carry excess food and bury it for another meal.

There is a big difference between having a dog who will pick up and carry and one who will bring to hand. Although it is natural for a dog to carry when he sees the need it is not so natural to give. The instinct to carry is the instinct to keep and dogs in the wild soon learn to be protective over their possessions. Domestic canines, however, learn that their human friends are prepared to share and will give to hand when they fully understand that this is part of an enjoyable game.

A puppy tossing a ball in the air on his own might be imagining that it is a live mouse and he is having fun with it before the final kill. No wonder we have problems when we expect a dog to return immediately he has the retrieve article in his mouth.

Possesive Trait (Ps)	Submissive Trait (Sb)
strong (s)	strong (s)
weak (w)	weak (w)

	Ps	Sb
	s	s

situation A

	Ps	Sb
	w	w

situation B

	Ps	Sb
	s	
		w

situation C

	Ps	Sb
		s
	w	

situation D

The retrieve matrix.

It is easy to develop retrieving faults and at times difficult to appreciate their existence until they have a good hold. The full understanding of retrieve training is held within the RETRIEVE MATRIX and this is based on two of the principal canine traits, those of POSSESSIVENESS and SUBMISSIVENESS.

Each dog has his natural level of either trait, from very strong in some dogs to very weak in others. It is the combination of these strengths which governs our progress in retrieve training.

A strong possessive trait should result in a dog having a very keen natural desire to go after a ball or other suitable article. However, a dog who is weak in this trait will require to be suitably induced to realize the pleasures of controlled possessiveness.

A strong submissive trait will result in an easy recall unless unsympathetic handling has created apprehension or fear and the negation of a natural response. A weak submissive trait will undoubtedly result in a very independent dog unless this factor is properly controlled.

Therefore, we have four combinations within the matrix to give us a variety of basic training situations.

Situation A – The combination of two strong traits creates the easiest training conditions where the strong possessive trait ensures a natural desire to go out and take possession of the article and the strong submissive trait ensures an immediate return on the call.

Situation B – This combination of two

weak traits will create a situation where great patience will be required, with the timing and introduction of each training element being controlled to assure success. Here we have a dog with no desire to go out for the article and, when he has been induced to go out, will become too independent to return unless the handler has overcome the conflict-of-interests situation.

Situation C – The strength of possessiveness will achieve an enthusiastic run out for the article and simplify the initial training but the problems in handling the uncontrolled independent dog require to be tackled and cured before any further progress can be made. The failure to recognize this situation is often witnessed when a dog can be seen to run out for a thrown article and then run away to find his own form of amusement with his toy.

Situation D – As with Situation B the initial problem is to build up sufficient enthusiasm to carry the dog through the more difficult retrieve-based exercises which lie ahead. The time and effort put into a weak possessive trait will be well rewarded by the ease with which the strong submissive trait will fall into place.

The problems we see regularly with dogs who refuse to retrieve, or play up when they pick up their article, are generally due to a lack of understanding by the handler of the principal canine traits which affect this exercise.

The strengths or weaknesses of these principal traits may well be inherited, but environment can influence the situation enormously. A young dog who has spent an extended puppyhood in breeding kennels may not know how to enjoy the fun and games which can be had with toys of his own, especially when the owner is not prepared to play with him. A forced method used in the early stages of training can give the impression of weakness instead of a strong possessive trait. There can be many man-made reasons for failing to achieve a happy and responsive retrieving dog.

Man-made reasons for retrieving failures can be more difficult and time consuming to rectify than a straightforward programme used to train a dog from scratch.

A Training Technique

Before asking a dog to retrieve and give to hand he must be sound on the recall. He must also be capable of and reliable at picking up, holding and carrying the article, then releasing it into your hand when asked.

The recall element has already been covered but the full breakdown of training elements can be given:

1 Take, hold, then carry the article.
2 Pick up and present to hand.
3 Go out, pick up and return.

Many puppies are happy to take an article from their handler and carry it around, but quite a number of puppies become troublesome because a forceful approach has been applied to make the youngster return and give the article to hand. Puppies or dogs with this natural aptitude should be coaxed along to carry and have fun but never asked to return with the article until the recall has been consolidated, to avoid 'a clash of interests'.

The same basic approach for retrieve training can be applied to all dogs but progress through the various stages will differ tremendously. Some dogs with the most advantageous strength in the principal traits, the most suitable upbringing and an intelligent handler can accomplish the objective with the minimum training. Others who are not so fortunate may seem to take a lifetime.

Take, Hold, then Carry the Article

The article used during the initial training in this element is your index finger. Any puppy or dog should become familiar with your finger massaging his gums and be quite happy to accept your finger in his mouth. No owner is worthy of a dog if he cannot carry out this function without being bitten.

With your dog sitting, straddle him so that you are both facing in the same direction, show your affection by stroking his cheeks and place your index finger behind his canines. With your thumb over his muzzle and your fingers under his lower jaw hold his mouth shut. Give gentle praise, stroke his cheeks and ask him to 'Hold', but restrict this action to about three or four seconds during the first few occasions. Do not overdo it and do not lengthen the holding periods until he is happy to accept this procedure.

You are always in a position to know if there is any loose skin from the upper or lower lips being trapped by the finger and this should be released before any pressure is applied. Any attempt to apply excessive pressure when holding the dog's muzzle will hurt you long before it has any effect on your dog. When you wish to remove your finger release your grip over his muzzle and, as he opens his mouth to release the index finger, ask him to 'Give'.

It will not take him long to realize that

Holding the index finger.

your index finger behind his canines is quite an acceptable experience and he will hold without any pressure being applied to keep his mouth shut. Each time you put your finger in his mouth use a gentle 'Hold' as you praise and stroke him. Make sure the experience becomes a pleasant one but be ready to hold his mouth shut if he thinks of opening it before you ask him to give your finger back.

When you are perfectly happy with your dog's acceptance of this procedure prepare to teach him to carry your finger. Stand in front of your dog (he may be sitting or standing) and get him to hold your index finger again. With your thumb over his muzzle and the remaining fingers under his lower jaw encourage him to walk with you as you move backwards. Keep asking him to hold, encourage him and on occasions pull against his canines but make sure he does not open his mouth. Let him release your finger only when you are ready and request it.

The sensitivity of your finger prevents you from applying excess pressure when holding your dog's mouth shut and this ensures a gentle, considerate approach to the rudiments of retrieve training.

During this period of training you are in a position to control your dog's actions. If he is going to reject your finger you have the means of preventing it. You will be able to sense his actions much more quickly than if using some other object. You are in a position to comfort by stroking his cheeks and yet apply the correct amount of pressure as and when it is required with the knowledge that you cannot be hurting him.

Progress depends to a great extent on your approach and the dog's readiness to accept your actions. Dogs who have already been trained to retrieve but have mouthing problems or are reluctant to release the article can be trained by using this method.

The next stage is to use a suitable replacement for your index finger. A suitable folded sock, to make about four to five inches in length, or a glove, is probably the answer. Again it is preferable to straddle your dog so that you are both facing the same direction, and put the article in his mouth whilst you ask him to hold it. Praise and stroking his cheeks will help to dispel any anxiety.

Transfer from holding finger to a sock.

You will probably find that he will accept the change of 'article' and prove that the groundwork with your index finger has been worthwhile. You can then stand in front of him and with one hand under his chin get him to follow as you move backwards.

Keep the training sessions short and make sure he does not get bored. It should not take him long to realize there is great pleasure in strutting round with an article in his mouth.

When you have full confidence that your dog wants to walk round holding the article run away and call him to you. Get him excited but prepare to use a firm 'Hold' if he thinks of mouthing, chewing or even dropping the article. You may wish to carry out the initial part of this training whilst the dog is on the lead.

It is only when he holds with excitement that you can consider enticing him to take the article from you as you tease him with it. Having done this successfully on a few occasions you can 'accidentally' drop the article as he tries to grab it from you. In the excitement he should be ready to pick up the article and carry it as you induce the recall whilst moving away from him.

This is a critical stage in the training programme and it is important that he picks up from the 'accidental' drop before progressing to the next element.

Pick up and Present to Hand

The pick up should now be consolidated by dropping the article and on occasions by kicking it around to increase the dog's desire to get hold of it.

As he has been taught to hold and carry until you take the article from him there should not be any problems in getting him to present to hand although the excitement may have made your dog forget. If this happens it may be good policy to put him on the lead for a short spell to bring his mind back to the initial recall training element. Again, one hundred per cent success is required before considering instructions to go out and fetch.

Go out, Pick up and Return

The sight of the training article should now be sufficient to excite your dog and a short throw can be tried. Dogs with a strong response to the recall may find the excitement of a longer throw more to their liking. As soon as the dog picks up the article, revert to the recall procedure as you move backwards to bring him back as fast as possible.

Verbal instructions to 'Fetch it' are not necessary at this juncture. It is the desire to get the article which takes the dog out and not the command. The use of verbal instructions at this stage can result in a commanding voice which may put the dog off. When the verbal instruction is used it should be in a form of an excited request rather than a formal command. He can then learn the meaning of the phrase 'Fetch it' after he knows how to perform the act. A command, instruction or request verbally given to a dog means nothing until he knows how to perform the act.

When the pick up, hold, carry and deliver to hand is to your satisfaction the extended throw can then be developed so that your dog will go out any distance to pick up and return to you.

Your approach to date has created a situation of anticipation. It is more important to build up a keen desire to get the article and come straight back with it than to make him stay by your side and await a command. Running out before being verbally released to retrieve can be corrected at the next stage in training.

You can now teach your dog to sit and wait before release to go out and retrieve the article you have just thrown. Take a piece of cord seven to nine inches long and tie a knot to give a loop. Fix the loop through his collar in a manner which will not create a check action. Put your fingers through the loop and hold – this is the start of physical restraint whilst exciting him to go out when you have thrown the article. You then release your hold as you request him to fetch the article.

When your dog is accustomed to this approach and really enjoys his retrieve you can make him sit and keep him sitting until you release him to go out after the article. You have built up quite a reserve of enthusiasm and you can now start drawing on it with your more forceful approach in making him stay until you are ready to release him.

Eventually you can keep your fingers crooked in the loop attached to his collar and the time will not be so far off when he understands that he should sit and wait for the verbal release to go out and fetch your article. This will take a little time but the enthusiasm you have built in to the exercise will be rewarded during the stages of advanced training which have yet to come.

To sit in front of you on his return with the article is simply a development of the recall exercise, and your dog has been taught to hold the article until you take it from him.

The round to heel at the completion of the exercise is also part of the recall and these elements should be handled without any difficulty.

Chapters 3 and 4 are probably the most important in this book for owners who wish to develop into the field of competition. Without a proper understanding of the approach to training and a successful application of the foundation exercises the more advanced work will not be tackled in a manner which will achieve an efficient or successful conclusion.

At this stage many handlers are thinking of entering competitions, probably only at club level where much friendly advice will be given. Unfortunately much of this will be of a sympathetic nature, consoling the handler on the marks the dog has lost during his workout.

Many handlers are encouraged to enter competitions before they are ready. This can be a bad thing, but on the other hand if the handler is sensible and makes use of the occasion to gain experience, and applies constructive self-analysis after the event, he will feel greater satisfaction than he would have done by accepting sympathy for a so-called failure.

I would like to give an example of critical self-analysis after a competition. This was with Taurus in the C.D. Stake at Scarborough some years ago, when we had a 'field day'. Having qualified Taurus U.D.Ex. at the same trials and feeling very full of myself, I went in to do the C.D. work. The marking was as follows:

	Possible	Actual
Heel on lead	5	5
Heel Free	15	14
Send Away	10	9½
Recall	10	10
Sit/Stay	10	10
Down/Stay	10	10
Retrieve	10	9
Search	10	10
Scale Jump	10	10
Long Jump	5	2½
Clear Jump	5	2½
	100	92½

For the total loss of 7½ marks, who was to blame? If we go through the marks lost we can break it down and discover the main culprit.

Heel free: 14 out of 15 is good by any trials standard and I think we can share the responsibility. Send away: this was a beautiful send away, but being a little bit uncertain about his enthusiasm to do the full distance required that day I gave a little encouragement, which lost me the half mark – that was my loss. Retrieve: this was a beautiful retrieve, straight out, good clean pick up and straight back until he was two yards from me, when he stopped and dropped the dumb-bell. With one word he picked up the dumb-bell for a nice finish. Stupid dog – until we think back. He had already carried out a perfect retrieve in the U.D. Stake and this fellow was accustomed to a little encouragement in training. With a second retrieve that day without any encouragement he stopped and, thinking that there was something wrong, he dropped his dumbbell – proof that we had not consolidated on this exercise. Long Jump: as the jumps were set rather close to each other, I had witnessed one dog go for the Scale Jump when being sent out for the Long Jump. I could well imagine Taurus doing the same thing so I cut his run-up to the Long Jump. This was obviously too much, and he failed to clear. A second attempt proved to be no problem. Clear Jump: I was a little off-hand and let him go before we were ready. He failed to take the jump cleanly and knocked it flying. Again with the proper approach the second attempt was no problem and Taurus cleared it beautifully.

Therefore, out of the 7½ marks lost I was directly responsible for the loss of 5½ marks on the day, and I think we can put the other two marks lost down to lack of experience as a team. Still, we finished third and with another piece of experience behind us.

The only point I wish to bring home with this example is that handlers must be prepared to apply self-criticism before considering the dog to be at fault.

CHAPTER 5

Control Group of Exercises

General

The tests within the Kennel Club Regulations for Working Trials (I) and for Obedience Competitions (G) are given in Chapter 13. They were up to date at time of printing, but although the nature of the tests change very little over the years it is suggested that intending competitors obtain a current copy before entering any trials or shows. The full regulations should be read and digested very carefully.

As this section covers both working trials and obedience competitions, the training approach for any exercise will be given to suit the particular branch that requires the greatest depth, and it will be evident that certain exercises are for one branch of work only.

Before going into the training for the various control exercises, I feel it would be appropriate to quote from both the Working Trials and Obedience Regulations regarding handling.

Working Trial Regulations Regarding Handling

'A person handling a dog may speak, whistle or work it by hand signals as he wishes, but he can be called to order by the Judge or Judges for making unnecessary noise, and if he persists in doing so the Judge or Judges can disqualify the dog. No person shall carry out punitive correction or harsh handling of the dog.'

Obedience Regulations Regarding Handling.

'In all classes the dog should work in a happy natural manner and prime consideration should be given to judging the dog and handler as a team.'

My aim in this chapter is to continue the approach to training which will achieve results in keeping with the above requirements.

Heel Work – On and Off Lead

Basic loose lead walking is the foundation for good, competitive heel work and the objective required for loose lead walking in the previous chapter must be achieved before serious consideration is given to heel work.

Obedience competitions require a degree of precision which is extremely demanding on both dog and handler. Although working trials heel work does not demand such a precise approach many competitors have regretted their relaxed attitude when training for this exercise. In working trials it is so easy to lose marks on control exercises that every half mark can be vital to gaining a qualification at 'the end of the day.

However, it must be recognized that training for heel work can create a situation where the handler completely dominates the dog's behaviour. He can be overbearing and ruthless to the extreme and finish up with a first-class heel worker but with a dog of broken spirit. Although few handlers go as far as that there are degrees of dominance which affect the dog's approach to other and more independent exercises.

Let us consider the handler who has achieved apparent success by the overbearing and ruthless approach to heel work. A foundation has now been laid for this type of approach. This handler tends to believe that he has mastered his dog, and by a domineering method. He reckons that he can continue to teach the other exercises in the same manner. If he fails to meet with the success expected, then with each session of failure he reverts to heel work to restore the absolute control that he has mastered. It is the exercise he can do 'well'. This excessive heel work training inhibits the handler and dog to the extent that they are incapable of advancing to some of the more independent exercises. Handler and dog are so conditioned that every move is carried out to strict commands.

I have described an extreme condition that can be created by an obsession with heel work. It does happen, and to an extent that warrants a good hard look at the generally accepted training methods. This situation becomes very apparent when some obedience enthusiasts decide

to train for or enter working trials. It has been known for a dog to run into the long jump because he was too busy watching his handler. The handler had no idea how to condition the dog to become independent enough to see the jump. Tracking is another occasion which shows up excessive heel work control. The dog thinks that the tracking line is just a long lead and waits for commands, instructions, tugs and pulls to tell him he is right or wrong.

I remember one occasion when three obedience Class C workers were entered in a U.D. working trials stake and each one showed the effect of excessive obedience control. They were all top-flight obedience workers, but complete domination had killed any independence and initiative. As the handlers knew the starting direction of the track, they verbally pushed the dogs in the right direction. However, the dogs and handlers got completely lost before reaching the first corner. These same dogs gave a faultless display of heel work, gaining the full five out of five marks allotted to the test, but they lost practically every mark out of the 110 allotted for the track.

There are, however, dogs on record that were top-flight obedience workers who also retained their independence and initiative and proved themselves in the working trials field. This was only achieved because the handlers maintained a more appropriate balance between strict obedience control and the independent initiative that is required for a good working trials team.

Object of the Exercise
To have your dog walking close to and level with your left leg; he should be paying absolute attention to your movements, to ensure that he maintains the close to leg

Heel work with a very attentive German Shepherd.

position when you turn sharply to the right, left and about turn. He should also be prepared to move off from a sit position and also sit immediately you halt.

The precise and absolute attention you require from your dog is dependent on your own requirements. Your dog should always be capable of maintaining a satisfactory performance whilst on/off the lead.

The basic elements. Dog to:

1 Sit at your left side and await the instruction to move forward;
2 a Move with you promptly as you step forward and maintain the heel position;
  b Respond immediately to each sharp right, left or about turn;

3 Sit immediately at heel when you halt and remain in that position to await further heel work or release from the exercise.

As loose lead walking has been achieved through the training described in Chapter 4 we only require to develop the following:

1 Precision with lengthy periods of absolute attention.
2 The mastering of right, left and about turns.

We should now recap on the principal factor relating to the basis for control, recall and loose lead walking, i.e. to get your dog's attention, keep it and make use of it. Any failure in this basic foundation principle will certainly become evident during precise and lengthy heel work training.

It is, therefore, important that at the start of, or during, any training session the attention-getting routine should be applied in a manner which is appropriate to the stage of training.

It should also be adopted during a training heel work round when the slightest indication of inattention is noted. During 'heel free' training sessions the same form of attention-getting applies without reverting to lead control. In the earlier stages of 'heel free' a return to the use of the lead may well be required to ensure that full attention is attained.

Attention-getting can be performed with the stimulation of full verbal encouragement and visual signals from hands, arms and body along with use of titbits or toys, but at the end of the day the backward and forward routine without verbal assistance and only the minimal use of visual reinforcement is the real answer for sustained attention in advanced heel work routines.

Lead control in training is identical to that of loose lead walking but the minimum length of lead between dog and handler must be achieved in training. This minimum length, however, must be accomplished without any continuous tension on the dog's neck.

While walking with the lead both arms should be reasonably straight with each hand in front of the respective leg, and six or seven inches of lead between each hand is sufficient. Whilst walking each hand should be firmly against your legs and any use of the check collar can be applied via a twist of your left wrist and a sharp stop or backward body movement. This ensures the sharpness which cannot be attained through arm and shoulder movement for close work. When there is a need for continued backward movement the short check can be followed by the dropping of the lead except for the loop which is in the right hand. You have actually reverted to the attention-getting routine.

Periods of heel work should be built upon success. Up to the novice stage of obedience verbal encouragement is in order, but beyond this stage periods without verbal control or apparent inducements must be attained. Initially ten seconds of concentrated heel work is sufficient with a build-up to thirty seconds within each unbroken session. The occasional halt with continued attention does not constitute a break within my term of an unbroken session.

Corners and About Turns

Cornering should be carried out without any apparent loss of pace and, although the same may be said for about turns, it is difficult to imagine these being executed without remaining on the same spot whilst the direction is changed. It is, therefore, important to create a flowing movement and in a manner which assists rather than hampers your dog.

The factors which help to achieve smart close turns relative to your own footwork can be taken as follows.

1 A couple of short steps into and out of each turn. This helps to maintain closer attention from your dog by way of changed movements.
2 Positioning and pivoting of feet on each turn. The ball of your foot becomes the important point of pivot.

Footwork for turns.

Right Turns – The final step is with your right leg forward and your right foot turned out to the right as it touches the ground. The left foot can then be brought round and placed in line with the new direction. This allows the right foot to pivot before stepping out in the new direction.

Left Turns – The same process takes place but the final step is with your left leg and the left foot turned out to the left as it touches the ground. The right foot can then be brought round and placed in line with the new direction. This allows the left foot to pivot before stepping out in the new direction.

About Turns – The final step is with your right leg and with the right foot turned out to the right as far as comfort allows as it touches the ground. As your left leg comes close to the right a greater pivot of the right foot is required to complete the full turn.

These movements require practice and should be properly executed in practical sessions without the dog at your side before introducing them to the heel work routine.

Although footwork is important and should be applied in an effective manner on all turns your attitude towards your dog must not be neglected.

The right turn requires a quicker canine movement to ensure that a speedy response is attained. Left turn actions require a momentary pause from the dog while you turn into his path of movement. A slight but positive check on the lead as you turn will create that pause; this of course should be accompanied initially by a verbal attention-getting warning that you are going to turn. The use of your dog's name should be sufficient and, as you both become more proficient, the check can be stopped and a continued satisfactory performance can eliminate the verbal warning.

Good, tight and smart about turns lead to equally good right turns and it may be advisable to perfect about turns before considering right turns. Tightness and speed on about turns can be attained by taking your own body out of the dog's way and allowing him to make the tightest possible turn. This approach can be applied during basic training and at any later stage if tightness is lost.

When you decide to make the about turn change your own movement from forwards to quickly backwards with an urgent instruction for your dog to follow. If necessary give a short, sharp jerk on the lead as you give encouragement to follow you at speed. Your backward movement should take you between two and five paces. When you feel that he is fully attentive and with you, turn to carry on in the same direction as your dog so that he is now in the heel position for a continuation of your heel work routine. Good about turns in the proper manner should help to ensure good right turns.

It should be recognized that a dog learns to control our actions if you carry out the heel work to suit his pace. If you go slowly because it suits him or if you go fast to keep up with him you will never be able to control his pace. Creating variations in pace is very important.

Change of Pace

Although fast- and slow-pace heel work is required for more advanced competitions it is very useful to apply changes in pace from the earlier stages of training, and in their own way both paces create situations for attentiveness.

A fast pace keeps a dog lively and short bursts from time to time should create an enjoyable reaction, although encouragement should be applied in a manner which will suit the dog. Too much encouragement can cause uncontrolled excitement and this should be avoided.

Heel work at a slow pace gives a dog time to think about distractions, but it also gives the handler more time to concentrate on his dog's reactions. Short sessions of slow pace with periods of right, left and about turns can keep a dog very attentive. Build up with variations of speed and this can prevent boredom from affecting your own and your dog's performance.

Heel Free

Heel free is built on sound, attentive lead work, but sound heel on lead is not sufficient to ensure the type of performance which is required for competitive situations. The ability to apply the attention-getting routine without the use of the lead should also be considered an invaluable aid to a sound heel free performance.

Everything which has already been described about attention-getting and heel on lead applies to heel free, but periods of heel free training should be built up slowly and in conjunction with a good standard of heel on lead.

With some dogs, and particularly with adaptable handlers, heel free can be introduced at an early stage of training. However, any indication of faults must be countered as soon as they become evident. This may well mean a return to lead work or reintroduction of inducements.

Temperament Test

As this is a test and not an exercise, training should not be necessary. In fact, training a dog of unsound temperament to stand up to this test would be against the principal objective of the test.

The least that is expected of a dog is for him to stand his ground whilst the judge approaches from the front and then runs his hand over the dog's back. A dog that will not accept this certainly requires help to lead a less apprehensive life in the outside world, and that concerns me more than being trained to stand up to a temperament test. Almost any dog can be trained to stand firm and accept the approach of strangers, but this does not make him at ease in their presence. A dog who normally reacts with uncertainty needs to be conditioned into a more friendly state of mind to accept the world at large. That means introducing him to varying situations that will help in the long run. He requires gradual mixing – to be taken shopping, and to the local training club, where he will get the opportunity to meet people with other dogs. He should not be protected against the outside world but, at the same time, he should not be forced into situations he is not ready for.

One conditioning method that can be of great help is the giving of titbits, especially when the dog is hungry. Always carry titbits with you, then when you meet somebody the dog is uncertain about give them some titbits so that they can entice your dog to them. Let them feed your dog and make real friends. This approach can easily be extended to the training club, where 'doggy' people are more understanding. You can make use of a small number of people, say the same four or five until your dog has more than accepted

Temperament test. Your dog should be accustomed to being handled.

making your dog more socially acceptable and thereby conditioned to the outside environment. He will, however, be suitably at ease and in a state of mind in which the temperament test will not have any effect on him. He will also be temperamentally conditioned to enjoy fully an obedience-showing career.

I have judged dogs that have been 'trained' to withstand a temperament test, but these dogs were not conditioned to be socially acceptable animals. The trainers of these dogs are making a complete farce of the test and the reason for its introduction. I have certainly no intention of describing the training method that would achieve this kind of result.

The Stay Exercises – Sit, Down and Stand

The basic requirement for each of the stay exercises is the same: that the dog should remain in the position instructed and should not move, even on return of the handler, until the judge has indicated that the exercise is finished.

Each of the stay exercises is taught in the same manner, although the final duration of the stay differs with each position. The sit/stay calls for two minutes in that position with the handler out of sight, the down requires ten minutes with handler out of sight, and the stand requires up to two minutes with the handler remaining in sight, although he will normally be required to turn his back towards the dog. Although the stay exercises are very important in themselves, they are also the foundation of many other exercises, such as the agility, advance stand, sit and down, distance control and the send away.

them, is looking for them and going forward to meet them as they approach. When they can approach your dog individually and stroke him at will without the use of titbits you are ready to extend his circle of friends. Add a couple of new ones and start afresh with the titbits. Remember this is more effective with a hungry dog than with a dog that is fed before going to the training club. As this friendliness through titbits will only be taking place during your presence you are in a position to give backing or support to your dog, and this will not affect his guarding instincts in the car or at home.

The approach suggested is not a means of beating the temperament test but one of

Drawing a dog into the STAND position.

With all the stay exercises it is very important that the dog is never allowed to break a stay, either by coming out or by changing position. Hidings or tellings off after the event are of little or no value. Anticipation and prevention on the part of the handler will do a lot more good. A handler can only anticipate movement if he gives total attention to his dog during training for the stays. It is quite common to see handlers at a training club treating the stay exercise as an opportunity to have a good old chat. Then when they are told by the trainer that the dog has moved they tend to take it out on the dog for not obeying the instruction to stay. This, unfortunately, is a very common sight.

Sit / Stay

The basic training for this exercise has already been given in the foundation section. As it is now necessary to build up to two minutes with the handler in or out of sight, it is a good idea to extend the final time in training to a little beyond the two minutes to create a more stable situation. To ask a dog to sit perfectly still for a longer period is not very fair and quite unnecessary. Whilst still at the stage of staying in sight, get some member of the family or friend of the dog to entice the dog gently to get up. He should not use the dog's name or a command but use a sensible approach to tempt your dog to relax from the exercise in hand. At the same time you must tell your dog to stay sitting where he is and make sure that he does not move. During the use of deliberate distractions your dog must not be allowed to move and you must be in a position to ensure that he knows you will note and prevent any tendency to move. When you are certain of your dog's ability to stay you can move out of sight, by which we mean that you are out of his sight, not he out of your sight. Whilst out of sight you can occasionally speak to him to let him know you have not left him. Build up trust; give him full faith in you. He must understand that you will always return to him. As described in the foundation section, always use the same instruction, and the one most suited is 'Sit/Stay'. The stay should mean to him that you will be back for him. If distractions are used when you are out of sight make sure that you are in a position to see exactly what is going on, then anticipate any move and get in quickly with your voice to prevent it.

Down / Stay

The dog must initially be trained to go down and be relaxed before we can consider making him stay for a period.

Initial training should be carried out from the sit position. It is much easier to teach a dog to go down from the sit than from the stand, as putting the dog into the down can be a very submissive situation.

Have your dog sitting at your left side and get down to his level – it may be easier to kneel. Put your left arm over his shoulder so that your left hand is placed behind his left pastern. At the same time put your right hand behind his right pastern and push his front feet forward from underneath him, or just lift his front

Hand signal for DOWN *in preparation for a* STAY.

feet forward so that he will drop onto his chest and at the same time let your own body drop and rest on your left elbow.

Other methods can also be used. A natural method is one of using the verbal and visual indication to go down while the dog is lying down of his own free will. Another approach is by inducement. With food or a favourite toy, get down on the floor beside your dog and when you are kneeling encourage him down by means of the inducement. Food is particularly useful in this instance and the reward can be given as soon as he is down. Any or all of

Putting a dog into the DOWN position by lifting left leg and pushing off balance.

these methods can be used during a training programme until your dog understands your requirements.

The procedure for the stay in the down is identical to that of the sit, but this time you want your dog completely relaxed – he can go to sleep if he wishes. If you want him to stay for ten, fifteen or twenty minutes he must be completely relaxed and again have great faith in your return. Dogs move from the set stay positions for one of three main reasons. They may be:

1 Worried and concerned about something.
2 Bored with the whole procedure.
3 Just not understand the requirements.

As any of these reasons can probably be attributed to the handler's approach they can only be corrected by him giving full consideration to his own general attitude and modifying it to establish a more suitable pattern.

Stand/Stay

It is very unnatural to ask a dog to stand still for one minute. Admittedly you are not asked to go out of sight. Again this exercise is taught in precisely the same manner as the 'sit' and 'down' stay. When you have reached the stage of turning your back on your dog you should still be in a position to watch him for any sign of movement. When you turn your head to watch him he will know and probably stand still, but he may soon learn to make a move when you are not looking. This is easily overcome by the use of a mirror, as you can then keep him in full view the whole of the time your back is turned towards him.

All Stay Exercises

When attending obedience shows and watching handlers give the final command before leaving their dogs in the stay exercises, I sometimes get the impression that most of the dogs must be deaf. Practically every handler seems to shout at the top of his voice commanding the dog to stay. If he is deaf he cannot hear you. If he is not deaf, why shout? If you train for obedience shows or working trials please try to break away from the traditional approach of shouting at the dog who is sitting, standing or lying by your side. It is quite unnecessary.

Class 'A' Recall

The object of the exercise is to ensure that your dog will respond immediately to the call by coming to you whilst you are walking. He should also fall into the heel free situation until you halt.

The recall is also the finish for the send away exercise in Obedience Class 'B' and Class 'C'.

The basic elements. Dog to:

1 Sit at your left side and stay sitting after you have moved away;
2 Come to you when instructed and join you in the heel free situation;
3 Carry out a limited heel free routine with the probability of turns prior to a halt.

The 'A' recall must be considered the easiest exercise to teach in the obedience repertoire, provided that it is based on a good and happy novice recall and good heel work, as it is really just a combination of both exercises.

However, the easiest way of starting the exercise without inhibiting the dog with the stay is to make use of a free recall whilst out for a walk. Call him in with great excitement and encouragement, use a hand signal to slap your side, and see that you are walking away from him as he comes running in. As soon as he reaches your side maintain the control through a dozen or so paces of heel work, halt with the sit as normal and then release him for fun and games. If you carry out this once only during your daily walk it will be surprising how quickly the main part of the 'A' recall has been accomplished.

All that is left to complete the training is to leave the dog at the sit, or down if preferred, walk away with the instruction to wait as with the novice recall, then call him in as before. In the early stages of this final part of training it may well be necessary to turn your head to give him all the encouragement necessary to get him to break the stay.

It is a simple exercise, simply trained, with the minimum of 'obedience' training.

Retrieving the dumb-bell at a nice steady pace.

Retrieve the Dumb-bell

Dogs should not be taught to retrieve with the dumb-bell, but should be taught to retrieve the dumb-bell after they have been instructed in the art of retrieving with basic articles as described in the chapter on foundation training.

I have seen so many handlers who have retrieve problems with the dumb-bell and these problems are generally caused by mistakes which have been made while teaching to retrieve with a dumb-bell. If a mistake is being made while using a basic article it can be disposed of and a new one of a different type can be used instead.

Retrieve training with a novice handler can be full of mistakes. The dumb-bell is essential for competitive work and it is advisable to minimise the risk of dumb-bell problems.

Changing from certain basic articles to the dumb-bell is simple and it is advisable to have the dog accustomed to your chosen basic article before using the dumb-bell. Here are some suggestions.

1 Wooden dowelling can have ends fitted to make up your first dumb-bell after he is happy to retrieve the dowelling on its own.
2 A piece of rubber or plastic tubing which is happily retrieved can be fitted over the centre of the dumb-bell.
3 A folded sock can be tied round the centre of the dumb-bell.

Any of these basic articles can be used for retrieve training and the most suitable can be applied with the dumb-bell for the change over.

Treasure your dumb-bell, it should be the most important piece of equipment to your dog.

Advanced Retrieve

By this we mean the retrieving of any article of reasonable proportions and composition, and it is remarkable what a dog can retrieve if he has the will to carry. I

Taking the dumb-bell when properly presented by the dog.

have had one dog retrieve a bucket full of water, and also a raw egg. I have had great fun with my dogs trying to retrieve an old motor tyre. I did not expect them to retrieve the tyre and did not make them, but every time we found an old tyre on the beach my dogs all enjoyed trying to bring it back to me. I think it gets a lot of frustration out of their system, and they would get most annoyed if I walked away and left them still trying to retrieve it.

The training for advanced retrieving should be a time for relaxed enjoyment, when the dog should be encouraged to pick up any article thrown or even kicked. I just have to kick an empty beer can and the first dog there picks it up. Start it all as fun and games and then on the odd occasions carry out the recall whilst he is running free with the article in his mouth. A good, solid recall is, of course, necessary. When you do call him in he must respond as you would expect with the obedience retrieve. After finishing give him his article back and let him continue with his fun and games. He will soon learn the difference between fun and the need for an immediate and proper response to your instructions. Restrict the strictly controlled recall with an article to possibly two occasions on one outing. During these fun sessions one full obedience retrieve should be included, with particular attention to steadiness. If anticipation does occur repeat the exercise with firmer control and then get back to fun and games.

It would be impossible to go through all the types of article one could expect to get in obedience shows or trials but I have found that a motor car sparking plug, being very heavy for its size, can cause problems, while a rubber balloon, not blown up of course, is very light and at times a dog wonders if he has anything in

A Zimbabwe prison dog in competition.

his mouth. Care should be taken to ensure that nothing is used that will be injurious to the dog.

If your foundation training is up to scratch, any attempt to mouth or chew articles can generally be stopped by the strength of your voice. He may chew whilst he is playing but as soon as you command his attention for a recall then the chewing must stop immediately until he is released from the controlled position.

With this approach to advanced retrieving your dog will respond to any article an obedience or working trials judge may use.

Distance Control

Object of the exercise – to achieve such control that your dog will make six positional changes involving SIT, STAND and DOWN from a distance of up to twenty paces, these changes to be made without appreciable directional movement by your dog. Movement of up to the dog's body length is permitted. Your dog must also remain in the final position until his release after you return to his right side.

The basic elements. Dog to:

1 Take up the starting position at your left side, i.e. sit, stand or down;
2 Stay in that position whilst you walk away, halt and turn to face your dog;
3 Change from a series of selected positions to others when instructed and without appreciable movement;
4 Remain in the final position whilst you return to your dog's right side, and await his release.

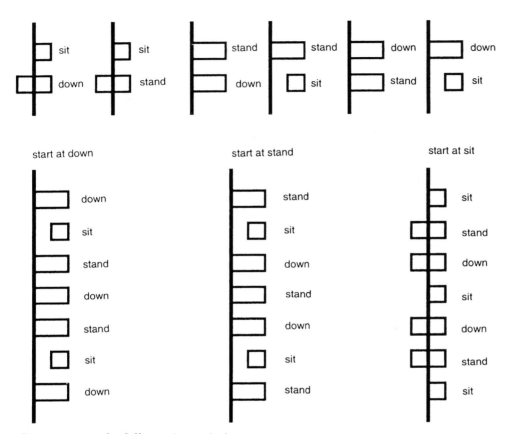

Distance control – full exercise variations.

Distance control is a very unnatural exercise to teach a dog and is probably the least purposeful exercise in the complete obedience routine. Its only value would appear to be to show the amount of precise control that can be achieved at a distance. The working distance is, however, very limited and is controlled by the size of the ring at obedience shows.

With this exercise we must firstly consider how to make it seem natural to the dog and have him enjoy it. If we watch the antics at training classes and also listen to the 'shouting' of commands at obedience shows it is obvious that some dogs do not enjoy it and their joy on completion shows in their relief when it is over. It is treated by some trainers and handlers as a completely submissive exercise, one that requires an overbearing approach where the commands are given in a manner of 'Thou must – or else'. It is quite easy to train a dog in a natural manner to sit, stand or down but quite another matter to obtain the main objective of the exercise.

The important and unnatural part of the exercise is the restriction on forward movement, and it is this restriction on movement by the dog that seems to bring out the worst in some handlers.

To obtain this basic requirement we should forget about the commitment to prevent the front feet from passing the designated point and concentrate our efforts on maintaining the original position of the dog's rear feet. If we can maintain the position of the rear feet of the dog throughout the six positional changes there can be no danger of the front feet moving beyond the designated point on completion of the sixth positional change. If the judge uses all possible changes in position during the six changes the dog will aways finish back in the starting position – i.e. start at sit will finish at sit.

The training about to be described is centred on the sit position, moving into and out of the sit. The method of obtaining these changes in position should be taught as a way of life and become second nature to the dog. If you are contemplating training for Class C Obedience then the approach to achieving the sit, stand or down should start with training for the stay. When positioning the dog for the sit/stay the method should be applied which will achieve the movement required in taking up the position for distance control.

As the dog's area of contact with the ground in the sit position is approximately half that of the down or stand, it is obvious that foot movement is essential to move from the down or stand to the sit position. The most natural method for a

Training for distance control. Hand signal for SIT.

Hand signal for STAND.

dog to employ of his own volition is to draw his haunches towards his front feet as he sits, and then in standing up he will step forward into the stand; this movement alone will cost half a body length. Training should commence using the sit as the main position with movements to the stand and back to the sit, and also down and back to the sit. These positional changes should be performed before advancing to the next stage. The stand to the down and reversed should be left until the other positions are being carried out with immediate response when you are standing no further than about three feet in front of the dog.

Stand / Sit / Stand

The purpose behind this is to get the dog to move his front feet back as he sits on his haunches, and this can be achieved by standing in front of him with your hand under his chin and stepping in to him to assist him gently back into the sit position. Whilst you are doing this tell him to sit and lavish praise on him once it is accomplished. A titbit the instant he sits can be quite a booster and will help to reinforce your praise. Give him ten to fifteen seconds in this position whilst you stroke and praise him.

You want your dog completely relaxed and not worried about being pushed into a submissive position. To change back to the stand change your own position to stand at the side of him and draw him back up into the stand position, if necessary putting your hand under his stomach to help him. There is every possibility that he

Hand signal for DOWN.

will not like this approach, so care must be taken not to make it any more unpleasant than necessary. His front feet will have moved forward into the original stand position, and any slight backward movement of his hind legs can be ignored. Again, when implementing this change of position tell him to stand and give plenty of praise on completion of the positional change. However, do not let him step forward during this praise: a titbit may well be in order, but again beware of forward movement in his desire to obtain the titbit. In the early stages always keep him in the changed position for ten to fifteen seconds with praise and comforting before moving into the next position. Remember that those movements are all being carried out in an unusual manner to the dog, and he should be made perfectly at ease between each stage. Repeat the full process three or four times before going on to some other part of your training programme.

Sit / Down / Sit

It should not be difficult to get a dog to go down from the sit position, since nothing unnatural is being asked of him and he just has to let his front feet slide forward. With a little encouragement and the aid of a titbit to entice him there should not be a problem, although care should be taken to ensure that he does not edge forward. However, I have found that the quickest drops into the down position have been gained by the more forceful method already described in the down/stay training technique.

To go from the down to the sit a titbit can be the best enticement. This time you are standing in front of your dog, pressing forwards with the instruction to sit whilst he is drawn up by the titbit. Without a titbit it will require your hand under his chin to help him back into the sit position.

The four positional changes already described take a bit of time to develop and training should continue until you can get instant response with each change from a distance of about three feet in front of the dog. When you are working from the front of the dog without any need to handle him you should have developed your own body and hand movements to reinforce the verbal instruction as to which position is required. In fact your movements will tell your dog what the next position will be and he can move into it before the verbal instruction is out. When all this becomes natural to him we can now consider teaching the stand to down and reverse.

Stand / Down / Stand

These positional changes can now be tackled whilst standing in front of your dog. He is already accustomed to you standing about three feet in front of him, so you can try to maintain that distance, as it gives him a good chance to assess your movements and anticipate the next change in position. At this stage you wish to take advantage of anticipation. Now put your dog into the stand and position yourself in front of him. Move as if you are to give the sit position and, as he is moving into the sit position, continue your movement and verbal instruction for the down. As he has been well trained to go from the sit to down the continued movement should become automatic. From the down to stand a similar procedure should be adopted.

Move forward as if to give the sit instruction and, as he is moving into the sit position, move back to draw him to stand, giving the verbal instruction at the same time. This approach makes the stand/down/stand positional changes very easy and simple without any need for a demanding or overbearing attitude.

However, it is now necessary to consider the effect of the stand/down/stand training on the stand/sit and down/sit positions. The dog has been conditioned to move right through from stand to down and from down to stand via the sit. When requesting the dog to go into the sit position from the down or stand it will now be necessary to instruct a 'Stay' as he reaches the sit position to prevent a continuation of the movement.

Throughout the training in all changes to the dog's position, your own physical movements have enticed and indicated the changes of position required. Your physical movements have been ahead of your verbal instructions which have acted as a reinforcement to these physical movements. Verbal instructions should now be timed to coincide with your physical movements.

The physical movement of enticement can now be minimized and then eliminated as an indication to the dog of the change of position. The verbal instruction will then become the motivation for the dog to change from one position to another.

Remember after each positional change to take the time and trouble to give him plenty of praise and let him know how clever he has been. Do not move more than three feet from him until complete perfection with immediate response is attained. Only then should you start increasing distance at a slow rate. Even with the increase in distance between yourself and the dog this distance should only be used on occasions, with the bulk of the training to keep in trim being carried out at a distance of three to six feet from the dog.

The diagrams will show the movements from the starting line, or designated point, for each individual change of position and also examples of the complete set of changes throughout the full exercise. The vertical base lines indicate the position of the dog's front feet at the start of the exercise. It will be noted that on occasions the front of the dog does go beyond the designated point but always comes back to the original position, so long as the hind legs are not permitted to move forward.

Advanced Stand/Sit/Down

Object of the Exercise: During a heel free routine at normal pace your dog to stop in the selected positions when instructed and without any change of pace from yourself. Also to regain the heel position when instructed as you pass him, having approached him from behind.

The basic elements. Dog to:

1 Perform normal heel free routine;
2 Stop when instructed and go into the selected position;
3 Regain the heel position;
4 Carry out repeat of (2) and (3) in each position.

Having trained for distance control and a good round of heel work, the introduction of this exercise, to the obedience heel work should not be a problem, but again, like all the other exercises, an easy introduction is essential until the dog fully understands the routine.

During a heel on lead session, stop and indicate to your dog the position required, praise him, tell him to stay and walk away from him. You can either go round in a circle or turn and pass him, turn again and walk back to his side from behind him. Stop, praise him, pick up the lead and walk forward with him at heel. Each time give him the instruction as you stop and ensure he goes immediately into that position before you leave him. When the pattern has been established drop the lead as you give the positional instruction and carry on walking, but look back to ensure he has carried out the instruction correctly and promptly. Do not bother about completing the circuit, go right back and tell him how good and clever he is. When you are quite satisfied with the results remove the lead and repeat the process but carry out the full routine by calling him to heel as you pass him. He will probably lack the understanding at first, so get him excited as you pass and give all the encouragement you can to take up the position at heel.

Send Away

Object of the Exercise:
To have your dog move away from you in a straight line and at a good pace in the direction indicated. On reaching the predetermined location he should go into the nominated position when you give the instruction. He should also remain in this position until that part of the exercise has been terminated.

Competitive obedience – Distance of up to twenty-five yards and to go down at the location can be expected, with a Class 'A' style of recall to complete the exercise.

Preparing a Send Away from the DOWN *position.*

Working trials – Distance of eighty to one hundred yards can normally be expected although distances outside this range have often been experienced. Your dog to stop when instructed and go into the position nominated by yourself.

The basic elements. Dog to:

1 Sit, stand or down at your left side, facing the direction in which he should move away. NOTE: In obedience shows the dog must be sitting;
2 Move out when instructed in the correct direction at a steady or fast pace;
3 Stop immediately he is instructed and go into the nominated position.

NOTE: In obedience shows the dog must go down;
4 Although (3) completes the exercise, in working trials the dog is recalled as in Class 'A' when competing in obedience shows.

The send away can be rather a slow and tedious exercise to teach a dog, especially in working trials, where considerable distances can be expected. As redirects are added to the send away in open stakes for working trials we must give very serious consideration to the approach which is going to create a happy and responsive dog. It should also be appreciated that to

Preparing a send away from the SIT position.

obtain the correct canine attitude we must create a purpose in the dog's mind. Once the habit has been formed and consolidated the reason for wanting to go out can be put into the background and finally eliminated.

Directional control is an additional feature at the end of the send away for open stakes in working trials. Although the instructions for teaching directional control are catered for in the pages which follow the send away, it is often found that handlers try to combine the teaching of the send away and directional control at too early a stage. Care must be taken to avoid this temptation.

My approach to training lends itself to putting the dog down at the end of both the send away and directional control, and the method of training which follows is based on applying that selected position. With

this in mind your dog should be able to give an immediate response to the instruction to go down at any time and within a reasonable distance from yourself, initially up to ten yards. This response should be taught quite separately and prior to send away training.

The most effective inducement to go down when required is generally food. Most dogs respond eagerly to small, juicy and tasty morsels. However, they should be stored in a suitable container, one which can be opened quickly and of a size which can eventually be kept in your pocket.

Three send away markers are also advisable. Pieces of sacking, or an old jacket which can be cut to make more than one marker, will be of value. There will be a time when the inducement – your container of titbits – will require to be hidden under the marker.

You now create the incentive for your dog to go away from you. It is the real desire to go out fast and go down for his reward of food. Initially your dog is taken on the lead to one of the markers; only use one at this stage. As soon as you reach the marker with the container of food on it, he is put down on or right beside the marker. Immediately he 'hits the deck' you produce food and give him a titbit whilst in the down position. Call him up, walk round with him, then return to the marker and drop him again. Immediately open your container and give him another titbit.

At the same time you are giving him plenty of praise every time he goes down at the marker. When he knows that he must drop immediately he is at the marker, and looks at you as much as to say 'Well, I'm waiting, where's the titbit', you are winning. Note that your food container should be of a type that your dog cannot open; we do not wish to have him distracted before he goes into the down position. Continue with this procedure until your dog pulls you to the marker and goes down without instructions. This does not mean that you can leave them out. Just test him by occasionally leaving out the instruction to go down and watch for his reaction.

You will find that he learns very quickly at this stage and a foundation is being built up on something he wants to do. To carry out this training after your dog has been fed for the day will probably have limited success, but to base this procedure on a hungry dog can be very effective. We shall assume that all training is being carried out prior to the main meal of the day.

Although this procedure is based on the use of food, and I do on occasions change to a play toy at a later stage, play toys can be used from the start. However, it is important to ensure that the toy is a strong enough inducement and that your dog is only allowed to play with it after he has gone into the desired position at the send away marker. To achieve this it may be advisable to have the toy in a container and take it out for fun and games on completion of each send away.

When you have reached the stage of having your dog pulling you on the lead to the marker every time, you have the basis for the send away. Now is the time to give him the gentle instruction to 'Go' as he is moving towards the marker. He is going away and does not require an instruction but this is the build up for the instruction which will be necessary at a later date. This is the conditioning process in action. The desire for his reward is strong and he knows that he must drop at the marker before he receives it. When you are com-

pletely satisfied that his desire is strong you can then take him the usual distance from the marker – this should be somewhere between five and ten paces away. Slip the lead and let him go. Again, as he is going, use the instruction 'Go, on you go, son' and 'Down' as he reaches the marker. Follow up and give him his reward – the titbit or the toy. Do not overdo any single session, but stop whilst he is still very keen.

It will now be appreciated that you have conditioned the dog to wish to go out at speed to a place of your choice and immediately go down at that spot. When this has been fully achieved with a great desire to be released to get there you can consider training the send away as an exercise. You therefore continue to put your marker with the container of food on it and continue as before, but instead of releasing him make him stay for a few seconds, facing the direction of the marker and built up for the release, which you accompany with the encouragement to 'Go, on you go, son'. You can make him stay in any position you wish although for obedience competition you will eventually require to make him sit and wait.

At this stage accept your dog's impatience, as you have been building this up and creating it. You can now make further use of the loop of cord attached to the slip collar as with the basic retrieve. It is important to maintain the desire to get out to the chosen area. You are physically restraining your dog and at the same time gently encouraging him with a build up for the release.

Your distance at this stage can be built up to about twenty-five yards and his marker with the container will be in full view. Each time you position your dog before releasing him he is facing directly towards his marker. You are conditioning him to go straight out in the direction he has been facing. It is important that each time you send your dog out, although you may wish to stand still until he is down, you always go out to him and give him his reward from the container.

There is no need at any stage to take time in setting your dog up to go out in a particular direction. Many dogs have been put off by their owners pulling and pushing at their heads to make them face in the direction they wish to be sent. If your conditioning is correct your dog will expect to be going straight out in the direction you position him.

You can now introduce two new factors to your training by changing the direction to the marker. This is done by applying the 'round the clock' technique with the marker as the central point. Distances of twenty to twenty-five yards should be satisfactory. The two new factors when using 'round the clock' techniques are:

1 Changing background without having to move your marker. The confidence of a known base to the dog can be important.
2 The send away without a scent path known to the dog.

After placing your marker send your dog out along the same route, making use of your scent path. Collect your dog and return to the same 'send from' spot, then move round the periphery of an imaginary circle for some ninety degrees. Face your marker and start walking in its direction and watch your dog's head. When you are certain that he has sighted his marker release him with the instruction to 'Go'. You may wish to stop or sit him before releasing him to go to his marker. The choice is yours but it is important that you do not disrupt his attention or take away his enthusiasm. This procedure can be repeated until you have completed the circle.

Now is the time to prepare for the day when his container is not to be left on the marker. You can put the container under a corner of the marker but let your dog see you do it. He therefore knows it will be there when he arrives. When he is accustomed to this and does not expect to see the container you can then keep it in your pocket and only take it out and give him his reward as usual when he is in position at the marker. If you are asking your dog to go forward and then back in training the least you can do is to cover the same distance. It is important to go out to him every time to give him his reward.

Although you are now in the position where it is unnecessary to leave the container at or under the marker you should be prepared to leave it at the marker on occasions to bolster any flagging of enthusiasm.

There are now a few points to consider at this stage:

1 You can occasionally take away your marker after carrying out a send away to a particular spot and send your dog to the unmarked but already used spot. Although you can occasionally work without a marker it should be used at least ninety per cent of the time.
2 You can vary your send away areas but always start with the marker at this stage.
3 Enthusiasm to reach the marker or unmarked spot is of paramount importance. Any deviation or looking back at the handler from this short

distance of twenty yards must be considered undesirable and a cause for concern. If this happens return to an earlier stage in training.

4 Encouragement to keep going out should not be necessary in training but should be utilized on occasions. It will be of value if required during a lengthy send away in a competitive situation.

5 Do not attempt to send your dog beyond a chosen and already used spot. If you wish to extend your send away distance, move backwards. Initially use a single send away area to build up on distance. At the end of the day you may wish to achieve two hundred yards or more.

6 Remember that this is a long-term exercise and short cuts should be avoided.

When sending dogs away to unseen markers where there is no scent path or previous knowledge to help the dogs it is common to see them deviating from the intended route. Many of them seem to pick out a natural background marker of their own choice. To help counter this type of situation it is important to use purposeful distractions at short distances whilst you are in a position to control your dog's direction.

At the beginning of this section I recommended the use of three send away markers. To date, we have only used one of them. We now require all three and they should be placed at each corner of a triangle with sides approximately twenty-five yards in length.

Place your container for his reward on marker 'B' and move back to marker 'A' to use it as a 'send from' spot. Send your dog to marker 'B' which has the container in view, follow up, reward and finish. Leave your dog at 'B' and place your container at 'C'. Carry out the send away routine from 'B' to 'C', reward and finish, then repeat the process from 'C' to 'A'.

This process round the triangle can be

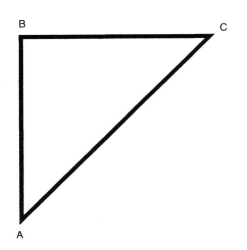
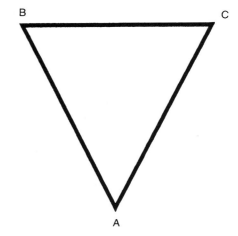

Send away triangles.

repeated at various times until your dog can accomplish the full procedure without the container at the markers.

The movement up to now has been in a clockwise direction and can now be repeated in an anti-clockwise direction, again starting with the container in view, as initially your dog may wish to go in the wrong direction.

It should be recognized that the first indication of a dog intending to take the incorrect route is the direction in which he is looking. You may turn his head in any direction you wish but he is likely to set off in the direction in which he chooses to look. To move his head round with your hands is seldom of any value and this practice should be avoided.

If at any time your dog is looking at the wrong marker, walk forward with him at heel in the correct direction until he is looking in the direction of your choice before releasing him to 'Go'. Initially this may mean walking most of the way to your chosen marker but this avoids incorrect directions and consequent failures.

When your dog is happy to carry out triangle send aways in either direction without a container on or under the marker you can concentrate on sending alternately from 'A' to 'B' then 'A' to 'C'. You must watch for the direction in which the dog is looking and if it is towards the incorrect marker you must walk forward in the correct direction until he is looking in the direction you desire before releasing him.

Patience and perseverance at this stage will prove to be extremely beneficial as distances increase. If problems do arise at a later stage you should refer back to this stage of training and consolidate.

As a great deal of training has been carried out using a send away distance of approximately twenty-five yards your dog will now be well conditioned to such a distance and a break away from this habit may take a little time. It is, therefore, preferable to build up on distances by using the same training area until at least one hundred yards has become a very acceptable distance. Each increase in distance should be in the region of fifteen per cent from the previous stage.

The increase in distances will create the situation where your marker is not going to be visible to your dog until he is well on his way out. It is the knowledge that the marker is normally there which will take him out and in a straight line.

The alternative send away markers can still be used at the greater distances and it is recommended that the markers be set at a distance apart which is approximately half the distance of the send away. A fifty-yard send away would be to one of two markers twenty-five yards apart. After carrying out one such send away go out to your dog, walk him to the other marker and then send him straight back to your 'send from' spot. You have now completed your own and your dog's scent path round the triangle.

Send aways to alternate markers can at times be made without the full scent path round the triangle during the build-up of distances, but great care must be taken to ensure that you continue walking your dog in the desired direction if he is not looking in that direction when you are preparing to send him. There may be occasions when you are forced to walk most of the way before sending him. It is better to do this than cause confusion in the dog's mind. Do not overstretch your dog's mental ability at this stage of training.

The effect of scent paths and the use of markers must always be kept in mind.

Acknowledge the use of them and the possible effect of their absence.

When building up in your well-used send away area occasionally do your first send away of the day to the well-known spot without a marker or scent path, but only apply about three quarters of your normal distance. This will help to give guidance on your progress.

On achieving one hundred yards of consolidated send aways in your usual area without a marker or scent path, build up distances in other areas. You may require to start with your marker and a scent path, also to reduce your starting distance. Always be prepared to return to your original training area to give your dog a boost of confidence.

Breaking in to the use of new ground without the help of a marker and a scent path takes time. Distances achieved will normally be much shorter than those attained in areas known to the dog. Two hundred-yard send aways in a well-used area may result in one hundred yards or less in a new area to the dog. Time, patience and versatility are required to achieve sound competitive performances.

The final distances you wish to achieve are up to yourself. The training to go out beyond one hundred yards is just a continuation of the routine already described but it takes time and patience.

The send away for obedience shows can be relatively short. Few are over twenty yards in distance although great accuracy is generally required. Obvious markers can be and often are set up for the benefit of judging but they can also act as homing devices to dogs which are trained for such marked areas. It is, therefore, advisable to include training for a variety of such markers in your obedience send away programme.

Directional Control

Although directional control, or redirecting as it is sometimes called, is only a corrective factor which could save a few points in the obedience ring, it is an important continuation of the send away exercise in the advanced stakes in working trials. The training principles for redirecting are identical to those of the send away.

Object of the Exercise

To have your dog move in a straight line to the right or left at a good pace and at a distance from you. On reaching the location of your choice he shall go into the position nominated when you give the instruction. He should also remain in that position until he is recalled. This exercise is carried out at the end of a send away as required by the open stakes schedule in working trials. It is also a very useful correcting factor when required in the send away for the lower stakes in working trials or obedience shows.

The basic elements. Dog to:

1 Be attentive at the end of the send away;
2 Move across when instructed in the direction intended at a steady to fast pace;
3 Stop immediately he is instructed and go into the position nominated;
4 Remain in the position nominated until he is called or collected.

It is important not to carry out redirection at the end of the send away until both have been perfected quite separately at the distances being applied.

The triangular approach to send away was developed for the purpose given but this development opened the door to a great advancement in directional control training. It is essential that the triangle send away training at a distance of twenty-five yards be perfected and be second nature to the dog before introducing directional control training.

To prevent any confusion all redirecting should be carried out in a line, left or right, and parallel to the direction you are facing, with outstretched left or right arm to indicate the direction to your dog. As the instruction to 'Go' is used in the send away it is recommended that this word be avoided when redirecting. To say 'Go Left' or 'Go Right' can be confusing to the dog but the instruction 'Left, son, good boy, left' would be more appropriate.

Return to the twenty-five yard triangular set up with your markers at each corner and signified, as before, 'A', 'B' and 'C'. With your container as a reward fully on view at marker 'C' do a send away from 'B'. Reward as usual and repeat the send away from 'C' to 'B'. Carry out the send away procedure two or three times each way with the container at the appropriate marker to create maximum inducement.

Now leave your dog on marker 'B' and move into a position about five yards directly in front of and facing 'C', which also has the container on top of the marker. Your dog should be very keen to get to his container and you just require the instruction to release him. At the same time direct with your arm and bring in the 'Right, son, good boy, right'. If necessary move forward to arrive at the marker at the same time as your dog. After reward and praise repeat the process from 'C' to 'B'. Your dog is just carrying out the send away routine as before, but with yourself in a different position to effect the redirect.

You can start to move back and away from the area of redirection without affecting your dog's performance. At each training session another yard or two can be created between yourself and the line of redirection until you have moved back the twenty-five yards to point 'A' of your triangular send away area. At each training session you can start with a send away between markers 'B' and 'C' before carrying out redirections to prevent your dog from deviating from the intended line.

Maintain your redirect distance of twenty-five yards until you have created a good sense of responsibility. On occasions remove your markers after the first redirect or send away and watch for a positive response from your dog when he moves to the unmarked spot. Gentle encouragement whilst he is moving along the correct line will be of value so long as the encouragement does not distract him.

The triangular send away and redirect routine to markers, with and then without the reward container, should now be the pattern of training. When the send away, redirect and then recall can be carried out both clockwise and anti-clockwise with markers the routine can then be performed to the same spots after the markers have been taken away.

Increased distances for redirecting can now be developed which are based on a sound send away and with markers in place to maintain confidence at these greater distances. Markers again to be utilized for at least ninety per cent of the time and with changes in training areas which are compatible with the send away training programme.

Consolidation at intervals is very important and the reintroduction of the reward container on the marker from time to time will boost your dog's confidence.

Beware of any indication of your dog deviating from the intended line, either on the send away or the redirect. Do not try to correct the situation during a badly executed attempt. It is much better to go back to a simple routine which creates success. This can be either one or a combination of the following:

1 Creating scent paths.
2 Shorter distances.
3 Replacing markers.
4 Reward container on marker.
5 More encouragement.

There are no quick methods of training for send away and directional control. Short cuts will affect a competitive performance when you need it most.

Speak and Cease Speaking on Command

Who needs to teach a normal and healthy dog to speak? It is the most natural activity for a dog to give voice, and yet we can have so much trouble getting some German Shepherds to speak when we want them to. It is reasonable to say that one German Shepherd takes more easily to 'speak on command' than another, but I think that most of our problems in teaching 'on command' are caused by our own failures. One of these is the very use of the phrase 'speak on command' – if we try to teach a dog by commands we are on to a loser right away. There are only two ways that I know of to teach a dog to speak when required, and they are:

1 By encouragement when he starts of his own accord.
2 By inducing him to speak and cre-

ating the situation where he will want to speak.

Both methods can be used together, but it depends a great deal on his upbringing whether the second approach is worth pursuing during the early stages. Firstly, we should recognize that we cannot 'command' a dog to speak until he has been fully trained, and even then it is doubtful if the use of commands would meet with much success. We can, however, ask, request or induce a trained dog to speak when we desire it.

Our main problems are caused by telling an untrained dog in this exercise to be quiet every time he feels he has some reason to bark. He becomes inhibited, and when the time comes for you to want him to speak he is so inhibited that it becomes impossible to induce him to speak when required. I made a mistake of this nature with one bitch. The older dog in the house had been taught to speak when required, and if he had reason to bark of his own accord, say somebody coming to the door, there was no problem in telling him to 'shut up'. However, the young bitch, who did not bark very much anyway, obviously took this to mean her as well. She was inhibited from the start. Admittedly I left it a bit late, but when I decided to start getting her to speak I would make use of a visitor to the house, the postman, milk boy, anybody, and when she barked I would encourage her. Initially, as soon as I said anything, even with the greatest of encouragement, she would immediately go quiet. For too long she had been conditioned to stop as soon as she heard me tell the old fellow to be quiet. It took a great deal of gentle encouragement to get her to continue barking when she started on her own. It proved to be a long, hard

Encouraging the speak on command.

main words are emphasized to create the main inducement. As time goes on you will be able to use the main word or words on their own – in fact they can be of great assistance as an inducement – but if you are also training for obedience competitions be careful not to use hand signals that can be confused with distance control instructions.

In the early stages go up to your dog when you encourage him to speak, because you do not want him to come to you. The value of this will be realized when you start training him to speak at a distance and he must stay there.

When you feel that he has progressed sufficiently, encourage him to think there is cause to speak, for instance somebody coming up to the door. Do not play on that one too often: he may well get wise to it. Praise him from the start and always let him know how pleased you are with him – again titbits can be a help. Inciting him to speak for his supper can be of great assistance. Holding a piece of meat in a clenched fist can also be very useful, so long as he knows it is there. When it comes to competing he does not need to know it is not there. The objective is conditioning and forming the desired habit or response to your verbal or physical incitement. A satisfactory speak is only of value if you can stop it. This may require a two-second, overbearing outburst of 'Enough' from yourself – two seconds of shock treatment, and this must be made effective – but immediately incite him to start again and then the same to stop again. The successful application of this approach can lead on to a slightly longer delay between stopping and restarting.

slog to get over the problem I had created with a bitch that should have been helped from the start and not hindered.

If we now look at the working trials exercise we see that not only are we being asked to get the dog to speak but we are also required to make him stop when required. We may be required to get him to speak again and then stop again. As with all other exercises, we break the exercise into elements and work through each stage.

Initially we make use of voluntary speaking and encourage him for a few seconds only, then distract him from the cause. The words you use are less important than the way you use them. The phrase used, however, should include the main word or two words that you wish to use finally, and as training develops the

Achieving distance between yourself and your dog should not be any problem but, if it is, hook him on to a fence and get him used to speaking from a distance. Use the same spot until he makes no attempt to strain on the lead, then leave him at the same spot with the lead attached to his slip collar but with the other end loose. Let him believe he is attached. When you are satisfied that he is going to make no attempt to come forward try with the lead off. If there is any attempt at any time to come forward hook him to the fence again and consolidate through each stage. The next move is to use a new spot and assess his reaction when tied. From then on use different places and without the fence behind him.

A dog who has been taught to speak and cease speaking is generally much easier to quieten than a dog that has not had the benefit of this training.

Steadiness to Gunshot

Like the temperament test in obedience, this is not an exercise that requires training but a test to assess the dog's stability. Although no training should be necessary, in fact I think it would be very difficult to train some dogs to stand up to close gunshot. However, most dogs may well require to be conditioned to accept and ignore the noise of a gun. It is, of course, quite acceptable if the dog just turns to note the origin of the noise.

No dog should be initiated to the gun from close up. His reaction must be tested from a distance. A starting pistol is very useful: although the noise is not so great, especially at a distance, the crack is very sharp and effective from close up.

Carrying out a steadiness to gunshot test.

I have found the best approach to initiating the further conditioning for steadiness is to make use of the gun whilst out for a walk with the dog loose and enjoying himself. Wait until there is quite a distance between yourself and the dog and let the gun off once. Immediately call your dog in and run away from him as if you were having a game with him. The number of occasions you can do this depends entirely on his reactions. Once on the first outing may be enough. In fact if your dog is not happy at all you may only be able to do this once on each outing until it bothers him no more.

Remember that a dog that is frightened by a close-up shot may never get over it. This is one form of conditioning where it pays to be overcautious. During conditioning do not leave him at a stay whilst firing the gun – you could ruin the stay exercises and it is preferable, at this stage, not to let a friend fire the gun. You can control the timing and your own reactions better when you fire it yourself. It is also better to have the dog coming towards the noise rather than cringing away from it. When you can walk with the dog at your left side and fire the gun in your right hand you are ready for the 'steadiness to gunshot' test and then somebody else can fire the gun for you.

CHAPTER 6

Agility Exercises

General

Agility exercises of the type we are about to discuss are generally confined to working trials but the same principles should be considered when training for agility competitions. The exercises consist of three different types of jumps with the details as required for German Shepherds.

1 The Scale Jump – a vertical scramble jump at six feet high and returning back over the jump.
2 The Long Jump – a low obstacle nine feet in length.
3 The Clear Jump – a plain framework to be cleared at three feet high.

A mature and fit dog who has been trained properly will find these jumps easy to negotiate and a very enjoyable way of expending a build-up of energy. Some people seem to feel that the Scale Jump of six feet is asking too much for the various breeds which take part in working trials and objections come to the surface from time to time with the complaint that it is a potentially dangerous exercise and should be dropped from the schedule. It must be recognized that all breeds are not suitably constructed for this type of agility but the working breeds, and in particular a fit, mature and well-constructed German Shepherd, are built for the job.

We have from time to time had the pleasure of watching the R.A.F. Demonstration Team of German Shepherds at work and it is good to see the enthusiasm these dogs have in negotiating eight feet or more on the Scale Jump. I remember witnessing a handler in Zimbabwe putting his prison dog over a Scale Jump which was in excess of eleven feet in height. This dog at one time held the world record. This shows the physical capabilities of our breed and also the mental approach when channelled in the correct direction. It should also be noted that the R.A.F. and Zimbabwe Prison Service do not allow their dogs to drop on the other side of the scale from these heights. They have a platform constructed to ensure that the drop is taken in stages.

There are, however, a few considerations which are common to all three exercises where attention to the following details is of importance:

1 Age and fitness of the dog is of little consequence in the early stages of training where the learning of a routine is the principal objective, but as the height and length are increased the physical fitness of the dog is a necessity and age must also be given due consideration. With the older dog fitness is an obvious criterion, but with the younger dog or puppy permanent physical damage

can be sustained by asking too much from such a youngster.

Dogs can be trained to the full agility requirements by the time they are twelve months of age but most German Shepherds require time to mature before their limbs and joints are asked to accept the full load from maximum requirements.

A reasonable guide would be two thirds of the maximum heights or lengths for a twelve-month youngster and a gradual build up to the maximum at an age between fifteen and eighteen months.

2 Training sessions should be kept short and in the earlier stages of training dogs can easily become bored or apprehensive if asked to jump too often. During the later stages of training the physical requirements must be given due consideration. Two to five jumps over each piece of equipment are quite sufficient for most dogs during one session with at least half an hour between each agility training session. Minimum of jumps to take place when maximum effort is required.

Two or three sessions in any single day should also be a maximum. Handlers with limited facilities are tempted to overtrain when they have the opportunity to use agility equipment. The failure to resist the temptation has ruined many a dog.

3 Training starts with the most elementary stage of control although greater control is required as training progresses. Control training is not part of this procedure but the measures of control will be mentioned at the appropriate stages.

4 Control equipment can be as important as the jumps themselves. The regular four-foot lead is probably satisfactory in the very early stages but a lead of some five to seven feet in length is advisable during the intermediate stages in training. A good nylon cord with a trigger hook can be used instead of a long lead.

Although agility training can be carried out with a check chain great care must be taken to avoid unintentional or harsh checking. The use of the dead ring would be advisable. A buckled collar or a combi-collar would also be suitable. During the later stages of training a loop of cord could be used as a means of restraining your dog. Take a length of cord about seven to nine inches in length and tie the ends together to create a loop. Fix the loop through your dog's collar, not the pulling ring of the check collar. Put your finger, or fingers, through the loop to restrain your dog. Full control is achieved when you can drop the loop and he will await your verbal release.

5 Encouragement and praise are vital ingredients for achieving an enthusiastic agility dog. During the full training procedure with all jumps it is preferable to refrain from single-word commands, but to use an appropriate phrase with emphasis on a key word. If you wish the phrase can be reduced to a single word when you have successfully achieved an enthusiastic agility dog. The application of the appropriate phrases will be discussed at the relevant stages.

The Scale Jump

Equipment

The Scale Jump should be a vertical wall of wooden boards which are well supported at each end. These boards may have narrow slats evenly distributed on the top half of the jump to give a measure of assistance which can help to achieve a successful scale.

It should be appreciated that this equipment MUST be built from good sturdy materials which are capable of taking the full weight of a big German Shepherd. The dog should feel that the jump can take the full force of his weight; he is putting his trust in this equipment and any uncertainty will affect his performance.

It is common practice to have the woodwork treated with creosote or painted. Some handlers paint one side white and the other black to accustom their dogs to some of the varying conditions experienced in working trials. Note that gloss paint should not be used as this can create a slippery surface, especially in wet conditions.

To achieve a progression through training the wooden boards should be approximately six inches in depth with one at three inches to give the option of a three-inch increase in height, which can be advisable in the middle to later stages of training. The sketch can be used as a basis for constructing a Scale Jump.

Location of the jump in training is very important. The jump should be placed on level ground to ensure that it will feel secure to the dog: many dogs have been put off by jumps which feel unsafe.

A good thick carpet of grass on even ground will give the best take-off and landing conditions. Soft conditions may give a good cushion on landing, but if the ground is too soft the take-off can be affected.

Object of the Exercise

To have your dog scale a six-foot vertical wall of wooden planks, stay at the other side in the position of your choice (Sit, Stand or Down), return over the jump on command and sit in front, then go round to heel. To be carried out to Kennel Club Working Trials Regulations. NOTE: The six-foot scale jump is the standard height for German Shepherds.

The basic elements. Dog to:

1 Sit at your left side at a maximum distance of nine feet from the jump;
2 Scale the jump;
3 Stay in the desired position;
4 Return over the jump;
5 Sit in front of you and go round to heel.

Training starts with the most elementary stage of control, although greater control is required as training progresses. At the earlier stages, it is only necessary that your dog is responsive whilst on the lead. He should be prepared to give you his full attention without the need to tug at the end of the lead when you call his name.

Now, fun is the name of the game. The training routine is based on achieving the desired mental approach. Your dog should enjoy jumping and a height of six to nine inches can be cleared by yourself and your dog whilst he is on the lead. The excitement coming from you soon achieves the desired reaction. You are also conditioning him to go between the uprights and then come back. You are ready to progress when your dog is happy to jump ahead of you whilst still on the lead.

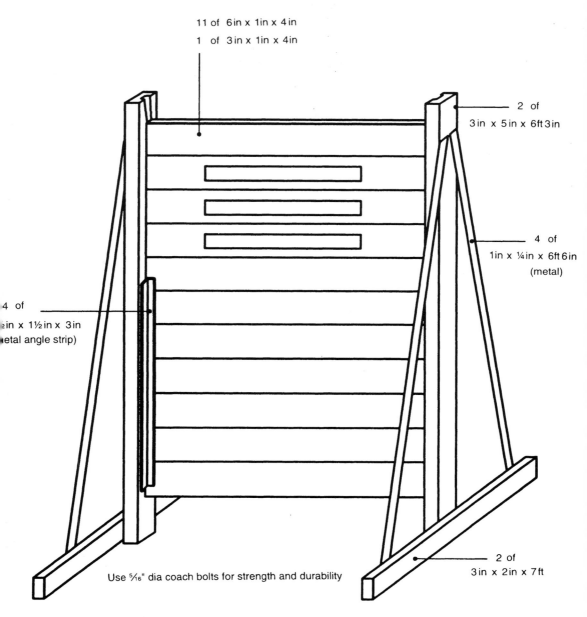

11 of 6in x 1in x 4in
1 of 3in x 1in x 4in

2 of
3in x 5in x 6ft 3in

4 of
1in x ¼in x 6ft 6in
(metal)

4 of
2in x 1½in x 3in
(metal angle strip)

Use ⁵⁄₁₆" dia coach bolts for strength and durability

2 of
3in x 2in x 7ft

The Scale Jump.

Handler enthusiasm is an essential ingredient, resulting in the dog's determination.

An encouraging tone of voice will help your dog, especially if any verbal expressions are in the form of a question, such as 'Are you going OVER?' and then 'Come on, son, BACK you come'.

It is quite unnecessary at this stage or later stages to take a long run to the jump. To do so gives the dog time to think of opting out. At all stages it is preferable to approach the scale from the side, some six to nine feet from the base, then turn to face the jump and carry out the routine which has just been described.

The value of basic control is an important feature and your dog should also have great enthusiasm for jumping this minor obstacle whilst on the lead, but he must learn to turn immediately he hits the ground and return to you.

To achieve this immediate attention and return it will probably be necessary to call his name as for the recall along with a sharp tug on the lead and move backwards to achieve the bounding return over the board. Never forget to give enthusiastic praise, even after such an elementary stage. Do not progress until your dog can automatically return without a tug on the lead or a verbal command.

The enthusiasm which has now been

built up can be the basis for progressing to a height of about two feet and this is achieved by height increases of three inches at a time. Your dog will probably be able to clear this height; just let him as it is not necessary to create a scaling action at this stage.

The gradual increase in height to about three feet brings about a change in approach. If a standard four-foot lead has been used it is now time to change to a longer lead or length of cord of some five to seven feet, which should be held in a manner which allows you to drop the excess and yet maintain a hold of the end to achieve effective control.

A little control should now be applied prior to jumping and this is where your control training for the sit is of value. Your dog may require to be physically restrained in the sit position before he is released to jump. Anticipation can be accepted as normal at this stage and it is preferable to use physical rather than verbal restraint.

Have your dog sitting about two or three feet from the base of the jump. Distance from dog to base should be equivalent to the height to the top of the boards. As height is increased the distance from the base of the jump to the dog's sitting position is suitably adjusted. It is important that the correct distance from the base of the jump is maintained. The habit of distance developed through the remainder of the training cycle will continue through your dog's working life.

If a dog is kept too close to the boards before jumping, fitness and enthusiasm may overcome the additional effort required, but as the years roll on the competitive life can be reduced by the dog's inability to scale from a close situation. The additional effort required in youth can no longer be drawn on during the later years in life.

If a dog is kept too far back he is likely to hit the jump, then scramble over. He is then likely to jump out at the other side and create the same problem on the return. At the lower heights this is no problem but the development of this habit can be detrimental at the full height.

Training prior to this stage has been based on an encouraging phrase such as 'Are you going OVER?' with the emphasis on the 'OVER' as he is going to take off.

As you are now starting to restrain your dog the phrase can be used as a preparation for the jump with the addition of 'Go on, son – OVER' as you release him. The sequence would, therefore, be – sit your dog as you say quietly 'Are you going OVER?' without emphasis on the 'over', then release him from the stay with 'Go on, son – OVER'. Make a forward movement yourself to encourage the jump. Time the 'OVER' to be a fraction of a second prior to take off. Be careful to use an encouraging tone of voice; a harsh command could put your dog off. From now onwards study your tone of voice and timing. Watch for adverse reaction as this will indicate a fault in either voice or timing.

When full control has been attained prior to jumping, with your dog prepared to sit and await his release, the jump can again be increased in stages to about four feet. By this stage your lead can be dispensed with. Consolidate at this height but ensure that your dog is perfectly happy to go over the jump and immediately return back over the jump. He should be responding to your verbal instruction to go 'over' and to the encouraging 'back' to come back to you.

As the training procedure has been based on anticipation you may have a problem in containing your dog at the sit for those few seconds prior to the jump. It would, therefore, be advisable to attach a loop of cord to his collar as previously advised.

You now wish to control the situation when your dog is at the other side of the jump. To date you have encouraged anticipation on the return over the jump, but by training in this manner you have a very attentive dog who will remain attentive when out of sight at the far side of the jump when it is eventually raised to six feet.

To stay in the desired position is now of great importance. The position of 'stand', 'sit' or 'down' is your own choice and this choice should be controlled by your dog's natural response. Is he happy to stand? Or does he prefer to sit or is he more contented in the down position?

Now, when you release your dog with the instruction to scale the jump at the height trained, immediately follow up so that you can stand hard against the jump as your dog lands and turns at the other side. Raise your hands and tell him to 'stay' for two or three seconds. If you are a small person you may need to reduce the height to something below the four feet.

Independent training for the stay exercise will certainly help to obtain the control you require. By standing against the jump with hands raised you have in effect blocked his normal return route for these few seconds. Before his interest and attention is lost move back quickly from the jump as you call him back. A suitable phrase to call him back could be 'Come on son – BACK you come' with encouraging emphasis on the 'back'.

If you wish to have him sit or go down at the far side of the jump walk round beside him, do not forget to praise your dog, put him in the desired position, then return to the starting side before recalling him. Training for sit or down on command at a distance should be carried out quite independently of the jumping if you wish to introduce either of these positions into the stay at the far side of the jump. Be careful not to lose your dog's desire to return over the jump immediately he is called.

Remember to control his position of staying at the actual point of landing. Any movement forwards can reduce distance between dog and jump. A young enthusiastic dog will be able to cope when jumping close but the effect of age will certainly reduce the ability to cope with such a situation.

In each training session increase your dog's stability at the far side of the jump by gradually extending the time delay before his return. Also maintain the control as you move back from the jump and wait for a few seconds before calling him back to you. Build up to a total of a ten-second delay on occasions. Dogs are seldom asked to stay at the far side of the jump for more than five seconds.

Do not proceed any further until complete control has been attained in this basic element of stay at the far side of the jump prior to the recall back.

On returning to you over the jump your dog should sit in front of you before going round to heel as in the recall and retrieve exercises.

Normal recall training now becomes an essential feature of this stage in training, where your dog is prepared to return on the flat, sit in front of you, then go round to heel. Do not try to improve or correct recall training in conjunction with scale training. Perfect recall training to front and finish as a separate training function.

To coordinate the sit in front and round to heel into the scale training, be prepared to move backwards some five to ten paces as your dog is on the downward stage of his return over the jump. Do not move too early or you will encourage him to jump from the top board instead of dropping down reasonably close. When he drops encourage him to finish in front of you as you move back, then round to heel as for the recall.

As your dog learns to expect a proper finish you can gradually minimize your backward movement until you remain at the correct distance from the jump and achieve the desired finish.

The full controlled exercise at the height of about four feet should now be accomplished. You have an immediate response to his release with 'Go on son – OVER' with a positive stay in the correct position at the point of landing. You also have an instant return on the instruction 'Come on son – BACK' followed by a sit in front before going round to heel. Although the verbal instructions have all been based on 'Go on, son' or 'Come on, son', this can easily be replaced at any time with your dog's name.

With your dog now well accustomed to scaling to a reasonable height and capable of doing the full routine in a keen and controlled manner, the increase in height from four feet should be taken in steps of three inches at a time, with a period of consolidation at five feet and again at five feet six inches, before increasing to the full six feet in height.

It must be remembered that, with the increasing height, you stand a little distance further back from the base of the jump. The distance from the base should be similar to the height being scaled, but the regulations allow a distance of nine feet from base of jump to dog and handler.

At working trials it is possible that the jumps may be set close together and this can cause confusion in a dog's mind, especially if he has a distinct preference for a particular jump.

To counter this possibility it is advisable in the later stages of training to place the Long and Clear jumps relatively close to the Scale. You can then take your dog right up to the Scale Jump and let him see it, then move back a few paces and prepare him in the normal manner. This should let him understand which jump is to be taken. To keep your fully trained, scale-jumping dog in trim without causing any over-stress, the jump should be maintained at a height of about five feet six inches, then occasionally raised to the full six feet to ensure that his judgement is sound enough for competitive work.

The Long Jump

Equipment

The Long Jump is usually made up of a minimum of five boards about eight inches wide and supported at an angle so that at the full length of spread it gives the impression, at dog's eye level, of one continuous board. The sketch shows the typical construction which also helps to achieve suitable storage. This sketch also illustrates a typical spread for action. To ensure that the full jump is clearly visible to the dog it is normally painted white.

The location of the jump in training should be on level ground, with sufficient space at each end for take-off and run out on landing. The take-off and landing areas should also be reasonably level.

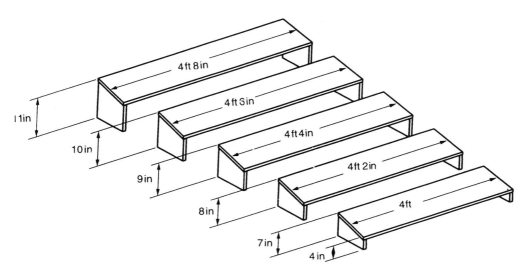

The Long Jump.

The siting of a board on uneven ground, or a badly constructed or damaged jump, has affected the capabilities of many dogs. It is advisable to take up a position some four to six paces in front of the jump and to view it at dog's eye level before asking the dog to carry out this agility test.

Object of the Exercise

To have your dog clear a nine-foot-long spread of boards to create length of jump rather than height and to remain under control on completion of the exercise. To be carried out in accordance with the Kennel Club Working Trials Regulations. NOTE: The nine-foot-long jump is standard for dogs exceeding fifteen inches at the shoulder.

The basic elements. Dog to:

1 Remain under control at a suitable distance from the front of the jump;
2 Run and clear the jump;
3 Remain under control on landing.

NOTE: The Long Jump is normally made up of five or six supported boards about seven to eight inches wide and spaced with a gap between each board. As the boards rise from the front to the back one it would be appropriate to start training with the rear board, which is the highest.

As with the Scale Jump, fun is the name of the game and the training routine is based on achieving the desired mental approach.

Whilst on the lead your dog should enjoy jumping over a single board. It is preferable that you jump with him whilst you create an excited atmosphere. Do not at this stage, or later stages, allow him to step on the top of the board. This would only encourage him to continue using the board for support as training progresses through greater lengths. The excitement you generate will help to give your dog the lift he will require for the more strenuous jumps to come.

It would be preferable to refrain from

using a single word command at this stage. 'Go on, son – OVER you go' is probably quite appropriate, but put the emphasis on the 'over'. If you wish, the phrase can be reduced to a single word at a much later stage in training. Although I use the word 'over' for both Scale and Long the remainder of the phrase is different. So long as the two routines are quite different and there is no doubt in the dog's mind as to which jump he is going to tackle, the similarity of the verbal instructions is quite unimportant. Remember, dogs learn from actions and not words. There are individual words in the English language which have double meanings, but they are never confused unless taken out of context.

It is quite unnecessary, at this stage, to give your dog a long run up to the board. To do so would give your dog time to think of opting out. At the various stages of training, the approach to the jump should be from the side and at a suitable distance from the front board. This distance will be dependent on the set length of the jump and the following gives a rough guide:

2 yards from the front board for 3 feet length
5 yards from the front board for 6 feet length
7 yards from the front board for 9 feet length

These figures should be used as a guide only and may be modified slightly to suit individual dogs.

Progressing to a second board which is placed close to the first can create the temptation for a dog to step on the top of the board. This is the time to appreciate that your dog requires enthusiasm and purpose to clear the slightly broader jump.

As your dog is still on the lead for this stage of training, it may be necessary to give a short but quick jerk with the lead as he is taking off, to obtain clearance over the jump. With two boards placed close together handlers are normally fit enough to clear the jump along with the dog, and progression to greater things should not be attempted until your dog is happy to clear these boards ahead of you.

It will also be appreciated that a good length of lead or cord will be required, probably five to seven feet in length. The lead should also be held in a manner which allows you to drop the excess and yet to maintain a hold of the end to achieve effective control on landing. On every occasion follow your dog to the other side of the jump, initially by jumping over but eventually by going round the side, then call your dog to you. Create the habit of moving to join your dog and also having him come back to join you for praise and any other kind of reward which will give him a feeling of satisfaction.

When you are satisfied with your dog's keenness, and ability to clear the boards without putting a foot on them and come right back to you, a gap of some eight or nine inches can be made between the two boards. Any attempt to put his feet on or between the boards should be countered in the manner described earlier.

Three and then four boards can now be used close together and possibly extended a little to give a three-foot spread. By this time, and with the proper encouragement, your dog should be eagerly anticipating the jump and you will have to follow smartly round the side of the jump to prevent a tight-lead situation.

The lead should now be discarded and the jump reduced to two or three boards and about two feet in length. Your dog

Concentration to complete the Long Jump.

should now be prepared to clear them when released, and you join him as you follow round the side of the jump.

Consolidate on a good, keen, free but controlled jump at this stage before progressing. It should be sufficient to hold your dog by the loop of cord previously described before you release him to jump.

Verbal control prior to release is not important at this stage, in fact anticipation shows keenness, ability and understanding of the routine. These factors are of paramount importance.

Progression to four and then five or six boards can be made by placing them together, then creating a gap between them to obtain four feet or a little greater length. During this extension your dog's run-up to the jump can be lengthened to four or five paces.

The longer the jump, the shorter the training sessions. It is important to maintain your dog's enthusiasm and not to overdo it. Three or four jumps each session should now be sufficient.

It is also important to hold back on the collar by means of the cord loop rather than make him stay prior to the jump. Every little extension in length should be accompanied by greater encouragement with the follow through and praise as you join him. As you increase the length of the jump to nine feet you increase the length of the run-up as previously described.

Your dog may find it more difficult to adjust to increased lengths but if you make each increase about three inches and consolidate at every additional foot there should not be any problems.

Training prior to this stage has been based on an encouraging phrase such as 'Go on son – OVER you go' with the emphasis on the 'over'. The timing of 'over' and also your tone of voice is now very important. As you increase the length of the jump any error in timing or tone can upset your dog's momentum.

Study your dog's normal take-off point and time the 'over' to be a fraction of a second prior to take-off. The tone to be used should not be given as a harsh command, but as an urgent word of encouragement. Assess the effects of your own approach so that adjustments can be made before extending the boards beyond six feet.

During this period of training it is presumed that other control training has been carried out and that your dog has been taught to stay in at least one position. Now is the time to have your dog stay, by means of verbal control only, at a suitable distance from the jump. The position is your choice; make it the position which suits your dog best.

Keep him in the stay position for a few seconds only, then carry out the full Long Jump routine, follow through quickly but maintain a controlled completion of the exercise – do not forget the praise.

Only when the full length is achieved and consolidated can you consider the final requirement of the schedule – that the handler must not proceed beyond any part of the jump ahead of his dog. The fact that you now stop at the jump should not have any effect on your German Shepherd, but in training you only require to stop occasionally to ensure that it does not affect him.

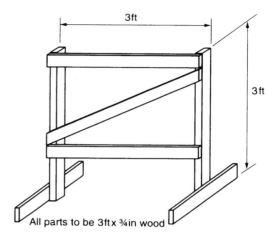

The Clear Jump.

fitted bottom bar and intermediate bar with a supported top bar which can easily be dislodged if touched by the dog.

This training sequence is based on a type of hurdle with a fixed top bar as illustrated. Also illustrated is a hurdle with a swivel base which has been specifically designed by Ardfern Canine Training Services for adjustability during training and for easy storage.

The Clear Jump

Equipment

The Clear Jump is normally constructed in the same manner as a hurdle but the variations in style are much greater than those experienced with the Scale or Long Jump. Some have a fixed bar at the top and a very low crossbar which encourages a dog to step through, whilst others have an intermediate crossbar which effectively minimizes the gap. Still others have a

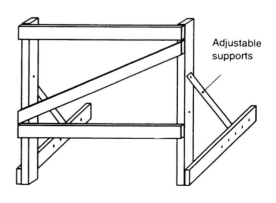

An alternative Clear Jump.

The top bar of the jump should be very distinctive and be painted white to ensure the dog is given every opportunity of assessing the effort required to clear the bar.

Even ground is again desirable for a satisfactory take-off and a safe landing.

Object of the Exercise

To have your dog clear a hurdle which is three feet in height and to remain under control on completion of the exercise. To be carried out in accordance with the Kennel Club Working Trials Regulations. NOTE: The three-foot clear jump is standard for German Shepherds.

The basic elements. Dog to:

1 Remain under control at a suitable distance from the hurdle;
2 Clear the hurdle;
3 Remain under control on landing.

NOTE: This routine requires a hurdle with a top bar fixed at the three-foot height.

As with the other jumps, fun is the name of the game and the training routine is based on achieving the desired mental approach.

The hurdle should be laid on its side to make it the easiest possible obstacle to clear. When deciding on the direction of jumping the hurdle should be pushed away from the dog's starting position so that the top bar is resting on the ground.

Whilst your dog is on the lead he should enjoy jumping over the hurdle in the 'flat' position. Do not let your dog step between any intermediate and top bar. If this does become a problem, lace string or tape between the bars to break the gap. The excitement you generate should help to give your dog the lift to clear the obstacle.

Chat your dog into an excited and willing frame of mind and as you are timing his take-off use the phrase 'Go on – UP you go, son' but put the emphasis on the 'up'.

A long run at this stage or any other stage of training is quite unnecessary. A long run-up would give your dog time to think of opting out, but it is just as important to recognize that such a run-up would encourage a dog to jump flat, that is, with length rather than height. Failure to develop an upward spring as heights increase would cause problems on reaching the full hurdle height. During the whole of the training sequence a starting distance of about four to six feet from the hurdle is probably about right. A single step forward before take-off is all that the dog requires.

When your dog is happy jumping ahead of you as you run past the right-hand side of the flattened hurdle you are in a position to consider raising the top bar from the ground to achieve a little height.

The top bar can now be supported at each end (not in the middle) to give a height of six to nine inches. Again this is a very simple jump and will not give any trouble if the initial stage has been accomplished with enthusiasm.

At this stage we are only consolidating a routine. Heights can now be increased in increments of approximately three to six inches until the top bar is some eighteen inches from the ground.

During this period your dog is still on the lead and it will be appreciated that he will require the full use of a good, long lead, probably five to seven feet in length. The lead should always be held in a manner which allows you to drop the excess and yet maintain a hold of the end to achieve effective control on landing. At this stage it is still advisable to follow your dog round the hurdle.

Create the habit of you moving to join your dog but also maintain his attention and control. Follow up with praise and any other kind of reward which will give him plenty of satisfaction.

Do not progress beyond this stage until your dog is returning to you with verbal instructions only. Any need to tug or pull on the lead when your dog has cleared the hurdle indicates a lack of verbal control.

As anticipation is the essence of a keen jumper, control prior to a jump can be maintained by means of a finger in the cord loop attached to the collar to hold him back for a second or two before releasing him to clear the hurdle.

The hurdle can be maintained at a height of about eighteen inches until the 'off-lead' routine has been consolidated with a controlled finish.

Anticipation should still be used as a measure of your dog's keenness to jump and it can be quite important to physically restrain your dog from jumping rather than apply strong verbal control.

'Lift-off' for a successful Clear Jump.

Training prior to this stage has been based on an encouraging phrase such as 'Go on – UP you go' with emphasis on the 'up'. The timing of 'up' and your tone of voice is now very important.

Study your dog's normal point of take-off and time the 'up' to be a fraction of a second prior to that point. The tone of your voice to be used should not be given as a harsh command but as an urgent word of encouragement.

Assess the effects of your approach so that adjustments can be made before increasing the height beyond the two-foot mark. Control and an expression of your pleasure should still be part of the routine on his completion of every hurdle jump.

A progressive increase in height is now your objective. A two- or three-inch increase at a time is quite sufficient and will not be noticed if time is taken to consolidate, especially at the heights of two feet, two feet six inches and two feet nine inches before increasing to the full height of three feet.

During this period of training it is presumed that other control training has been carried out and that your dog has been taught to stay in at least the sit or stand position.

Now is the time to make use of this training and have your dog stay in the position which suits him best, and by means of verbal control only. This, of course, should be carried out at the appropriate distance from the jump.

As we are introducing a significant change in the element of restraint it is desirable to reduce the height of the hurdle considerably, probably to about half the full height. With a change of this nature, it is easy for a dog and handler to misjudge the situation and a failure or refusal at this stage could be disastrous. The reduced height should eliminate the possibility of failure.

Now you can position yourself at the distance from the hurdle which is used for clearing the full height and keep your dog in the stay position for a few seconds only before releasing him with the verbal 'Go on – UP you go'. Follow through quickly by rounding the hurdle and execute the controlled return to you – do not forget to give him praise.

In competition you are usually permitted to release your dog to jump in your own time and as such it is not necessary to make him await your release for too long.

Up to a maximum of five seconds is quite long enough. To extend this period may result in a mistimed jump or even a refusal.

When you are satisfied that the control and timing are satisfactory you can gradually increase the height of the hurdle again. As your dog already has the ability and judgement to achieve the full height this stage should be completed in a very short time.

Remember that in competition you are not allowed to move past the hurdle until your dog has landed at the other side. Make sure that you restrain your movements occasionally in training.

Further training to keep your dog up to scratch should be carried out at full height unless there has been a long lay off or a lack of fitness. It may then be advisable to return to half height for a short period, then make a gradual increase in height as previously described.

CHAPTER 7

The Principles of Nosework

General

Every German Shepherd loves to use his nose. He can be seen following the scent of a rabbit or some other game whilst his owner takes him for a walk through the countryside. He can also enjoy struggling through undergrowth to seek out a stick which has been thrown by his master or searching a pebbled beach for a thrown stone and confounding everybody by bringing back the correct one. These are some of the joys of the family German Shepherd, joys which have now been harnessed and controlled by man to aid the police forces, the services, mountain rescue operations and in the competitive field of working trials and obedience competitions. Trained German Shepherds can track down a fugitive, quarter an area in search of a criminal or missing person, can be used for the location of drugs, explosives or buried bodies. Searching through the undergrowth for lost property or discriminating and acknowledging articles with a selected individual's scent are additional functions for our canine friends.

Any dog's greatest asset is his inherited power of scenting. We cannot compete against our canine companions; even in this day of high technology there is not a piece of equipment which can replace a German Shepherd's ability to follow the track of a human being or differentiate between the scents of one person and another.

This chapter has been written primarily for those wishing to make use of their German Shepherd's inherited scenting instinct, either in a professional capacity or as an owner with a competitive spirit who wishes to train for working trials or obedience competitions. The training principles should also prove to be of value and interest to the family German Shepherd owner who is looking for greater companionship through a fuller development of his dog's character.

The contents are also based on the applications involving human scent only, with a full understanding of tracking as a basis for all other scenting applications. A German Shepherd's sense of smell must have taken many centuries through the breeding of many types to develop to its present standard. Let us help him enjoy and pass on his inheritance to future generations.

Before domestication a dog's nose was a major part of his survival kit; the uses of his nose, ears and eyes were developed in varying degrees to cater for local requirements. He had to eat to live, and to eat generally meant locating and catching each meal.

Although the senses which controlled his hearing were mainly developed as part of the defence warning system, they also served to let him know that a meal ticket might well be in the vicinity. Eyesight became an important factor where the countryside afforded little or no cover and the visual movement of game was the first indication of a prospective meal. Keen eyesight could pick out movement at a distance and survival would depend on the ability to detect this. Dogs in this category were the forerunners of our present group of breeds known as Gazehounds.

With most types of dog, however, his sense of smell was the main tool in his kit for survival. When an animal was close enough on the windward side of the dog, the animal could easily be located and considered as suitable prey. Experience told him if the particular scent warranted investigation or if the animal was healthy and belonged to a stronger family.

Tracking down an animal, be it weak, injured or a type easily overcome, was the main approach to securing food for most dogs. The scent such an animal left on the ground, the scent of crushed vegetation or disturbed soil from its foot or hoof prints was followed by these dogs until they could catch up with their prey. To locate the ground scent of an animal and to track in the wrong direction would end in frustration and hunger. Sensitivity was, therefore, developed through the survival of the keenest noseworkers who knew when a faint track was present and were able to detect the correct direction. Centuries of survival of these highly developed scenting instincts have created the forerunners of our present-day tracking breeds.

Since dogs became more attached to man, domestication has created a situation where survival has been less dependent on the dog's own abilities. However, the instincts built up over the centuries do not disappear very easily.

For many years now, breeding has been taken out of the hands of mother nature, and man's manipulation of matings has secured the strengths of inherited instincts to suit his own requirements. Unfortunately over the years the introduction of breed exhibiting has brought a new dimension to the breed characteristics and, although this has helped to standardize and improve the construction within our breed, the working qualities seem to have been ignored by many breeders in various countries. This does not mean that German Shepherds bred for the show ring are not suited for work but it does mean that a higher proportion may have an ever-diminishing aptitude for nosework. Puppies who finish up as family pets, whether they come from show stock or working lines, may well prove to have exceptionally strong scenting instincts or may, by canine standards, have little interest in using their ever-diminishing natural instincts.

Each dog owner can, however, capitalize on what natural ability his dog does possess. This natural instinct may not be particularly evident but the correct inducements may reveal hidden talents.

Outlets for his Scenting Activity

The outlets for scenting activities are numerous and varied; these activities may require a brief introduction and can be placed into the following categories:

Tracking: To follow the scent left on the ground by a person walking over that ground. To track down a criminal, to find a missing person, or to locate articles dropped en route.

Seek back: To track back and find an article dropped or lost by the dog owner whilst out for a walk.

Property search: To find articles which have been lost by a person in either light or heavy undergrowth.

Quartering: Air or wind scenting to quarter over open ground, through thickets or buildings, to locate criminals or missing persons.

Scent discrimination: This is basically an application for obedience competitions where the dog is required to pick out an article amongst many others after being given the scent from the individual who initially scented the wanted article.

The outlets for these applications can also be put into the following general categories: professional, competitive or household pleasure.

An Introduction To Scenting Theories

Scents and a dog's ability to differentiate between such a variety of scents are very much a mystery. We may have our theories, the results of various experiments, or we may have analysed the products of an intensive study on the subject, but in the end we are left with theories and little more.

Only the dog knows what scent or odour he is following on a track, or the difference between one person's scent and another's when he is discriminating between articles which have been handled by different people. If a dog loses a track or fails to discriminate, who are we to censure him for

an inferior performance without an understanding of the cause?

I shall define a number of theories: some with substantial backing from the experience of many people, others a shot in the dark based on logical thinking. Although, as yet, we do not seem to know the logic or development of the various scent patterns.

I suppose that the various scents can be broken down into three basic types and there will generally be a mixture of these around. They are:

1 Animal scents.
2 Ground odours.
3 Material odours.

To the human scenting organs there seems to be difficulty in recognizing the presence of more than one scent source at any particular time. The scent of new-mown grass will mask all others. The aroma from bacon frying in a pan obliterates all others and the odour from disturbed farmyard manure extinguishes the many other scents from our olfactory organs. We seem to be quite incapable of appreciating anything other than the most dominant scent at any given time.

It would seem, however, that the canine olfactory system is capable of concentrating on scents or odours other than the dominating scent in any particular set of conditions.

I have watched dogs track across fields with newly scattered farmyard manure when the odour was rather nauseating to the human nose and yet the dogs were quite oblivious to its presence as they concentrated on the scent which we as human beings could never hope to distinguish.

I tend to consider canine scenting and human powers of vision to be on a similar level. We can see any number of objects at one time, can then focus on one item and follow its course. At the same time we can visually monitor the surrounding objects. Ability and training can help to determine our powers of general observation, even when we are concentrating on an individual item.

Our canine friends seem to have the same power in the form of scent focusing. It would appear that they can be well aware of many scents or odours whilst concentrating on one. They seem to be able to ignore dominant odours whilst giving their full attention to particular subordinate scents.

It is this ability to focus on a single subordinate scent or a particular combination of scents and odours which makes a dog of unique value to man.

Animal Scents

We can start by considering animal scent, and our main interest is in the scent of the human being, although other animal scents cannot be ignored.

When we ask a dog to track he is expected to follow the scent path created by the various personal scents and ground odours left behind by a person having walked across a piece of ground. He is not being asked to follow the scent of a particular person but of the last person to be in the particular area where he began to track. Once he has located the track he is expected to maintain contact and not transfer to another, either more recent or older than the one he decided to follow.

A dog being asked to quarter the ground for a missing person or a criminal is expected to indicate the presence and location of any human being in the area without the need to discriminate between one person and another.

A dog who is expected to apply the art of scent discrimination is given the scent from a particular person and he should indicate an article containing that person's scent from a collection of articles contaminated with the scents of various other people.

So conditioned are we to the success of a well-trained dog in the art of scent discrimination that we seem to find the occasional failure from these experts is due to one of a number of theoretical causes. However, there is one possible cause which seems to be ignored.

In theory every person carries a distinctive scent of his or her own and this scent is basically a result of perspiration. Like fingerprints, each scent is unique to each individual and with a population of fifty million people in the U.K. there must be fifty million different distinctive sets of fingerprints and human scents.

A fingerprint expert in his attempt to match prints may well discard the majority with ease but can require time and all his expert training to determine the exact similarity between matching sets. With fifty million human scents, is it not possible that there are occasions when scents of two people are so similar that any slight masking by surrounding odours can negate the difference so that they appear to be the same?

Fingerprint records are grouped with each section containing basic similarities in the same manner that other human characteristics can be grouped: for example each one of us falls into a particular blood group. If necessary the same sort of classification can be done with height, the colour of a person's hair or eyes, or for that matter any other human characteristic. It is, therefore, more than probable that human scents can be classified and with knowledge we could well find that scent is related to more physical properties of the human being, such as blood or saliva groups.

Comparing scents from different classifications will no doubt be a simple exercise for any self-respecting dog and the discrimination of scents within a classification may not be too difficult unless they are very similar. Some scent classifications may well be tied within a very narrow band, thereby creating major problems for a dog lacking in the expertise or concentration necessary for the very finest discrimination of scents.

Ground Odours

The effect of odours from vegetation can be of major importance when we come to discuss the art of tracking and we may even find that it has an effect on the scent discrimination exercise at open-air obedience shows.

Walking across a piece of ground disturbs the surface to some extent and there is no doubt that any sign of vegetation affects the strength of the track odour. Bruised vegetation appears to emit relatively strong odours and it would seem that these odours change through chemical reaction at varying times and under differing conditions.

Each different type of vegetation will have its own particular odour, and this odour will vary in accordance with the stage of growth. Vegetation full of growth in the spring will maintain a high concentration of odour when released by the effect of feet treading on the surface and crushing or bruising it. In the late autumn when the growth has well passed its peak the vegetation will be drying out and this concentration of odour will be less dominant but will still be strongest in the immediate area of any footprints.

Material Odours

This can generally be taken to mean any matter not directly related to the previously discussed origins. It can relate to the articles of clothing being worn, either of man-made fibres or of an animal base. Or it can relate to articles left on the track or used for searching or scent discrimination.

Although each material will emit its own odour it will harbour human scents after being in contact with a person. A porous material will hold a human scent for some considerable time, whereas non-porous material such as metals and some plastics will not be so conducive to retaining human scents.

Most, if not all, materials have some odour of their own and some are strong enough to be apparent to the human sense of smell. Leather is a good example of a smell that humans can identify and yet a dog can discriminate between human scents on different pieces of leather.

Scent Life

Scent life and thereby the strength of a scent or odour at any particular time is dependent, to a great extent, on the moisture in the atmosphere. The ambient temperature and wind conditions are also important factors.

When dealing with a short time cycle such as the normally accepted periods of time in searching, quartering for a missing person or carrying out a scent discrimination, the scent life is a minor factor. In the cases where longer periods of time are involved the scent will disperse according to the prevailing conditions.

Moisture seems to be the basic controlling factor; it would appear that scent cannot be maintained in the atmosphere without it. The ease or difficulty of a dog following a track is dependent on the moisture and the conditions which control the rate of evaporation. The moisture from crushed or bruised vegetation creates a strong odour at the moment it is damaged by the tread of a footprint. The result of a dry atmosphere, the heat of the sun and the effect of the wind will be to disperse the moisture and the odour it carries. The drier the atmosphere with supporting conditions the quicker the ground odour and body scent will disperse. A damp, cool, still day will ensure that scent odours linger on in strength for a considerable period.

A good dog may well find that to follow the movements of a person across a pasture field three hours after the event could be difficult in a very hot, drying wind. However, the same movements late at night may be much easier to follow some eight or ten hours later because of the overnight dampness.

As competitors, tracklayers or judges, colleagues and I have often discussed and assessed the prevailing tracking conditions, the type of ground and the weather. We have often come to firm conclusions on the probability of achieving a successful track under these conditions, only to find that the dogs know better. Sometimes they prove that the conditions are much better than our assessment and at other times the conditions are apparently much worse.

I recall judging at one trial, on the second day of continuous rain, when the conditions were extremely bad and yet many dogs completed the track with ease. At another trial on the same ground when I was competing there was a tremendous cloudburst just after my track had been laid. Half an hour later my dog could not detect any scent at the starting stake. This was the only time this dog failed even to start on a given track. The scent of the tracklayer and the odour from the crushed vegetation had been completely washed away by this deluge of rain.

I have also judged tracking events in South Africa and Zimbabwe where atmospheric and ground conditions seemed to be devoid of moisture. Conditions were difficult and there were failures, but there were also some very notable and encouraging successes.

The police at their National Trials run a hard-surface track as one exercise and it is commonly recognized as a lottery. A section of the track is laid on a tarmacadam or concrete road or airfield runway. If a dog works during damp or wet conditions he has a chance but if the surface is dry there is little hope of locating a scent after half an hour.

To illustrate this point I laid an experimental track on the beach one day. The tide was out and I walked alternately along stretches of damp sand just below the high-water level and the dry sand above this level. About twenty minutes later the dog was put on to the track and worked the sections on damp sand with no problems but the dry sand conditions proved very difficult. This was further proof of the effects of moisture.

We can theorize much about scents and prove some theories, but there is so much we do not know.

CHAPTER 8

Tracking

General

Tracking is probably the most natural use we can make of a German Shepherd's scenting powers, his ability to focus on particular scents, to relate one scent or odour to another and to follow the related scents created by a person walking across a piece of ground. Tracking is an instinctive art; only the dog knows how it is done, only the dog knows which scent or odour is taking his attention and only the dog knows the strength of that scent.

All German Shepherds have this inherited art, but not all of them realize it, nor do they all have the power of concentration or the scenting sensitivity to make a first-class tracker dog. Any German Shepherd will track when he wants, but only on the scents which take his interest and only for as long as he maintains an interest in that particular scent. If one member of the family goes out for a walk just ahead of another and the second party has the dog, one finds invariably that the dog's nose is down at ground level tracking that member of the family ahead of him.

There is no need to teach a German Shepherd to track and I believe that we are showing a gross lack of understanding if we try, but we can, however, induce and encourage a German Shepherd to use this unique and natural ability. We can create situations where he will gain experience and improve on his ability, but we cannot teach him to track. This does not mean that a sound standard of tracking can be achieved without a great deal of thought, and a good natural tracker can be ruined by lack of thought or misguided planning. A less strongly motivated German Shepherd can easily become a non-starter if insufficient consideration has been given to the task of inducing the correct attitude of mind.

We, as handlers, have much to learn in the art of tracking. We have no inherited instincts to help us; we must learn from our dogs through observation, by watching their reactions and by monitoring their progress. A dog will only track at the request of his human companion if there is sufficient incentive and the best long-term incentive is the sheer joy of tracking plus the pleasure of his handler on completion of the track.

An operational or competitive dog will normally wear a special harness when tracking with a thirty to forty-foot line connecting harness to handler. This helps to ensure that the dog tracks with responsibility and also ensures that the handler is nearby when the dog reaches his objective.

Free tracking, without a harness, can be fun, especially with the family dog. However, this has limited application unless it is used as a back track, that is having your dog retrace your footsteps to find and return with some lost article such as a dropped glove, the car keys or some such personal possession.

The Track

Wherever a person walks he leaves a trail of body scents and odours from his clothing. These scents float freely in the atmosphere and will drift and cling to the vegetation as they drop to the ground. There are also odours from shoes and trousers in contact with the ground or vegetation, but most important of all are the odours from bruised or crushed vegetation or even the soil disturbed by each footstep.

On a fresh track most scents and odours will be prominent and the dog will probably focus on the human scent because his incentives are based on this use of body scents. As the time lag between a person walking across a piece of ground and the dog investigating the area increases, the airborne scents of a man and his clothing will diminish and eventually disappear. The ground odours, from shoes or the bruised vegetation, will continue to be emitted into the atmosphere for some considerable time until they too are of little significance.

Fresh tracks will appear to a dog as a continuous scent path, and with a wide band of scent he may even track one or two yards on the windward side of the actual footsteps. In time, as the odours become weaker they will only be located in the immediate area of each footprint with a twelve to fifteen-inch space between one toe mark and the heel of the next step.

When a person turns to walk in another direction this creates a dead end in that particular direction; the dog will realize that the scent path does not just stop, instinct will tell him to cast around until

he locates the change of direction. The scent path from one such turn to another will in future be referred to as a 'leg' of a track and each turn will be termed a 'corner'.

The start of a track is the area or point where a dog is expected to pick up the scent. On an operational track the point of pick up can be anywhere, the flower bed outside an open window after a burglary, the side of a field where a suspect was spotted from a distance, or at the roadside beside an abandoned car. A competitive track will normally start at a definite point and will probably be marked by a post put into the ground for that purpose.

The end of the track is where the dog has reached his objective. With an operational dog this may be at the home of a suspect or at the roadside where the getaway car had been parked. On a competitive track the end will be indicated by the last article dropped on the track by the tracklayer.

A dog is expected to indicate the presence of any article dropped on a track and any such article can be used as evidence against a suspect or can confirm the route taken by a missing child.

No two tracks are alike, nor do the conditions on a single track remain constant. It may be practical to compare this with a panoramic view as seen by the human eye, where a passing cloud can cause the texture of the hillside to change and the sun, lowering itself in the evening sky, will create a changing sequence of colours or tones so that certain features lose their distinction and others become more clear for a period.

A track changes along its course in accordance with the terrain; the odours from crushed vegetation will alter from one area to another, the edge of a field can be rich in grass or weed vegetation whereas the rest of the field could be newly cut stubble or may even be ploughed. The pasture at the bottom of the field may be very damp and sheltered ensuring good scenting conditions for some hours, yet the top of the field may be open to the wind where the drying atmosphere can shorten the life of the track odours considerably.

The track to be followed may be that of a missing child, carrying little weight on a pair of small feet, thereby leaving minimal impression on the undergrowth and a short-lived scent, or it could be two hundred pounds of sweating thug in full flight whose heavy boots will leave a very distinctive and long-lasting scenting impression.

Every single footstep on a track differs from the one before it. How else could a dog determine the correct direction of a track? Admittedly on an ageing track the difference must be minute and it is open to debate whether a dog can tell the difference when introduced to these ageing tracks. I believe that, generally, dogs can detect the correct direction and may backtrack some five or ten paces before sizing up the situation, then turning to follow in the correct direction.

I did, however, witness one trial with three-hours-cold tracks where the dogs were taken across 'clean' ground at right angles to the track with the choice of going right or left. Every dog was a proven top-class tracker and yet half of them went in the wrong direction. It may have been the conditions on that day, I do not know, but these failures were left unexplained.

Although ground conditions are very important, it is the combinaton of ground and atmospheric conditions which govern the changing dominance of the various

scents or odours on a track. There may well be critical periods in the life of a track when a dog finds it easier to focus on the odour from crushed vegetation rather than the human scent which must be the initial incentive to follow a track, yet the dog must realize that this ground odour is a reliable substitute and will lead him to his objective.

Interference on the Track

Every track will probably be affected by some sort of interference. This interference may be caused, for example, by sheep, cattle, rabbits or members of the rodent family. I wonder what scent is left by a flock of seagulls which take to the air as a tracklayer approaches, or a flock which land and take rest on top of a newly laid track. To lay a track in a field without knowing that a herd of dairy cattle has been taken in for milking a little earlier can create unsolved and worrying problems because the dog will not settle to his usual steady track.

A German Shepherd who has had the freedom to chase rabbits or birds at his leisure may well consider it to be his right to leave a track for the more interesting scent of game.

The interference from human cross tracks can create a bigger problem, especially when somebody walks across the ground after the track has been laid, thereby creating a fresher track across the intended line the dog should take.

I have watched a family of four walk straight up the first leg of a track, but if I had not seen them how would I have reacted to my dog's inability to start on an otherwise simple track?

On another occasion I had just finished

laying a track and looked around to assess my bearings to find that two youths were walking across the tracking area carrying my marker post from the start of the track.

Tracking interferences are natural hazards and there is a great need to appreciate the existence and significance of such hazards before blaming the dog for failure.

Our Overall Objective

The Dog and Handler

Our objective is to create a keen, reliable track-sure dog, one who responds to the sight of his tracking harness, who does not require commands to track but patiently waits for the harness to be fitted round his body and who, as soon as he feels or hears the tracking line being clipped on to the ring, puts his nose down to seek out that track. By means of a build-up in experience and time delays such a dog will eventually be competent to follow a track three hours after it was laid (three hours cold) and of at least half a mile in length.

Ideal conditions can greatly lengthen the workable life of a track and the three-hour period is given as the requirement for the most exacting competition work. To attain a competent and reliable performance under these conditions, however, a dog must be experienced and capable of working out colder and longer tracks.

A dog should be capable of distinguishing between the correct track and cross tracks; cattle or game tracks should not be a problem but the existence of a human cross track can create difficulties and careful conditioning is required to obtain sound results.

Our tracker dog should also be capable of encountering obstacles such as fences, hedges or walls. Did the tracklayer negotiate the obstacle or did he walk along beside it? The dog should be prepared to investigate round or across a 'dead' area. A stream will not hold scent and he should be prepared to investigate until the track has been located; on colder tracks a road may cause the same problem. The important point is that the dog should have sufficient enthusiasm to investigate and check out all possibilities. The handler must learn to understand the principles of tracking and be prepared to accept that the dog knows a great deal more than he does.

He must build up a trust in his dog whereby each successful track further consolidates the confidence which a handler has in his dog and the dog has in himself. The handler must learn to be patient and should accept that he does not know everything about each single track – even if he lays it himself.

Failures will occur which are no fault of the dog. The dog should NEVER be blamed for a failure. His skill is a reflection of the handler's knowledge, ability and effort.

Each dog has his limits and so does each handler. Train and practise up to these limits and you can do no better.

Motivation to Track

Tracking requires one hundred per cent concentration from a dog. The best trackers can cut themselves off completely from the outside world whilst they are working and this means fully committed concentration for an unspecified period.

A competitive track will probably take ten to twenty minutes to complete, but a practical track can take a dog across fields, through fences, along ditches and through thickets for two miles or more. If we take a normal walking pace of three miles an hour as our guide there are forty minutes of concentration involved in a track of this nature but many operational dogs are asked to work for longer periods and this requires unstinted dedication.

Consider our own capabilities; how long can we concentrate on a subject without taking a few seconds relaxation? Think of high-speed motorway driving, especially during a busy period; consider the mental and, at times, physical exhaustion caused by a lengthy spell of fully committed concentration just to stay on the road.

This sort of concentration cannot be achieved without motivation. A dog must have a burning desire to track; he must experience a great sense of enjoyment and satisfaction. At one time hunger gave him the motivation. Hunger and the kill were the incentives which created the instinct which is inherited in our present-day canine companion. We must, however, use or find the forms of motivation which can build up the degree of concentration required for our final objective. In the long run the inducement to track will be the sheer joy of finding and following the specified scent path.

Competition Requirements

Competitive tracking is a worldwide activity with at least three basic sets of regulations affecting various countries and most breeds of dogs.

British working trials regulations are the basis for the South African approach; other countries in that locality, such as Zimbabwe, have developed via the Kennel Union of South Africa (K.U.S.A.).

European regulations are based on the Federation Cynologique Internationale (F.C.I.) and Schutzhund, which are very similar. This type of competition has now spread to South Africa, Zimbabwe, United States of America and many other countries. America and Canada also have tracking tests which differ from all others.

Although the regulations for the various styles of competition all differ, tracking is tracking, and the basic requirements are the same wherever you are. The objective is to locate and follow the scent of the tracklayer at the post which marks the start and to follow this track with the greatest accuracy, also to indicate the articles left on the track by the tracklayer.

Full details for the tracking requirements in U.K. working trials are given in the KENNEL CLUB (1) schedule but a brief summary of the various requirements is given here.

Utility Dog (U.D.) Stake [K.U.S.A. Equivalent T.D.I.]

The initial direction of the track is indicated by a second post which is placed about twenty paces from the start. The track will be approximately half an hour cold and half a mile in length. One article will be placed somewhere on the track and another at the half mile distance to indicate the end of the track. At least one article must be recovered to qualify.

Working Dog (W.D.) – 1½ Hours Cold Patrol Dog (P.D.) – 2 Hours [K.U.S.A. Equivalent T.D.II And P.D.]

One post is used to indicate the start of the track with no assistance being given to locate the direction of the first leg. The track will be approximately half a mile in length and two articles will be placed on the track with the second indicating the finish. At least one article must be recovered to qualify.

TRACKER DOG (T.D.) STAKE [K.U.S.A. EQUIVALENT T.D.III.]

Again one post is used to indicate the start of the track with no assistance being given to locate the direction of the first leg. The track will be approximately three hours cold and half a mile in length. Three articles will be evenly spaced along the track with the third indicating the finish. Two articles must be recovered to qualify.

In the U.K. the judge has full discretion in the decision of his track shape and this will probably include anything from four to fifteen corners. Although the distance between each corner (the legs) is normally walked in a reasonably straight line the judge may well decide to include a curve. Within the K.U.S.A. Regulations the T.D.I. track is kept very simple.

Normal competition track articles can vary tremendously in both size and composition. They can be as small as a golf tee or as large as a shoe, although the size of a matchbox may be more appropriate.

The article may be symmetrical and specially cut for the purpose or may be of an odd shape which could appear to be litter, such as a used shotgun cartridge, an empty cigarette packet or a crumpled page from a book.

One further tracking event in the U.K. which is restricted to the police and is part of the schedule for the National Police Dog Trials is the hard-surface track. This is approximately half a mile in length and half an hour cold. The track length has to be laid on a hard surface such as a road or a path without vegetation.

In America and Canada, tracking is an exercise on its own where dogs do not normally compete against each other and the only objective is to gain a tracking title. A T.D. (Tracker Dog) title is available where the track can be between half an hour and two hours cold. The length of the track is between 440 yards and 500 yards with a dark-coloured glove or wallet at the end of the track which has to be identified by the dog. There is also a more complicated track for the T.D.X. title. This is probably the most advanced stage in competitive tracking within the English-speaking countries. The track is a minimum of three hours cold, at least 1000 yards in length and will probably traverse fences, hedges or suchlike and will cross at least one road. A fresh cross track is also introduced as an additional hazard.

The F.C.I. and Schutzhund trials are very similar and have sets of tests at three different levels. At each level the track takes up one third of the total marks available and although the track conditions are much less arduous than the competitive tracks already indicated the general approach and precision is much more demanding. A very brief description of the tracking levels is as follows:

F.C.I. I.

The dog follows a track laid by the handler which is around 450 paces long and includes two right angles. The track to be worked immediately after it has been laid. Two everyday objects to be left on the track.

F.C.I. II.

The dog follows a track laid by a stranger, which is around 600 paces long, thirty minutes old and includes two right angles. Two everyday objects to be left on the track.

F.C.I. III.

The dog to follow a track laid by a stranger, which is around 800 paces long, one hour old and includes three right angles. Three everyday objects to be left on the track.

Equipment for Tracking

Very little equipment is required for tracking but the most important and costly is the harness. Controlled tracking can be carried out best with a properly constructed harness which has been designed for comfort and freedom of head and neck movement so that the dog can take the strain of a tight tracking line through the harness shoulder straps whilst his nose is down at ground level.

My very first tracking harness was made out of our younger daughter's pram harness; it was very effective and well used until my father bought me a purpose-made leather harness when I qualified my first dog to the level of U.D.Ex.

Although harnesses made from canvas or nylon webbing can be obtained, one made from good bridle leather is far superior and worth buying when one considers the hours of pleasure obtained from this chosen pastime. A good well-preserved leather harness will outlast a number of dogs and may outlast the handler as well.

A harness made from canvas webbing can be quite satisfactory but will have a much shorter life and although a nylon harness will certainly last for many years there is always a tendency for the straps to slip and cause discomfort from the resultant poor fit round the dog's body whilst he is tracking.

The sketch shows a harness made to suit a German Shepherd with the

An adjustable tracking harness for a German Shepherd Dog.

adjustability to suit the variations within the breed. Any good saddler will make a harness to your requirements.

The connecting link between a tracker dog and his handler is the tracking line. This line should be approximately thirty-six feet in length and it should have a dog lead type of clip at one end for attachment to the harness and preferably a loop at the other end for holding. The most suitable lines can be obtained from any hardware shop. A good quality cotton clothes rope or waxed cotton sash-window cord is ideal. Polypropylene or nylon ropes of similar weight are also suitable but are more likely to cause rope burns on your hand if you have an enthusiastic tracking dog.

Proper marking posts are not essential and a garden cane may be sufficient to mark the start of a track. However, a good, pointed post can prevent a fair amount of frustration when trying to push it into dry, hard ground. Many people find a broom shaft with a nail in the bottom to be a useful piece of equipment.

Articles to find are another necessity, to provide the real incentive to track. In the early stages they should be of a good size: a glove, a ball, a 'doggy' toy or a slipper. These can make ideal articles to start with; later on, items similar to competition requirements should be at hand.

Although the general requirements of tracking have already been discussed the objective and basic elements now require to be given.

Object of the Exercise

To have your dog follow a scent path which has been created by a person having walked over a piece of ground and having changed direction on a number of occasions; also to indicate the presence of any articles which have been dropped by that person. To build up time delay and experience to suit the requirements of the appropriate competitive standard or practical working conditions.

The basic elements. Dog to:

1 Locate the track;
2 Maintain a concentrated approach to following the track;
3 Identify a change in track direction;
4 Locate and indicate any articles which have been dropped by the tracklayer;
5 Continue to follow the track after finding an article.

It is now necessary to assess the approach

to tracking. Your objective is to condition your German Shepherd in such a manner that he will know, without commands, when and where he is expected to locate a track; he is not being asked or told, but is being released and given permission to track. The sight of the tracking harness should be sufficient to excite a German Shepherd and his expression should be one of expectancy and joy.

Progress may well be slow, but full of promise and pleasure. Even with a good, natural beginner and a handler who knows the ropes the progress should be controlled at a pace which will ensure that each step is firmly instilled in the dog's mind.

The natural tracking desire varies considerably from German Shepherd to

Fitting the harness on to an eager dog.

German Shepherd. Some are so keen that it is uncanny to see how they can progress so far beyond their handler's capacity to understand the complexity of the task in hand, and it is often the handler's shortcomings which ruin a good dog. Other German Shepherds are much less motivated and may require a fair amount of inducement before they discover that their olfactory system is much more effective and efficient than their eyes.

German Shepherds who have had strict obedience instilled into their system may find it difficult to acquire the independence required for tracking and may well find that their obedience-orientated handler is less capable of appreciating the completely different approach required for this form of work. The obedience enthusiast must be prepared to start thinking afresh, discard his obedience training and return to the status of a novice.

Although the approach to conditioning a German Shepherd for tracking may be similar, the purpose for one dog may be quite different from another.

The natural tracker can be built up to a high degree of efficiency without the introduction of articles on a track; he will probably consider any such articles as a hindrance and is likely to ignore their presence. The objective with a dog like this is to influence him, from the beginning, to stop for an article. He requires no inducement to track but he does require an inducement to stop for articles.

At the other end of the scale we have the German Shepherd without any interest in tracking; we would call him the less motivated tracking dog. He requires a strong inducement to enlist nature's gift to achieve HIS objective.

It is important to know whether a dog is a 'natural' or not, as this affects the handler's outlook and his ability to control the progress of training to achieve the prime objectives. To determine a dog's natural response a very simple, unsophisticated test can be applied. Whilst out for a walk with your German Shepherd go into a field or park at a time when there are absolutely no distractions and use a piece of ground on which you have not already walked during your present visit to the area. Tie your dog up to a fence post or other suitable object; do not tell him to stay or inhibit him in any way, but just leave him and walk out some fifty paces and then return down wind in a semicircle.

Whilst you are doing this your dog may jump around and bark; just let him. Do not shout or scold him as you may find that his excitement is a good indication of his desire to sniff out your scent path.

When you return to your dog, untie him and repeat the walk with him on the lead. If he is a 'natural' he will be curious to know where you have been and he will put his nose to the ground to follow your scent path. Your dog may show interest only for twenty or thirty yards or he may track you right round to your starting point.

The extent of his interest is dependent on the strength of his inherited instinct. A German Shepherd who has been trained to walk on a loose lead at all times, however, may well be too inhibited by the lead to show any natural response. With a dog so conditioned to the lead a truer picture can be obtained by letting him go free to see what reaction comes naturally.

Many German Shepherds will not show any interest in the scent path and may well be saying 'I do not need to follow that scent to find him; he is on the other end of the lead.' These dogs may have very little tracking ability in their inheritance and some may not have the ability to concentrate for long enough periods, yet others can have a strong tracking instinct lying dormant, waiting for somebody with the correct understanding to bring this potential to the fore.

Inducements for the Less Motivated German Shepherd

A German Shepherd who retrieves or loves to run out for a thrown toy, even if he does not return with it, has a distinct advantage; he has a strong possessive trait and as previously described with the retrieve matrix we are dependent on using or cultivating that possessive trait. The submissive trait is not important; it may be an inhibiting factor, but we do wish to capitalize on this possessiveness to achieve our objective.

There is no single approach towards cultivating possessiveness, although the basic principle of fun and games should be foremost in a handler's mind. Each handler should observe his dog or puppy. Is there a favourite toy? Will food have to be used as an inducement? Would the help of an assistant be an advantage? I can give a few ideas on cultivating this possessiveness, but it is up to the handler to use a specific idea or to develop his own.

The initial inducement can be carried out by using sight instead of scent to obtain the desired reaction. Tie your dog to something suitable or have somebody hold him on his lead. He must not be told to stay or to be quiet as he must not be inhibited in any way. Tease him a little with his toy, then walk out and place it in full sight of your dog; this may be five, ten or twenty paces from him, depending on

your dog. Return to him, take the lead and let him take you out to his toy, then let him off the lead for fun and games with his prized possession. The secret at this early stage is to have him desperate to go out and claim his own toy. This can be anything which takes his fancy and if you are fortunate you may have a variety of such toys which are equally valuable to him.

Some dogs like squeaky rubber or plastic toys; with others a rubber bone or ball may take their fancy. One dog I know of could only be excited with a ball in the toe of a nylon stocking.

My own German Shepherd bitch, Jeza, was a real country girl who did not know family life until she was six months of age. She did not know what toys were for and nothing excited her sufficiently to induce an enjoyable game until I used a hardboard disc about six inches in diameter. With a backhand flip I could make that disc float through the air like a bird in flight. That was enough for my little country lass; she would go out like a shot to make the 'kill'. I had a plentiful supply of discs at that time and certainly needed them, not only for Jeza but also for friends who realized what an inducement they could be.

When the sight of the disc was sufficient to stimulate natural excitement I would walk out twenty yards and place it on the grass, return to Jeza and let her take me out to it on the end of her lead. I would then release her, pick up the disc and throw it for her. These discs became her incentive to track.

Young Caro, another German Shepherd, joined our household at the age of fifteen weeks. He was a character and, like his father, was a natural carrier. By the time he was five months old he was picking up any piece of wood he could carry and although he was not retrieving, he was carrying articles of his own choice. At that time we had a favourite walk through a country park where timber operations gave young Caro a tremendous selection of tree cuttings. After Caro had selected his article for the day and had run around with it, also teasing Jeza into chasing him with his piece of wood, this piece of wood became his valued possession. That was the time to tie Jeza up and for Irene, my wife, to hold Caro on the lead whilst I took his piece of wood and walked into the wind for some thirty paces or so and let Caro see me drop it. I then returned by exactly the same route, took the lead, then let Caro take me at top speed to get his stick. The stick was then thrown for him and he was again in possession of his precious piece of wood. Half a dozen such outings with increasing distances each time had Caro doing one hundred yards before I thought of introducing him to the tracking harness.

Although I had labelled Caro as a less motivated tracker after applying my usual test, he responded magnificently to the correct inducement for him. Many dogs take much longer and it is a case of progressing at the rate which suits that particular dog.

Another approach which was used to develop Caro's enthusiasm, and is used extensively, with variations, by police dog handlers, is also a basis for manwork training. A piece of leather, canvas, sacking or some such material is ideal for having a tug-of-war with a dog. The excitement of such a game can be a very strong incentive to track for an article. It must be said, at this stage, that personal aggression is not necessary and it is not advisable to mix full manwork training with tracking.

When the dog has accepted this exciting game a short track can be laid in the same manner as with Caro and his piece of wood or Jeza with her disc, but in this instance the dog is given the full satisfaction of a tug-of-war after finding his article.

A novel variation to this tug-of-war is an old trick which suits a dog who enjoys pulling at the exposed roots of a tree. Hammer a wooden peg into the ground so that the dog can enjoy pulling it out. I have never used this form of incentive but I believe it can be very effective with some dogs.

There are dogs of various breeds that show no interest in the standard approach to tracking inducements and German Shepherds are no exception. At one time using food as an inducement was frowned upon by the majority of enthusiasts, but its use is now becoming a commonplace activity and not only with the reluctant tracker.

Over the years I have tried a number of methods using food and I shall now describe the approach that seems to be most successful. It will be realized that there is no point in using food as an inducement after the dog has had his major meal of the day. At the same time, I do not believe in starving a dog for the purpose of training.

This method involves a piece of tripe, or some mince, in the toe of an old stocking, or a piece of muslin, tied to a length of string. This can be dragged along the ground to leave a food scent path. Little containers with the same food can be placed on the track as a reward. As with other methods, the tracks should be short to begin with and gradually lengthened with experience. A container of food should be placed at the end of the track.

To wean the dog from food orientation

the food drag can be lifted for five to ten paces then dragged again. Distances can be built up without the drag and short tracks laid without any drag but with the food reward at the end.

This is a method which can be stopped and then reintroduced at any stage of training. Food drags can even be used to help achieve a good working inducement on tracks that have been given a lengthy time delay.

There is no limit to the use of food but, like any other method, common sense must prevail and the dog's responses must be taken into consideration.

A Foundation for Tracking

Each stage of conditioning a dog to track must blend with the previous and the following stages. There are practices to be encouraged at certain stages which are considered to be decidedly harmful at others. Some trainers will have thrown up their hands in horror at a few of my comments in the previous pages, but I hope that the following notes will dispel any apprehension.

I have given details which involve double tracking, i.e. walking straight out then back along the same line, thereby creating tracks in opposite directions and superimposed on each other. When one considers that the alternative involves walking round in a box or circle to create a single track the dog may well be distracted from the objective by having a choice and he may backtrack round to the article. In the earlier stages it is also imperative that the time factor between dropping the article and allowing the dog to go out after it is kept to a minimum.

Although this practice is decidedly helpful in the early stages it must be stopped as soon as possible to ensure that a forward-tracking attitude is developed.

It is also believed by some trainers that the introduction to tracking must be made with the correct equipment, i.e. a tracking harness and line. Many good dogs have been introduced at the start without a harness and I have found it easier to maintain a fun-and-games approach without the formality of a harness and only introduce the use of this equipment when the dog is capable of concentrating for a sixty- to one-hundred yard track. Also I believe that in Germany, the home of present-day tracking, some top-class dogs are tracking whilst attached to an ordinary collar and line and some others without lead or line.

A number of authoritative voices say that a handler should not lay any tracks for his own dog, even in the earliest stages. At the same time I know of a few top-class handlers in the past who would NEVER allow any other person to lay commissioning tracks for them. In laying all their own tracks they turned out good, practical, working police dogs or competition dogs of some note. This subject will be discussed in greater detail at a later stage.

Although the natural tracker does not require the inducements of the less motivated dog he must realize that the purpose of the exercise is to find the articles on the track. If the reader has skipped over the earlier details on inducements for the less motivated dog because he has a 'natural', he would be well advised to go back and read again so that he can coordinate the natural desire to track with the need to find articles.

The natural tracker can always be a problem to his handler if he is not induced, from the beginning, to stop for the articles.

134

Stopping for an article.

Even the less motivated dog who has been properly induced to go out for his article will eventually enjoy his tracking so much that he can, at a later stage, ignore articles because they interrupt the enjoyment of tracking. He can become a 'natural' and the handler will have to ensure that there is always sufficient inducement to stop until it becomes second nature for the dog to become rooted to the spot as soon as he has located an article.

The procedure is now identical for both the natural and the less motivated dogs, but the purposes differ greatly. The 'natural' is induced to stop at the article and the 'less motivated' is induced to go out for the article.

The first tracks should be of a length to suit your dog – they may be ten yards or they may be fifty – but it is important that the working of each track be carried out by the dog without any break in concentration. His mind must be fixed on his objective from start to finish. Keenness at the end of the track is as important as keenness at the beginning.

With these initial tracks the dog will normally be on the lead, but make sure that a slip chain, if used, is not on the choke. It may be desirable even to use a leather collar. German Shepherds who are inhibited by the lead and slip chain may well perform better if released to track free during the foundation stages.

A nice, quiet field away from all distractions is the ideal setting for your foundation work. Position yourself so that you lay your tracks into the wind. Tracking into the wind serves the useful purpose of helping the less motivated dog

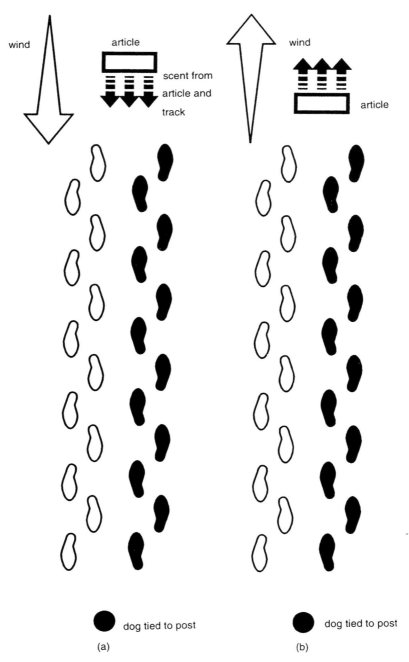

wind

article

scent from article and track

dog tied to post

(a)

wind

article

dog tied to post

(b)

Double tracklaying. Return by overlapping outgoing footprints.

to locate his article quickly, as he will probably wind it before he goes the full distance. This success encourages longer periods of concentration and therefore more successes. Also, tracking into the wind with the article at the end ensures that no scent has travelled beyond the article, so there is no inducement for the natural tracker to go beyond that point.

To lay those foundation tracks, first tie your dog to a post or let somebody hold him; let him know you have his fun article and walk or run out the required distance. Let the dog see you place his article but ensure that it is suitably hidden from view until he is almost on top of it. We now wish to avoid the dog catching sight of the article so that achievement through scenting will increase his confidence. Return to your dog by the same route, then encourage him to go out as you follow at the end of the lead. The scent of his article will reach him before he has gone the full distance and he should 'home' in on it. He may start off by using his eyes having seen you walk out, but his nose will soon take control and prove to be much more reliable.

Whenever your dog reaches the article make the most of it. Give him plenty of praise with fun and games, titbits, if you wish, a fun retrieve or a tug-of-war; anything so long as your dog finds tremendous pleasure in stopping at the article.

The next stage is to try carrying out this foundation work with a following wind. Although the track does not go beyond the article the wind will certainly carry the scent on for some distance. Your dog may well overshoot the article by a yard or so before realizing it is there but he should turn back to indicate its presence. If he carries on much further without a positive indication of the article he is not ready to

progress and more tracks into the wind are necessary.

Developing a Tracking Routine

Your German Shepherd should always know when he is expected to track. The sight of the harness, your own actions and the routine you develop should be sufficient to let him know he is being allowed to track. The only verbal support he should require is a few words of encouragement as he puts his nose to the ground to locate the scent. His reactions, however, can only meet your requirements if you plan each stage and develop the routine gradually so that one stage is in harmony with the next.

The tracking harness is the key: the dog should automatically seek out the track when the harness is fitted and then realize that the job is finished when the harness is removed. To have a dog wandering round with the harness on before he is being asked to track will take away this key to motivation. To leave the harness on the dog after the completion of the track will have the same effect. Some trainers advocate that the dog should become accustomed to the harness before he is given his first track. This may well work with good dogs and well-disciplined handlers, but it tends to introduce a sloppy approach and thereby to negate a very natural form of motivation.

The complete development of this routine is based on full canine dedication to the job in hand from the moment the tracking harness is fitted round the dog's body. Recognize that the initial tracks in harness may be strange to the dog and can detract a little from his enthusiasm, but this should not be a problem if the foundation has been properly carried out.

1 Take your dog with the harness and line to the start of the track, or within five yards of it.
2 Put the harness on your dog, remove his lead and check chain and attach the line to the harness. Immediately release him to track with a few words of encouragement. 'That's a good boy, where is it?' is as good as anything.
3 On finding an article he may return

Complete dedication from a committed tracker.

to you with it, he may stand over it, or he may lie down beside it. These are only some of the options, but on finding the last article, or on recognizing that you are lost, you remove the harness immediately to let your dog know that he is not required to track any further.

We can bend a few of our rules in the early stages to build up the connections, so long as we do not forget our final objective. At this stage the foundation has been developed, your dog has great enthusiasm for his article and he recognizes that his nose is an ideal tool to locate the scent path and the article.

The harness can now be fitted round the dog immediately prior to laying another foundation track: straight out, drop the article and straight back. In the meantime your dog is tied to a post with his lead – a benching chain and leather collar is a good alternative – or he is held by a friend. Return to your dog, clip your lead to his harness and let him go out ahead of you to track down his article. The harness may distract him a little but give him an abundance of encouragement and follow at his speed. On reaching the article give him a few seconds of fun, remove the harness, then give him much more fun.

If you lay the track before fitting the harness at this stage of his education he may well lose some or all of his enthusiasm to track. You wish to have his mind firmly fixed on the track from the second you leave him to lay it. On finding the article, your enthusiasm with fun and games is again keeping his mind on the objective whilst the harness is still attached. At this early stage removing the harness immediately he finds the article can inhibit him at the moment he requires praise for successfully completing his assignment. The use of his lead instead of the tracking line has the purpose of maintaining the close contact of foundation tracking. If the full length of a long line is used he may well wonder why you are so far back, and this experience plus the new feeling of a tracking harness could well be too great a distraction.

Tracks can now be developed as a single scent path where the first leg only is used for tracking and finishing at the article. This first leg should be laid into the wind so that article finding is easy and positive. After dropping the article the tracklayer should carry on walking for some ten to fifteen paces, then return at some distance from, but parallel to, the working leg of the track to ensure that the track is not contaminated by the return. The tracking line can now be used and the applied length be extended as confidence is gained.

One or two tracks in a session are quite sufficient and, if you are laying a second immediately after working the first, remember to remove the harness for the short period and use a clean piece of ground well clear of your first track.

Although enthusiasm must be considered to be of top priority, the fitting of the harness prior to laying a track should be stopped as soon as possible, but not at the expense of lost enthusiasm to start a track.

The importance of a short time lag between laying and working the track can be vital. The time taken in preparing harness and line, etc. after a track has been laid can be critical if we wish to maintain the maximum of enthusiasm.

When we feel that the harness does not need to be fitted before the track has been laid, prepare the harness and line by having them laid out all ready before laying the track and make sure that the line is free from tangles or knots. When you have laid the track your dog should be impatient to start; do not disappoint him by taking too long to prepare him. Hamfisted or fussy handling at this stage can be the biggest cause of dogs going off the boil, and then handlers wonder why their dogs have lost enthusiasm.

When single-leg tracks of one hundred yards or so are being worked, a change to tracks with a following wind can be laid to give the dog experience of realizing that an article can be present without prior warning. Crosswind tracks can also be added to his repertoire. On these very fresh tracks with a crosswind he may well track some three to six feet off the track – and on occasions may track even wider. Come back on the track and then work wide again. Do not worry about this lack of accuracy because he will work much closer to the scent surface as he becomes more experienced and the tracks are older.

A corner can now be included in the track, but again the first leg should be walked into the wind to ensure that no scent has drifted beyond the corner (see figure on page 140). A first leg of some hundred or one hundred and fifty yards will give the dog a chance to settle in before reaching the corner; he will then cast round until he finds the new direction. This is where the importance of enthusiasm becomes evident.

An enthusiastic dog will be very annoyed at losing the track and will busy himself to relocate it. He will probably learn the first lesson in finding a 'lost' track. However, a dog who is lacking in enthusiasm is likely to flounder at this first minor obstacle and will probably require a great deal of encouragement and help to continue round the first corner.

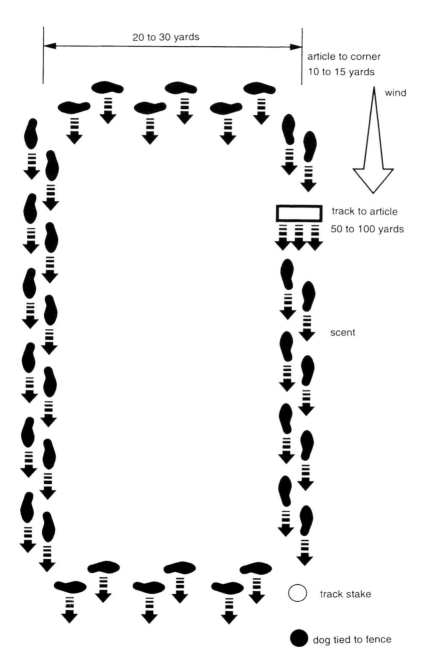

20 to 30 yards

article to corner
10 to 15 yards

wind

track to article
50 to 100 yards

scent

track stake

dog tied to fence

Creating a single scent path.

This kind of situation is a bad omen for the future and the handler must realize that he is on a 'loser' unless he goes back and achieves a greater response to the initial inducement.

With the article placed some twenty to twenty-five yards beyond the corner the effect of any slight wind change will not be sufficient to carry the scent on to the first leg. This could induce the dog to cross over and miss out on part of the track. This distance also ensures that a full cast does not take the dog beyond the article so that he misses it. To find his article some twenty yards or so after taking his first corner will give the dog great confidence in his own ability to think out a problem and meet with success, i.e. finding his favourite toy. Remember, a handler's confidence can only be a product of his dog's success.

Corners involving crosswinds should now be laid and it could be advisable to lay the first few with the second leg going into the wind, this gives your dog a choice of direction as the scent from the second leg will be carried beyond the corner. This should not cause a problem, but any attempt to go in the wrong direction by a greater distance than the length of the tracking line should be countered by your refusal to move until he recasts and picks up on the correct direction. A continuation of this type of difficulty will necessitate corners at a slight angle which is increased with every track so that the change in direction is gradually introduced.

Corners which create a following wind with the second leg should not cause any problems: so long as the dog has the enthusiasm to cast, there will be scent in only the one direction. Guaranteed success with crosswinds should make corners with a following wind on the first leg a simple conclusion to another stage of development.

The article can now be placed further from the corner until each of the two legs on the track has been lengthened to about one hundred and fifty yards.

During this period of development the dog has watched the tracks being laid and there has not been any need to use a starting post to indicate the start of the track, although there would have been no harm in using one. As competitive tracking necessitates a post at the start of the track, and it is essential to know exactly where the track can be located, it is advisable to introduce and use a starting post until the full routine has been developed. The post can then be considered as optional if other markers are available.

A time delay of a few minutes between laying the track and preparing to work it can now be introduced and this will have one of two possible effects.

1 A more enthusiastic dog because he is annoyed at being kept waiting.
2 A relatively uninterested dog because waiting has dampened his enthusiasm. He is no longer motivated and is just not ready to progress.

The time lag can now be extended to some ten minutes or so. The track length can be increased gradually to about four hundred yards and two or three corners introduced to create a build-up of experience whilst developing the routine.

Again the dog can be tied to a post so that he can watch the track being laid, or it may be more convenient to leave him in the car if it can be positioned so that he can watch the start of the track being laid.

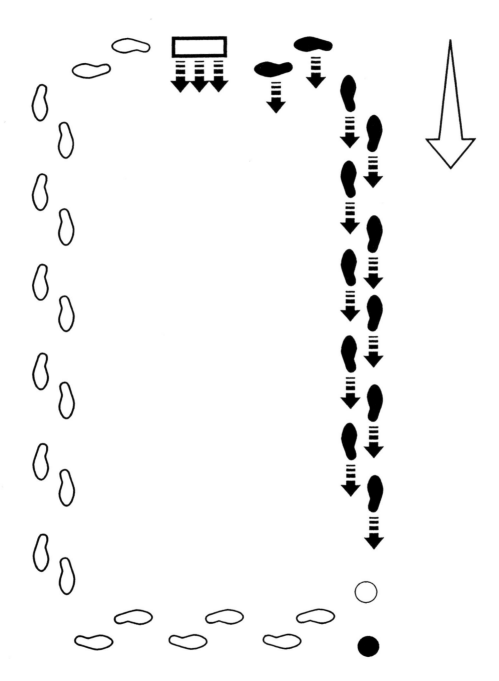

It is important to appreciate the effect of wind at corners.

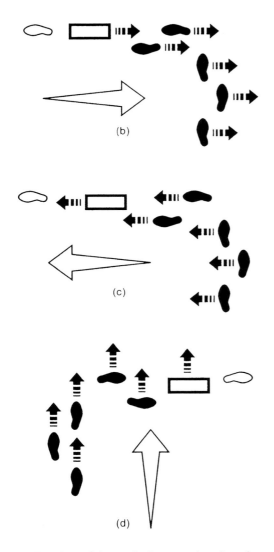

(b)

(c)

(d)

foundation followed by the development of the tracking routine in the dog's mind.

Your dog can now be left out of sight whilst you lay the track. Leave him in the car or in somebody's care, but as soon as you have laid the track take him to the starting post and prepare him in the normal manner.

Distance and age of the track can now be gradually extended to the full half mile in length and half an hour cold. Additional corners will have to be included – four to six should be sufficient, with most of them at right angles. An obtuse-angled corner should not create any problems but an acute-angled corner can encourage a dog to cross from one leg to another and it may be advisable to study the effects of wind before adding acute corners to his reper-toire. The distance between each corner can also be varied and track legs can vary between fifty and three hundred yards. There is little value in making a track leg any longer, and shorter legs at this stage may well cause confusion with some dogs.

Tracking Progress

Enthusiasm for tracking is much more important than working long tracks or extended time delays. Each dog pro-gresses at his own pace and achievements can only be assessed by determining the canine enthusiasm in conjunction with the length and age of the tracks. The last fifty yards of a track are just as important as the first fifty. If the dog's enthusiasm diminishes before he reaches the article at the end of the track, it is too long, too old or a combination of both.

The amount of concentration a dog can give is not limitless. It takes time to build up the amount of concentration which will

During this period a routine has been established where the dog knows that the presence of his harness means tracking, and your soft words of encouragement whilst fitting the harness will have helped to reinforce the routine. Unsighted tracks can now be introduced and this is a very important stage of development. It is the stage which proves the value of a sound finally be required. Every break in that concentration whilst tracking must be a cause for concern.

A programme for any form of canine training must be flexible, and a tracking programme is no exception. There are, however, a few guide lines which should be considered when planning your future work load.

1 Each stage from the initial foundation right through to the full competitive practical requirements should allow for the need to consolidate before progressing from one stage to the next. A qualification in one competitive stage does not necessarily mean that the dog is ready to progress to the next.

2 Although puppies can be introduced to tracking and benefit greatly from this form of activity, it must be remembered that their ability to concentrate should be related to their stage of maturity. I believe also that the sensitivity of the olfactory system is related to maturity, and it is safe to assume that mental and olfactory maturity is closely related to the dog's age. Any programme of progression involving young dogs must take any lack of maturity into consideration.

3 Some dogs thrive on tracking and can be given a track every day for a lengthy period before they become bored with a once enjoyable outlet for their enthusiasm. I wonder how many young brides have mistakenly served up their loved one's favourite dish every day in an attempt to make him happy. Even a dog can get too much of a good thing.

The police can take a new dog and a raw handler and have them comfortably working a full half-mile, half-hour-old track by the end of a three-month general training course, but other dogs will be discarded in the process because they will not make the grade in a reasonable time.

I find myself averaging two tracks per week during the first eighteen months to two years of my dog's working life. Starting at the age of four to six months the youngsters are given plenty of time to develop. Sometimes we manage as many as four tracks during one week, whilst for other periods of a few weeks at a time we may not track at all. I do not believe we have hindered our progress either way.

The track shape illustrated below is ideal to apply in segments for training. The full track may be considered as a typical competition track, starting from either end.

In training, any segment can be used to create a combination of short and long legs, acute or right-angled corners. A simple A to D with short legs may suit one session, with F to H

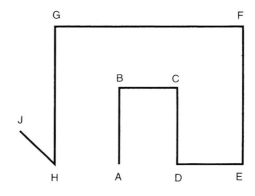

Sectional training tracks.

covering another. There are many possible combinations to suit your requirements on the day and you should not have to think up new track shapes.

4 The keeping of a tracking record which creates a history of progress is much more important than formulating a precisely timed programme for the future. It is a record of progress and this controls your attention on the future.

Handling Techniques

Although the foundation and routine development sections have concentrated on creating the sound basis of a tracking dog, this work can be jeopardized by inexperienced or inconsiderate handling.

Handlers must always remember that they are the weak link in a tracking partnership. If you are fortunate your dog may well be able to carry your deficiencies for a period but he will finally be brought down to your level of competence. It is up to the handler to learn as much as possible about his own function to ensure that his dog is given every opportunity to perform at his best, and the handler must bring his level of understanding nearer to the expertise of his German Shepherd when tracking.

The application of handler techniques involves the ability to plan and lay tracks suited to the dog's standard of work, also to apply sensible and sympathetic line control.

Good, thoughtful tracklaying generally goes unnoticed, but can go a long way towards avoiding unnecessary problems when the dog is working the track. Two legs of a track being laid rather close with a crosswind can entice an inexperienced dog away from the correct line. Any uncertainty over selected landmarks when laying the track can cause greater confusion, especially when the dog is considered to be wrong, and this situation can be aggravated still further by inconsiderate line control.

The handler who lays a track for his dog can easily affect his dog's attitude towards tracking if he makes incorrect use of his knowledge of the track. On the other hand he can prevent problems and assist his dog to gain experience by the skilful use of his knowledge combined with sensible line control.

The foundation and development of the tracking routine has been described with the handler laying tracks for his own dog. This is not essential if the assistance of a well-experienced tracker-dog handler is available. Such a person can be a vital factor in the development of a future tracking partnership. It must be said, however, that many good, experienced handlers are adamant in their view that a handler should refrain from laying tracks for his own dog. The reasons for this opinion do have some validity and they are:

1 If the handler knows exactly where the track is he is likely to transmit that information through the tracking line to his dog, possibly without realizing it.

2 If a dog is brought up on his own handler's track scent he may not know that he can track on other scents.

At this stage, I will only say that I have yet to meet an experienced handler who has ruined a dog of his own by laying his own tracks. The reasons are probably based on observations of the failures of some inexperienced handlers and the causes of these failures may well have been misinterpreted. I have handled eight German Shepherds through to tracking qualifications and in each case approximately eighty per cent of the tracks were laid by me. I have also been involved in helping quite a number of novice handlers as they learned the art of line control whilst they worked their dogs on their own tracks.

There is no doubt that you do need to apply a great deal of self-control whilst handling a dog who is working a track you have laid yourself. It is very easy for a handler to communicate his own knowledge through the tracking line when he knows exactly where the track goes, instead of encouraging the dog to develop his own tracking technique. A handler can apply a little extra tension on the line and thus inadvertently let his dog know that he is coming to an article or a corner, or indicate the correct direction when his dog is casting at a corner. The sensitivity of the tracking line can tell a good many things if it has been used as a means of communication from handler to dog.

The attentive handler can learn a great deal by studying his German Shepherd at work. How does he react to a corner? Does he normally cast wide? Does he overshoot, and by how much, with a following wind? Does he track parallel with the scent path when there is a crosswind and by how much? With the full, detailed knowledge of a track a handler is prepared for a dog's reaction and can study them as they arise. Without that knowledge during the initial learning period a handler can fail to recognize his partner's reactions and possibly fail to cooperate fully with his dog's requirements.

Those handlers who advocate the use of other people as tracklayers for novice dogs will probably agree that this approach is only practical if an experienced handler is available to help. This experience can then be used to control the handler and assist in teaching him to interpret his dog's reactions; this is what is meant by the expression 'learning to read your dog'. Those who have this kind of invaluable assistance available are unlikely, perhaps, to need this book.

The alternative is to use an inexperienced tracklayer and to my mind there is no poorer combination than a novice handler with an inexperienced tracklayer. A novice who cannot find a suitably experienced assistant is strongly advised to 'go it alone'. If I meet up with any tracking problem during my dog's working career I immediately revert to laying all the tracks for the dog myself until the problem has been overcome and we have again consolidated on successful tracks.

Referring to the other problems foreseen by some experienced handlers regarding the change over from the handler's scent to that of a stranger, the reintroduction of a few foundation tracks by an assistant can soon overcome any reluctance to change.

Tracklaying is not such a simple task that anybody can be asked and left to carry out the function. It is well known that there are a few experienced and successful handlers who seem to have little sense of direction. They may be reasonably competent on the end of the tracking line but have difficulty in applying the disciplines of a tracklayer.

I remember one experienced handler who offered to lay tracks at a competition. The judge's track shape was simple and perfectly clear but this tracklayer managed to cross the first leg of the track whilst laying the third leg. The ground was open and the starting post was quite visible, but he took the post marking the start of another track as his marker. The track was quite useless and resulted in the waste of valuable time and an excellent piece of ground.

Some tracklayers go armed with pencil and paper, which is very commendable. They note any landmarks and know precisely where the track has been laid, but back at the starting post it may become apparent that there are two landmarks which appear very similar and far enough apart to cause concern. There are times when a clump of heavy grass or a patch of heather used as an integral marker within the track may be completely out of sight when standing back at the starting post.

To walk a straight line when laying a track is not so easy unless the tracklayer applies a certain amount of self-discipline and also makes use of suitable landmarks. The most helpful approach is to choose an easily identified, distant marker, but make sure it cannot be confused with another. Walk straight out towards the marker for the appropriate distance, keeping your eyes fixed on it the whole time. If you take your eyes off the marker for five seconds you will probably find that you have changed direction slightly. At each turn choose another landmark, or a point between two suitable markers, and continue with your track. It is preferable to use distant markers where possible. To use a tree or bush within the tracking area is acceptable on isolated occasions, but to use them regularly would encourage the dog to cast at every bush or tree in expectation of a corner or an article.

Although distances are usually quoted in yards the number of average paces when walking is a satisfactory substitute. If the distance is quoted in metres an extra pace for every ten metres will accommodate the difference, i.e. 300 metres will require 330 paces.

A tracklayer stopping to drop an article will probably create a small area with a much stronger odour. With both feet relatively close together at that point and probably a slight twisting of the feet, especially if the tracklayer turned to note suitable landmarks, any vegetation will have received very severe crushing compared to the normal footprint. This change in odour strength can give an indication to a dog that there is something of note in that area. The very same effect can result when making a corner on a track. This additional odour strength can be used to help and encourage a young dog to expect an article or a corner. So long as the presence of these strong patches is realized by the handler they can be used to advantage; on the other hand, special care can be taken by the tracklayer to ensure that he continues walking when he drops an article or changes direction.

A tracklayer should study the effect of wind on any leg, corner or the positioning of articles. Two legs of a track being rather close with a crosswind can be inadvisable for a young dog working very fresh tracks, but these conditions should not affect a more experienced dog working a much older track. On older tracks most peripheral scents will have dispersed and the close proximity of the other leg will probably go unnoticed or be ignored by the dog.

A corner which is too acute can cause similar problems and the presence of an article can also be a strong inducement to leave one leg of the track and take a short cut across to the more interesting scent on the other leg.

It is important that a tracklayer should remember where the track has been laid, but it is equally important he should recognize that he is not infallible. If a dog seems to be tracking well the tracklayer should consider very deeply before condemning the dog for overshooting a corner or for deviating from a straight leg. We as humans are just as likely to be wrong, but at the same time it can do much harm to allow a dog to deviate far from the scent path he is working. A tracklayer should strike the correct balance and this again illustrates the value of a tracklayer who is also an experienced tracker-dog handler.

The control of a tracking line is an art and one which should be developed with the greatest respect for the dog's feelings. Sensitive and considerate line control will be rewarded by a dog who accepts the responsibility of being a senior partner.

The tracking line should be taut whenever possible, with the tension being applied by the dog, the handler maintaining sufficient steady resistance to ensure that the line remains taut. When preparing to track the line should be laid out or thrown out in such a manner that knots or tangles have been avoided, or at least sorted out before the harness is fitted to the dog, as connecting the line to the harness is the signal to track. The handler should allow tension to be applied from the start to ensure that the line remains taut and is allowed to run through both hands, which are as far apart as possible. When the looped end of the line reaches the hand at the rear it is time for the handler to move forward to ensure that a steady tension is maintained. If this function is carried out properly the dog will not feel any jerk on the line as you follow him on the track.

When the dog stops or casts, any loose line should be drawn in and, if necessary, be held up high to allow the dog to pass underneath and so avoid a tangle of line with the dog's legs as he casts. Some very enthusiastic dogs can cast at such a speed that there is little time to draw the line in and lift it up high enough. On these occasions it is much simpler to let the line drop to the ground so that the dog can cast right over it. There may be a chance of him getting caught up with the line, but a loose line just below body height would present much more of a problem. If your dog does get tangled in the line, do not blame him. Tell him to stay, go up to him and sort out the problem, then give him a few words of praise and encouragement to continue with the track.

Under normal tracking conditions the full length of the line should be used but your arm from elbow to shoulder should be used as part of a shock-absorbing unit to maintain steady tension on the line. During a steady track your arm should not be extended at full length but held with the elbow in line with your body. This allows for the full extension of your arm when it is necessary, together with a slight quickening of your feet to maintain the tension on the line and regain the neutral arm position. The presence of any bushes or high undergrowth may necessitate a raised arm position to keep the line clear.

There is a tendency with some handlers in the U.K. to work with a very short line, down to about six feet in length. I have heard it said that this is because of the short distance between some corners on competitive tracks. Perhaps these competitors know what to expect from a particular judge, but I am sure there are other advantages that are not permitted in other countries.

Schutzhund and F.C.I. tracking regulations require the line to be ten metres (approximately thirty-three feet) and to be used as such. American tracking regulations dictate that the line length will be between twenty and forty feet with a visible marker on the line twenty feet from the dog. Australian tracking regulations indicate that the line be between nine and eighteen metres (around sixty feet) in length and normally be fully utilized.

The full length of the line is there to be used but there are times, particularly during training or very difficult conditions, when it is wise to shorten the distance between you and your dog. A dog that weaves from side to side on a fresh track may require a shorter length of line for a period. A very strong crosswind may also indicate such a change, although a short line with a following wind can cause so great an overshoot on a corner that recovery becomes unlikely. One must learn from experience where and when a shorter length of line should be used on a particular section of track.

Obstacles such as a ditch, a fence or a wall should also be anticipated. When it looks as if an obstacle will have to be negotiated move in towards your dog to give yourself some free line to work with. I have seen a dog stopped in mid-air when jumping a ditch because the handler did not have line to spare.

A barbed-wire fence can cause its own problems, but it is best to hold the dog firm when he decides to investigate the other side. Keep the tension on the line as you move towards the dog, let him through the fence to investigate and when he decides that the track continues on the other side hold him verbally if you can whilst you negotiate the fence. A young, keen dog may be difficult to stop, however; in this case try to snarl the line on a barb until

you are successfully over the fence, clear the line, then proceed with praise for your dog. A barbed-wire fence is always an inconvenience and only practice will help to minimize any problem.

Although competition regulations only stipulate that a dog should indicate the presence of an article which must be recovered by the handler, it is essential to train the dog to stop at articles. He may pick up the article and return to you with it but it is better if he stays where the article is found. With a dog who is eager to continue tracking it is best to hold him firm, keep the tension on the line and move towards him. On securing the article allow him to proceed and let the line through your hands with a steady tension as you would at the start of the track.

In the early days of tracking I would recommend that the spare line at the start of the track or at any stage during the track is left to drag on the ground. Some experts advocate that any spare line should be coiled and held in your hand. Although I fully agree with this practice it may not be practical with a very enthusiastic dog and it does require much attention to become an expert at it. I believe that any attention to detail can be of far greater value if directed to watching your dog for indications. A handler must be alert to his dog's actions when the line is being drawn in or being played out and I do not believe that this is the time to be trying to coil or uncoil a tracking line. When a dog has settled down and is well experienced, and if the handler has the time to think about the finer points, coiling any spare line can prevent possible snagging of the end in undergrowth.

The tracking line is a one-way communication system from dog to handler, and this shows up to the greatest advantage when tracking at night. As most practical tracks are carried out during the hours of darkness, the handler of an operational dog knows exactly what his dog is doing by the 'feel' of the tracking line. He cannot see his dog for much of the time but that line of communication tells him all he wants to know. A handler trying to communicate back through the line will find that the messages will become scrambled with the information travelling in the opposite direction and this can only lead to a confused partnership.

Unfortunately many novice handlers treat the tracking line as an extra-long lead which they jerk, tug or pull when they are displeased with their dogs' performance. No wonder an unintentional jerk stops a dog in his tracks and has him saying 'What have I done wrong this time?' The line could be snagged on a bush, caught round a tree when casting or some other innocent cause, but to the dog it means 'I'm wrong again'. His enthusiasm is dented and he has taken another step towards confused bewilderment. However, a dog who is accustomed to a sensibly controlled tension on the line will accept the occasional snarled line without questioning the cause.

Other handlers, although studious in their approach, are quite unconscious of their line control failings. I knew of one handler who was having problems with her dog dashing out full of enthusiasm at the start of the track, then casting around at the end of the line with a diminishing inclination to continue. Observation highlighted the fault. This handler was not fully prepared to move forward as the end of the tracking line came into her hands, and the subsequent jerk before she moved broke the dog's concentration and ability to settle into the track.

Although I explained the cause of the problem on a number of occasions this handler could not seem to overcome her slow start until I gave her the harness with the line attached and asked her to run out at the speed of her dog as I took control of the line. In the first such experiment I let this handler experience her dog's reaction to the jerk from the line, then I let her experience the smooth take-off as I maintained tension on the line and moved forward before I became an extension of that line. The next lesson was a reversal of roles where I played the part of the dog and the student handler was asked to apply the necessary line control. We went through the same procedure until I could move out at a suitable pace without feeling any appreciable change in tension on the line as she moved to follow. When she started tracking again with her dog she controlled the line beautifully and the problem was resolved.

Another aspect of line control is to ensure that the dog feels his responsibility. A tracking line without sufficient tension can give some dogs the feeling of freedom to dart about or to develop a careless attitude to their task and this may result in grossly overshooting corners or meandering off the track for other interesting odours. The correct amount of tension does ensure that a responsible attitude prevails.

It is very important that verbal restraint should never be applied at any time on a track, and when extra tension is applied a few words of encouragement will ensure that the dog does not feel obliged to relax. The purpose of tension is to control the pace without reducing the dog's enthusiasm.

Many experienced handlers maintain that a handler should not speak to his dog whilst he is tracking. Basically this is sound advice but should not be considered as a golden rule. A good dog can shut out everything irrelevant happening round him whilst he is tracking. If the track is all-important to him, his concentration requires a direct challenge before it can be broken. I have watched rabbits and game birds emerge from under a dog's nose whilst he was tracking without a falter in his step. I have handled a dog who passed within a yard of two pipe band drummers at practice and it was the silence, with the astonished look, as we passed them which brought the dog's attention to their presence; he ignored the noise but noted the sudden silence. During another practice track this dog stepped over a very surprised and embarrassed courting couple who had taken refuge in a quiet secluded spot one summer evening.

All the events happened to my first tracking dog, Quest, and at that time I did not appreciate the significance of his powers of concentration and dedication. I did discover, however, that if I tried to instruct him during a track or disturbed his concentration with a reprimand of any sort, he lost interest completely. He would seem to say 'If you know better than me, you carry on and finish it'.

It is, of course, correct to say that a handler should not nag or natter away at a dog whilst he is tracking but there are times, especially in the earlier stages, when encouragement or praise given quietly can help to give a dog that little bit of extra confidence which can make a difference to the limit of his concentration.

Any factor which breaks the steady pace of a dog whilst tracking requires special attention from the handler. If he stops to investigate, casts round or changes direction the handler should ask himself 'What is the reason? Is he casting at a corner or is there some sort of interference?' If the handler knows the direction of the track he can ask himself if he could have read the situation without prior knowledge. How well can he trust his dog to stop at an article? Or how competent is his dog at sorting out the situation in the area of interference?

It is important that a dog should be given the opportunity of investigating until he is satisfied, and it is essential that a positive error on the part of the dog must be countered as soon as possible. Any dog who deviates from a track by more than the length of the tracking line (twelve yards) is heading for trouble and should certainly be corrected before he has increased the distance appreciably. (Competitive tracks are, of course, excluded from this statement.)

There are times when an error has been made and it can be more damaging to attempt recovery. If the dog has crossed from one leg of a track to another, has indicated the new leg and is intent on taking it, confusion will result from taking him off and going back to the area of his departure from the earlier part of the track. This is a problem for the handler and tracklayer only and should be sorted out without the involvement of the dog.

A sound handling technique can often help to prevent a dog from leaving the track, but there can be occasions when a dog may temporarily lose the scent path. The scent could be very faint in a particular area or there may be some sort of interference. As the dog searches round for the track he can only widen his area of search if you, as the handler, move to give him greater scope, and every step you take could be drawing your dog further from the track. You should stand still and give your dog every opportunity to work out the problem. If your dog has overshot the corner his chance of picking up the track is reduced by every yard he has gone beyond the corner and it can be a very useful practice to step back a few paces to give him a better chance of retrieving the situation.

Whilst your dog is exhausting all possibilities note exactly where you are and the route you have just taken; you may even find it helpful to make a heel mark in the ground. These are important points to keep in mind if you have to move in search of the track. It is so easy to wander away from a known spot on the track and fail to relocate it.

As one objective is to achieve a track-sure dog and to take pride in reaching that goal with the minimum of lost tracks, the most successful handlers in competitions are the least experienced at relocating these lost tracks. To blunder on to a leg of a track after wandering around lost may give some handlers some satisfaction, but there is no credit due to dog or handler. A track lost, then regained in this manner, must be considered as a total failure.

However, no practical tracker-dog handler can accept failure so easily and he must try to assess the region of error in an attempt to retrieve the situation.

When a track has been lost the handler must put his dog before any personal drive to complete the track, and this means a continuous reviewing of the situation until the track has been relocated or the decision has been made to call it a day. To overdo the searching to relocate a track, even with a keen dog, can eventually affect his enthusiasm and also his trust in the handler as a competent partner. To try and force a dog into continuing the track when it has eventually been relocated can have a few undesirable effects. Some dogs

will act as if they are tracking just because it seems to please their master and they can finish up taking a direct route to anywhere, irrespective of the right track. Other dogs will become more confused and will find themselves quite incapable of tracking.

Some handlers believe that, if they walk round the rest of the track with the track-layer and the dog, the dog may decide to restart, or when the article is pointed out to him he may realize that he should have tracked round to it. I do not think a dog understands these human thoughts and they may even inhibit future performances. When a track has been lost it is a failure: the sooner a new and easier track is laid and then worked the better.

Punishment or giving vent to one's feelings at the expense of the dog when a track is lost can do nothing but harm and will never induce more satisfactory results on future tracks. I have witnessed this sort of conduct and have seen the continued deterioration of good, natural tracking dogs at the hands of a few unsympathetic and inconsiderate handlers. Although the dog has become the scapegoat for these failures, the handler has also paid a high price for his attitude.

Tracking Articles

The foundation for tracking has been based on the inducement to find articles at the end of the track and so far the items used have been well-known favourites belonging to the dog. They have been well impregnated with the dog's and your own scent; they are fun articles – the reason for tracking.

The introduction of new and strange articles on the track may initially result in

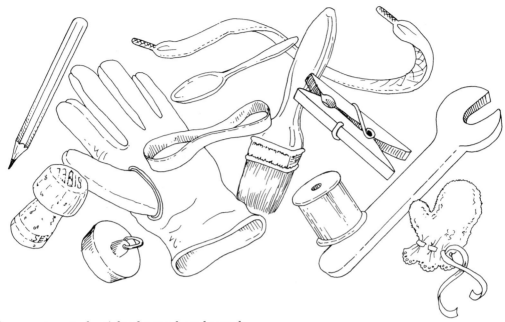

An assortment of articles for track and search.

the occasional failure to indicate their presence and it is important that one of the old favourites be placed at the end of the track to ensure a successful conclusion to a nicely worked track. This old favourite is now known as the 'saver', where the finding of it means fun and games and the maintenance of the tracking inducement.

The routine to date has built up the ability and concentration to a half-mile, half-hour-old track. A good sized, fresh article, probably the size of a glove with the tracklayer's scent only, can now be placed on the ground about ten to fifteen yards before the 'saver' is dropped. The last leg of the track should be laid into the wind to ensure that the dog picks up the scent of the article before he reaches it. By laying these tracks yourself you know

exactly where the article is and you can ensure that he does not overshoot the article until he recognizes that there are different articles as well as one of the old favourites on the track. On finding the article he is then encouraged to track the further few yards to get his 'saver'.

It is very important that your dog learns from the start that he should stop at a fresh, well-scented article and he may at first require verbal notice of its presence. The dog will know that it is on the track when he reaches it, and failure to stop is to ignore its presence. To use a small or poorly scented article at this stage would only create excuses for failure to locate it.

A routine can now be developed to establish the dog's reaction to finding an article. Should he stand over it, lie down beside it, pick it up and stay or bring it back to you? The choice is yours, but he should not be forced into any of them and if one approach stands out as natural to the dog, use it.

If you are undecided, the easiest method is to have your dog stand over the article until you go to him for it. This method only requires restraint. When the dog indicates the presence of an article, praise him and hold him at that spot whilst you walk towards him, drawing in the line to maintain tension and prevent him from moving forward. Keep praising your dog, pick up the article and, with encouragement, permit him to continue tracking for the final few yards to the 'saver', his favourite article.

It can be very impressive to watch a dog going into the down position when he finds the article. This, I believe, is the ultimate in control and can be well worth achieving, but not at the expense of canine enthusiasm. The down position is a submissive one and any attempt to apply a demanding attitude will certainly affect a dog's desire to indicate or stop at an article. If the dog can be induced into the down position with the reward of titbits or any other pleasant form of inducement then it can be well worth doing.

The moment a dog has the article in his mouth it becomes dual scented, although probably not as strongly as the well-used 'saver'. It is important, at this early stage, that you get the dog accustomed to articles without his scent; after all it was his scented 'saver' which induced him to stop and if his new articles became impregnated with his scent he might ignore the single-scented ones. The use of cross or following winds on the leg of the track containing the article will soon prove the dog's reaction to the lack of warning that an article is present. No attempt should be made to reduce the size of the articles until he is proficient at finding the larger ones.

To date the incentive to track has been built up on a single article at the end of the track, then the use of a 'saver' just beyond the article. The dog may well be conditioned to relaxing now, knowing that he has finished at this article or just beyond. If an additional item is placed in the middle of the track the dog may not want to go any further. How then do we introduce additional articles? This can be done by gradually increasing the distance between the article and the 'saver' until the article is about half way along the track. Another article can then be placed just prior to dropping the 'saver' and, if need be, the same procedure can be followed for introducing a third article.

When the process of adding articles to the track has been fully accomplished the 'saver' can, on occasions, be kept in the handler's pocket. The dog does not know that his favourite article is not at the end of the track but will be just as pleased to have his fun on production of the 'saver' after the last article.

The inclusion of smaller articles, especially metal or plastic ones which are less likely to hold the scent, should again be introduced whilst tracking into the wind. This approach will help you to meet with success. I always prefer to finish on a reasonably sized article which is also well scented. It is better that the dog finishes with success rather than failure.

Some handlers believe that failure to find the last article should be countered by withholding the fun article at the end. I doubt if this form of punishment serves any useful purpose and I do not think it helps the dog next time out. This attitude generally replaces the more constructive approach of trying to reason out the cause of failure.

Dogs who are initially classified as less motivated trackers, and have been fully induced by the use of fun articles, can become so dedicated to tracking that a stage may be reached when the presence of an article can become a hindrance, and some may even completely ignore them. This attitude must not be allowed to take a grip and the return to larger articles with the precise knowledge of their whereabouts is essential. The use of an 'into-the-wind' leg with an article should help to counter the developing situation.

There can be little value in stopping a dog when he has passed the article, then taking him back to find it. This discourages a searching attitude whilst in the harness; it also breaks the concentration in a manner which may create difficulties in getting the dog back to full tracking enthusiasm. The eventual finding of this lost article also gives the handler the feeling of partial success and he may not take the failure seriously enough. It must also be remembered that on a completely blind track the handler would have no idea where the articles were placed and would have no hope of recovery.

Dogs will fail to find or indicate articles on occasions and there can be a number of genuine reasons: the article may be of a type which does not hold scent very well; it may not have been scented well enough by the tracklayer; it may be in a hollow or a scent trap; there may be a very strong masking scent or there may be a combination of a number of causes which have prevented a good dog from realizing that a particular article was present on the track. However, these genuine reasons should not be used as an excuse for repeated failures.

Experience for Advancement

The groundwork for tracking has been built on enthusiasm and learning a basic routine. This gives a dog tremendous confidence in his ability to follow a scent path to its conclusion. Continued success on practice tracks will give a handler confidence and faith in his dog's ability.

Advancement on to completely blind tracks and the ability to overcome the various difficulties which make tracking such an interesting subject is very much dependent on a handler's ability to maintain enthusiasm and confidence within the partnership, also to add the third and vital ingredient – EXPERIENCE.

Experience can never be gained overnight and it takes many tracks under varying conditions with continued success to create a sound tracking dog. Although success will breed success in the future it must not be forgotten that experience of a single failure can, and will, contribute to failures in the future. If a dog has accidentally learned, on one occasion, that he can wind scent and cross over from one leg to another, he may well do it again, especially if he is in difficulty and this is the easy way out. If he has discovered that he can get out of working a difficult track by casting round and making it look as if he is working he may well do it again. It is therefore, important that the acquisition of experience should contain the minimum of failures and the maximum respect for the cause of each failure.

Completely blind tracks should now become part of the build-up. These are tracks which have been laid without the dog or handler being present. The handler will be shown the starting post and may also be shown the general direction of the first leg, but otherwise he will have no further knowledge of the track and will be fully dependent on the tracklayer being present to inform him if the dog has gone wrong. These blind tracks give the handler experience and confidence; also they ensure that the dog will track on the scent of various other people. At this and later stages I still believe that most of the tracks, probably an average of three or four out of every five, should be laid by the handler or a very experienced friend.

Colder Tracks

The time delay between laying and working a track is generally known as the age of the track but it is sometimes quoted as being a cold track: half an hour of time delay would be known as half an hour old or half an hour cold. Many handlers become impatient and wish to progress on to very cold tracks before the dog is ready but they must realize that it takes time and practice to consolidate through the time scale.

A rough guide for ageing tracks should be based on half-hour steps. Consider tracks of up to three quarters of an hour old as being within the half-hour stage, then vary tracks to a quarter of an hour on each side of one hour for the next stage.

When assessing the nature of a practice track, the age of it is only one of the factors to be considered: ground and weather conditions must be included in the assessment before finally deciding how long to leave the track. A damp day with little wind and a field of nice, lush grass can extend the normal one-hour-old track by a quarter to half an hour. A very hot, drying day with a breeze, combined with poor ground conditions, may well warrant a

half to three-quarters of an hour-old track instead.

Inexperienced dogs may well have the scenting ability to cope with tracks older than normal, but they may not appreciate that they are expected to work the older track and may use their energy trying to locate a fresher one. Some younger dogs may not have the necessary scenting ability for the older tracks – ability that maturity can give them. Both these considerations should be given due thought before trying to accelerate any tracking programme. Give an unprepared dog an hour-and-a-half-old track and he may work hard and complete it to your satisfaction, but give the same dog a three-month build-up from easy to progressively more difficult tracks and he will treat this hour-and-a-half-old track, under similar conditions, with a certain amount of contempt and make it appear to be too easy.

The combination of the age and length of a track is a factor which controls the total amount of concentration required from a dog and it is important that practice tracks should always be within the limits of the dog's powers of concentration. As an older track will probably have more than one article placed along its length a dog in difficulty should not be forced to complete the track but finish on the first available article on the track. It is much better to finish with success than to continue and court a failure.

Most experienced handlers will advise the novice not to enter a competition stake until his dog is ready. There is no doubt that this is very sound advice, but when is a dog ready? A dog which is competent on a fifteen- to twenty-minute-old track should not encounter problems on a half-hour-old U.D. track, though a dog which is competent on a one-hour-old track could well have problems when faced with a track one and a half hours old, especially if the weather or ground conditions are not ideal. A handler can be put in a spot if the only convenient working trial is due before the normal process of consolidation has had time to have full effect. The question is, 'Does the handler take short cuts in preparing for the trial or does he maintain a steady programme and take a chance on the day?' He could, of course, give the trials a miss, but that is usually too high a price to pay. From my own experience a dog will lift his performance on a single occasion and give a reasonable chance of success, but the dog which has been pushed to reach the required standard is likely to falter when the chips are down. No competition should alter the planned consolidation of the practice tracks.

Starting a Track

An essential ingredient for successful tracking is to make a good start; this helps to give the dog and handler confidence. When the direction of the first leg of a track is known to the handler there should not be any problems. However, the time I have spent in tracklaying and judging at competitive events has shown me that many dogs fail to give a convincing start and eventually fail through this lack of confidence or commitment.

If the routine which has been developed through the previous pages of this chapter has been systematically applied I would not expect problems. It is noticed, however, that some handlers like to take advantage of the track to the starting post but do so without a sense of purpose and then expect the dog to carry on from the post with enthusiasm. From the moment the harness is fitted to the dog there should be a sense of purpose from both dog and handler. This should be kept in mind at all times and the approach to starting any track should be one of dedication.

Although the handler knows the direction of the first leg on a competitive U.D. track there is no such guidance in the higher stakes. It is advisable that the start of some practice tracks be utilized to vary the direction of approach so that the dog is required to determine the correct direction to follow.

For practice tracks the tracklayer's approach, the positioning of the starting post and the direction of the first leg should be planned and discussed with the handler to ensure that variations in dog and handler approach can be applied. I would suggest that the handler should plan and lay most of his own tracks, or at least watch his tracklayer's start, so that he knows the exact details. Misunderstanding between the tracklayer and the handler has caused many a confused dog.

The development routine has encouraged the dog to put his nose to the ground in anticipation when he knows there is tracking afoot, and this attitude is now invaluable. Approach the tracklayer's lead-in to the starting post into the wind so that the dog can pick up the scent. This fortifies his enthusiasm to track. The dog, still on his lead, should be allowed to track a few yards to the post. It may also be helpful to let him indicate the correct direction for a lead length beyond the post. Praise your dog, call him back and put him into harness, ready to track. You are then confident of the direction of the track.

Any tendency to backtrack at the start can be countered by changing the direc-

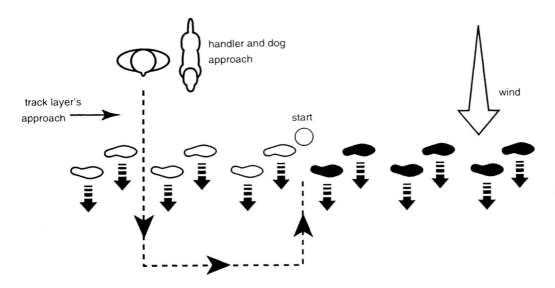

Countering a back track at the start.

tion of your approach so that you cross the tracklayer's approach about ten yards behind the post, then circle round to make the windward approach; this will create a break in the tracklayer's approach and should interrupt the dog's concentration on the backtrack. If he remains undecided, verbal encouragement to take the correct direction will then be required, but verbal assistance should be considered only as a last resort.

Locating a track without a starting post should also be considered and should not create any problem for a dog who is keen to start and has successfully located tracks at the lead-in to a starting post. But again the handler must initially know the exact location and direction of the first leg. It may be advisable to start by using two marker posts some fifty yards apart to indicate the line of the first leg and to introduce the dog, again into the wind, to the middle of this marked length of track. It can be very useful to educate a competitive dog in a similar manner, but without a marker. A starting post is generally left unattended for a period, especially with older tracks, and its presence seems to attract inquisitive people who invariably ruin the start of the track or walk away with the post. Starting a track without such a marker can minimize this type of hazard.

As the tracklayer in competitive working trials can indicate to the competitor the line he took to the start marker there is no danger of a dog being allowed to backtrack from the start of a working trials track. However, the training just described to give dogs the experience and choice of backtracking at the start can be invaluable to the practical working dog in picking up the start to a track. This conditioning can also help to prevent dogs from going in the wrong direction when relocating a lost track.

Interference and Cross Tracks

Game, cattle or other animals can cause untold problems on a track, and gaining experience of the inclusion of any such interference can only be carried out properly when the handler has full knowledge of the track or the close support of an experienced tracklayer. How else can a handler tell whether his dog is working the track or taking an interest in the irrelevant scents from those unwanted sources?

The movement of game cannot normally be controlled but experience can be gained by laying tracks in areas where game can be expected. Rabbits are very active at first light and a few early-morning tracks in an area of their burrows will give a dog plenty of experience under such conditions.

However, it can be rather inconsiderate to give a dog ageing tracks with an abundance of interference, and such interference should be introduced on easy tracks where the start is expected to be reasonably clear of game. The dog should have an opportunity to settle into an enthusiastic rhythm before encountering a game-infested area.

Cattle or sheep interference can cause greater problems. Some dogs will not track in the presence of cattle and I know of some superb trackers who will not entertain such an idea. For some unknown reason other dogs will ignore their existence and track on quite regardless of their attention. Dogs who have a 'hang-up' about cattle or any other animal can only overcome this tracking problem if they can be acclimatized to their presence outside a tracking environment.

Similarly a dog who is excited by the panicky movements of a few sheep will have a problem when trying to concentrate on a track if his eyes catch their fleeting movement. Again, acclimatization outside the tracking environment is the real answer.

Cattle or sheep are continously on the move during much of the daylight hours and to track where these animals have been can cause disastrous and discouraging failures, especially if it was not appreciated that the animals had been on the tracking ground. If your tracking ground does include the grazing of farm animals it would be wise to study their habits and movement routine.

Only experience will tell you how your dog will react to the interfering scents of animals but, again, familiarization should be carried out with easy and relatively fresh tracks and progress be geared to the dog's acceptance of the situation.

You may find that your dog has a tendency to cast continually in areas of heavy interference. A temporary shortening of the tracking line can help minimize this casting and often gives the dog greater confidence in his ability to overcome the problem.

It should be recognized that not all dogs have the ability to overcome many of the problems experienced when tracking and their limitations should be met with an understanding response from the handler.

Human cross tracks are inevitable, especially when tracks have been left for two hours or more. Even competition ground can be contaminated with a cross track without anyone being aware of it. Although U.K. working trials tracking does not include intentional cross tracks at any stage, Canadian, American and Australian T.D.X. qualifications build this requirement in to their schedule of work.

A few dogs do appear to be completely track sure but there are occasions when even they are likely to change over onto a scent path which crosses the track they are working. As we do not know precisely the scents or odours on which a dog is concentrating, or how often he refers to the subordinate scents or odours, we do not know why he ignores or takes a cross track. Experience suggests that a dog is unlikely to take a cross track which is older than the track he is following but can well be tempted to change over to the cross track if it is fresher than the track he is following. This helps to confirm the theory that as the track gets older the dog concentrates on the ground-based odours, crushed vegetation etc., because they are stronger and easier to follow than the human scent, which diminishes at a faster rate.

We do not know at what stage the human scent becomes subordinate on a track; it will vary considerably and be dependent on the strength of the track-layer's scent and the prevailing wind conditions.

My own impression is that the human scents become subordinate at somewhere between half an hour and an hour old.

Conditioning is based on cross tracks which are fresher than the main track although it would also be wise to assess the dog's reaction to slightly older cross tracks.

When planning the use of cross tracks there are a number of factors which must be kept in mind.

1 A dog will be tempted by a fresh human scent when the main track is old enough to have its human scent subordinated to the ground odours.
2 The distinctive scents from some people can be so much stronger and more tempting than others.
3 The ground odours from a person who is heavier than the tracklayer can be an inducement to change.
4 The wind direction can be, and may well be, the most deciding factor. If a dog is tracking into the wind and the cross track's scent is being carried to him, he is warned of its presence and has time to think about the value of a change. Instinct may tell him to abandon the older track. On the other hand, tracking on a leg with a following wind gives no warning of the cross track, and if he is tracking at a good confident pace he will probably be past the cross track by a yard or so before he fully realizes its presence. Then he may well find it much more convenient to continue on the main track.

Any one of these factors, or a combination of them, can affect a dog's reliance on a track and may well explain why a dog will ignore a cross track one day and eagerly follow one on another.

Experience with cross tracks must be gained with patience. Every time the cross track has been accepted by the dog it is a failure; in a sense it is a lost track and failures in practice should be few and far between.

The introduction of any difficulty on a track should be carried out with success in mind and cross tracks are no exception. Simple tracks should be laid by the handler and probably about half an hour old; a single cross track should be sufficient. The leg of the track used for crossing should have the dog working with the wind and the cross track at right angles. This cross track should be laid by an assistant and witnessed by the handler so that he knows when to expect it. The cross track can be laid just before the dog is worked or with a time gap of up to fifteen minutes, and it should intersect the track some fifty to one hundred yards from the start or from a previous corner to ensure that the dog is well settled in his work. An article some ten yards beyond the intersection can help to give a dog confidence in his decision to ignore the cross track, or if he requires help to negotiate the difficulty the article can assist in boosting his morale.

Confident in your dog's ability with a following wind, you can now include a track when the dog is working into the wind and he has the opportunity to think about the choice before he reaches the intersection. It may be worthwhile to place a well-scented article some two or three yards beyond the intersection; the scent of this article reaching him can encourage a singleminded attitude at a crucial moment.

The best way to pinpoint the exact spot of an intersection of the track and the cross track is to have the tracklayer put a post into the ground at the selected spot and have the cross tracklayer remove it as he crosses. This ensures that any article is placed at the intended distance from the crossing. The successful negotiation of cross tracks can allow the article to be placed progressively further from the intersection.

A shortage of experienced tracklayers to lay the cross tracks need not affect progress. A handler can lay his own tracks and the interference cross tracks. I have in fact laid tracks for my own dog where one leg of the track deliberately crossed another and on one occasion there was also an unintentional crossing by a com-plete stranger with his dog. This track was fully worked by Caro when he was fourteen months old.

If the same person lays the main track and the cross track there must be a tremendous temptation for the dog to accept the cross track. Continuing to use this technique must depend on the dog's reaction.

Building up on older tracks and altering the angles of intersections will conclude the normal requirements for cross track training. Reducing the angle between the cross track and the main track to about thirty degrees should be sufficient to determine the dog's ability to discriminate at intersections, and the timing of cross tracks up to half the age of the main track should also be sufficient. Success and plenty of time available may, however, induce some handlers to give their dogs more exacting experience.

Ground Variations

Dogs are asked to track on many different types of ground: heather, pasture, stubble, ploughed land or even hard surfaces such as cinder tracks or tarmacadam roads. Ground conditions can vary tremendously but the presence of good, green vegetation is required to give the greatest chance of success.

Heather can normally be considered as one of the easier types of tracking ground although articles can fall through to the base and dogs not accustomed to the depth of vegetation can miss them. When a dog indicates the presence of an article which blends in with the undergrowth the handler can then have a problem in finding it.

Stubble fields become readily available after the harvest and this type of ground may initially be a problem to the inexperienced dog, but vegetation seems to become evident very quickly and this improves the scent-holding properties of the ground. However, the present-day practice of burning the stubble does create major problems and a high proportion of tracking failures. The lines of stubble seem to have a fascination for inexperienced dogs and practice tracks must include legs diagonal to the lines of cultivation. On these diagonal legs dogs seem to zigzag off the track then back on to the scent path.

Tracking on ploughed land can be a completely new experience and generally creates many difficulties through the absence of vegetation, but the breaking up of the surface by each footprint does release the moisture, which seems to be adequate. Introduction to ploughed land should involve very fresh tracks, probably about fifteen minutes old, with progress determined by the dog's reaction. Although it is often difficult to obtain permission to track on ploughed land, the experience is a valuable addition to a dog's repertoire.

Ground spread over with farm manure seems to have a greater effect on handlers than on some of their dogs and experience has indicated that such rotting matter can sometimes be of little consequence as a possible distraction.

If I find at any stage of tracklaying that a piece of ground is liable to create more difficulty than intended, I give my feet a twist at each step to ensure greater disturbance of the soil or a more positive impression on the vegetation.

Hard-surface tracks are very much a lottery although nice, damp, cool conditions can make a half-hour time delay practicable. The absence of disturbed, moist soil or crushed vegetation removes the main scent or odour-holding source and any handler should be reasonable in his expectations of a dog working under these conditions.

CHAPTER 9

Scent Discrimination

Introduction

Scent discrimination is an exercise which is carried out as part of the working schedule in obedience competitions and, within the various English-speaking countries, this exercise seems to be based on either the British system or the American approach.

The British system provides for a graduation through the different stages of competition from a relatively simple test to one bearing the scent of a stranger to the dog. The American approach is based on a single, middle-of-the-road exercise where two different types of material are used and the articles to be located and retrieved carry the handler's scent only.

The general approach to training which is described in this chapter will be based on the British competition requirements, with additional information being given to cover the variations within the American exercises.

Scent discrimination can also be a very enjoyable party trick for the domestic pet owner who can have friends amazed at his dog's ability to pick out the correct article. A few examples will be given at the end of this chapter.

If a handler wishes to compete in both obedience and working trials special precautions must be taken to ensure that the dog understands the difference between scent discrimination and the search exercise which follows in Chapter 10. Although scent discrimination starts with a very free and easy introduction it is developed through to an exercise of precision. The search exercise can maintain a less formal approach and gives the handler more scope to apply a completely different attitude. I hope this will become evident in the differences between the relevant chapters.

Object of the Exercise

To have the dog discriminate between articles which have been handled by different people, and to locate and retrieve the article carrying the scent of the selected person. The three stages of competition have a natural progression from one to the next and this leads to a sensible approach to training. The competition stages are:

1. Class 'A' – Handler's scent to be on cloth provided by the judge. There must be six cloths set out in a straight line with the handler's scent on one cloth, with no decoys.
2. Class 'B' – Handler's scent to be on cloth provided by the judge. There should be a minimum of six and a maximum of ten cloths. This must include the judge's cloth, one with handler's scent and one decoy.
3. Class 'C' – Judge's scent on piece of marked cloth, minimum of six and maximum of ten. This must include the judge's cloth and one or two decoys. A decoy steward should not handle a cloth for a period of longer than the judge.

The basic elements. Dog to:

1 Sit at your left side, accept a masking of his nose to inhale the appropriate scent;
2 Go out and discriminate between the cloths in view;
3 Pick up the selected cloth and return to you;
4 Sit in front of you and keep hold of the cloth;
5 Give cloth to hand when required;
6 Go round to heel when instructed and remain at heel until released.

The procedure for each stage of competition is the same. The cloths, up to a maximum of ten, are placed on the ground some two feet apart to a pattern determined by the judge. The cloths should be clearly visible to the dog and probably about five to ten paces from the handler. The steward will take the cloth from the handler or judge and, without putting his own scent on it, place it amongst the other cloths whilst the handler prevents the dog from watching the cloth being placed. In Class 'A' and Class 'B' the scent of the cloth to be located is normally given to the dog by the handler cupping his hands over the dog's nose so that he can associate the handler's scent with the cloth he must select from the group. In Class 'C' a cloth with the judge's scent is usually draped over the dog's nose so that he can memorize the stranger's scent. In each case the dog is released with the instruction to go out and investigate the cloths laid out on the ground, then return with the appropriate cloth.

To save any confusion when reading this chapter the various cloths used in scent discrimination will now be clearly defined.

The expression 'scented cloth' will be used to indicate the cloth which should be located and returned by the dog. Cloths which have been deliberately scented by another party and should be ignored by the dog will be known as 'decoy cloths'. All others which do not carry any deliberate scenting will be known as 'neutral

Close investigation for the correct scent.

cloths'. Reference will also be made to cloths which are 'dual scented'; these are cloths which have been deliberately scented by a person and also previously retrieved by the dog, thereby carrying scent from a person's hands and also saliva from the dog's mouth. With dual-scented cloths we do not know whether it is the human scent or the dog's own scent which is being used for identification. I presume that the dog's own scent is the more prominent and will be the true inducement to retrieve the cloth.

The competitive scent-discrimination exercise must be conducted in the manner expected of all others in the obedience schedule of work. Every movement, from start to finish, should be performed with smartness and precision. It is not my intention within this chapter to detail the training requirements for such precision, as this can be considered to be part of the general training required for the competition retrieve exercise. My intention is to detail the principles of scent discrimination and a method of progression through each stage, from a straight-forward retrieve to the Class 'C' scenting requirements, so that a dog will continually work with purpose in his mind.

A dog should not be introduced to this field of work unless he is a good, keen retriever of the type of article to be used – a piece of cloth. Discriminating to the levels of Class 'A' and Class 'B' is relatively easy for a dog to understand if he has a keen desire to retrieve, but to attempt the schooling for this routine with a dog who lacks the enjoyment of a pleasant and smart retrieve is to encourage most of the bad habits which can be picked up at many of the training classes.

A successful discrimination.

Presenting the correct training cloth.

Developing the Routine

Class 'A' Routine

The Class 'A' routine sets the pattern and establishes the foundation for the more advanced exercises. Any faults which have been allowed to develop in this class of work will be difficult to eradicate during the more advanced stages.

Scent discrimination is a SIGHT and SCENT exercise in which the dog visually locates the group of scattered cloths, then identifies the correct cloth from within the group by scenting as required.

The pattern of association should, therefore, be developed with a well-used retrieve cloth, one the dog enjoys and with which he is perfectly capable of accom-

plishing a sound retrieve. If the dog is not proficient in the retrieve exercise it would be harmful and foolish to try and improve the finer points of retrieving during the sessions of schooling for scent discrimination. A dog who mouths a piece of cloth, plays around or pounces on it will only become confused if he is corrected for these faults during scent practice. The situation must be developed where no unpleasantness can be connected in his mind with the business of scent discrimination.

Many of the retrieving problems to be overcome at this stage can be caused by the over-excitement of certain naturally retrieving German Shepherds and some are liable to scatter everything before them whilst carrying out the scenting exercise. This is decidedly a retrieving problem; it must be treated as such and brought under control before attempting to develop the scenting routine. I repeat that the important point with any dog is to solve all retrieving problems first and Class 'A' scent will fall into place very quickly.

Discriminating between articles to find the one bearing his handler's scent is one of the most natural functions for any dog and to discriminate for an article which also bears his own scent can only simplify the task still further. Any family dog who enjoys a retrieve will search a pebbled beach for the particular stone his master threw for him and he will not be interested in bringing back any other. A piece of wood thrown in the same manner whilst out walking through woods will meet with a similar response. Yet these family pets have not been given the scent by their owner. They already know his scent and no self-respecting dog will mistake another scent for that of his master.

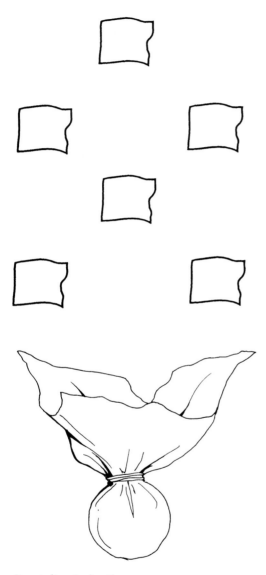

Scent discrimination.

that the dog does not realize that he is being asked to carry out an artificial exercise and he still thinks of it as a natural function. A number of dogs do achieve successful scenting and retrieving at the very first attempt when initially presented with the artificial conditions related to a competition set-up. These dogs have a natural ability and the preliminaries may be quite unnecessary although practice will be required to consolidate the routine.

The first step in the routine is to make use of a well-liked retrieve cloth which the dog can recognize by sight as his own. For convenience, this can be an old handkerchief with a golf ball, a stone or other article tied inside to give weight for throwing. This will be a dual-scented piece of cloth bearing his scent as well as your own. He should already be prepared to retrieve this cloth from anywhere, long grass, heavy undergrowth or any area where junk can be lying around. It is a piece of cloth he will search for until it is found.

Have a number of cloths, about five or six should be sufficient, scattered widely on the ground some four to six feet apart. These cloths will be clearly visible to the dog and must not carry your own scent. It is preferable that a stranger or a friend places the cloths for you. Even if it is not required for Class 'A' scent it is wise to introduce, early on, a decoy which has been well handled and thereby scented by another party, to ensure that your dog is acclimatized to this type of distraction from the start. This can be done by having some article of reasonable size scented by somebody else and placed on top of a cloth, but only partly covering it. If on occasions you do not have a friend available to put the cloths out for you, you can do this yourself so long as you do not touch them

It is only when we turn this natural function into an artificial exercise that we create 'hang-ups' in the minds of our dogs. The purpose of this development of a routine is to make the change so casual

– make use of a pair of tongs or a plastic bag with your hand inside before taking hold of the cloth. It may also be important that your dog does not see you place the cloth – even without your scent on it he may connect you with it. A decoy cloth can also be put into a plastic bag and used later in the day if an assistant is not going to be available during your training period.

During the development of this routine it is not necessary to give your dog the scent from a cupped hand round his nose to accomplish the exercise; he already knows that your scent will be on the cloth. The cupping of your hands gently round his nose is only to prepare him for more advanced scenting exercises to come and this can be introduced into the routine at a stage when it is felt that the action will not affect his performance. Commands should also be avoided, with gentle praise being used to express your requirements and also your pleasure. These phrases should include the key word which will eventually become the single-word instruction required for a competition performance. For example, the final word of instruction can initially be incorporated in the 'Good boy, you go and SEEK for it' until eventually a gentle but positive 'seek' will suffice.

To commence your schooling maintain a casual approach, as if you were about to give your dog a fun retrieve, and throw the weighted retrieve cloth beyond the cloths on the ground.

Look for and expect a normal retrieve under these conditions. If he has to search round and sniff at any of the cloths it shows that he is discriminating; so long as he is continually working to find his retrieve cloth you have no cause for complaint.

Now place the cloths closer together, two or three feet apart, so that they indicate a more definite area of distinctive objects, and throw your retrieve cloth amongst them whilst your dog is watching. Hold your dog until the retrieve cloth has landed and is stationary before releasing him for another fun retrieve. As the cloths have minimal scent except for the decoy he may well discriminate before returning with the correct cloth. Some dogs will only use their nose when their eyes cannot identify their own cloth; others are more at home using their olfactory system and prefer to identify in this manner, even if visual evidence is perfectly clear.

Success and complete satisfaction at this stage can encourage you to have the weighted retrieve cloth placed in amongst the other cloths whilst your dog is watching. You may on occasions wish to break his vision for a few seconds, by moving in front of him or turning him round in a complete circle, then letting him go out for his cloth. This momentary break of visual contact makes a dog lose sight of his cloth but the knowledge of its general location is sufficient incentive to go and seek it out in the correct area. It is important that the routine becomes firmly implanted in his mind and that he is required to investigate the area of visible cloths to locate the one he is trying to find. When retrieving the cloth after each discrimination your dog deserves genuine and freely given praise.

To this stage the weighted retrieve cloth has been used for discrimination. A cloth very similar to the others can now be used for a simple retrieve; it can be thrown or placed. The cloth will now be dual scented and can be placed into a line-up with five neutral cloths whilst the dog is watching. It may be advisable initially to have your dog set up at a right angle to the line-up of cloths and directly in the line with the dual-scented one to be retrieved. This will make the job easier for him.

Success can bring variations in position of the dual-scented cloth in relation to the others, the use of a decoy article placed on neutral cloths in various positions and the set-up position of the dog in relation to the line-up of cloths.

When these variations have been applied with success a single-scented cloth (your own scent) can now be used but again starting with the dog watching the cloth being placed in a line-up at a right angle to the dog's position so that he can go straight forwards to carry out a simple retrieve if he wishes. The variations already mentioned can then be put into operation.

To return with the wrong cloth when applying the handler's scent is the biggest crime in this exercise, but not a crime where the dog is blamed and punished. It indicates a failure in the process of education, and if such an error does occur the dog should not be made to feel that he has done wrong, but the correct cloth should be retrieved by the handler, immediately followed by a fun retrieve from within the scenting area. Consideration must then be given to the cause of the failure and the prevention of others.

Class 'B' Routine

In moving up to Class 'B' there are three principal differences from Class 'A' scent discrimination:

1 Increase to ten cloths being utilized.
2 Pattern of cloth positions on the ground can vary.
3 One cloth to be decoy scented.

The increase in number of cloths should not cause any problems, especially if a single straight line is maintained until the dog is accustomed to the additional cloths.

During Class 'A' scent training a decoy article was placed on top of one cloth. This can now be removed and the cloth scented by another party as decoy. The position of the decoy cloth in the line-up should be continually varied when it is recognized that it is of no interest to the dog.

The variable patterns of cloth positions on the ground should now be considered. It may be desirable to reduce the number of cloths to five or six until the dog becomes accustomed to the various set-ups. Competitive set-ups vary considerably but there are five basic patterns which can be used to prepare the dog for any pattern a judge may think of using.

These patterns are:

1 A single line of ten pieces.
2 A double line some four feet apart, five pieces in each.
3 Shape of a letter H.
4 Shape of a letter Y.
5 Pieces in a circle.

The scented cloth may be placed within the general formation of the pattern or it may be placed on its own within the general area. One common practice is to find the scented cloth placed in the centre of a circle of cloths. Some dogs will go round and round the cloths and never locate the obvious cloth in the centre.

Schooling for Class 'B' and the more advanced Class 'C' should be based on having your German Shepherd go out to investigate the obvious first.

In the earlier stages place your scented cloth in an obvious position and let him see it. This will bring in a straightforward

Various scent patterns.

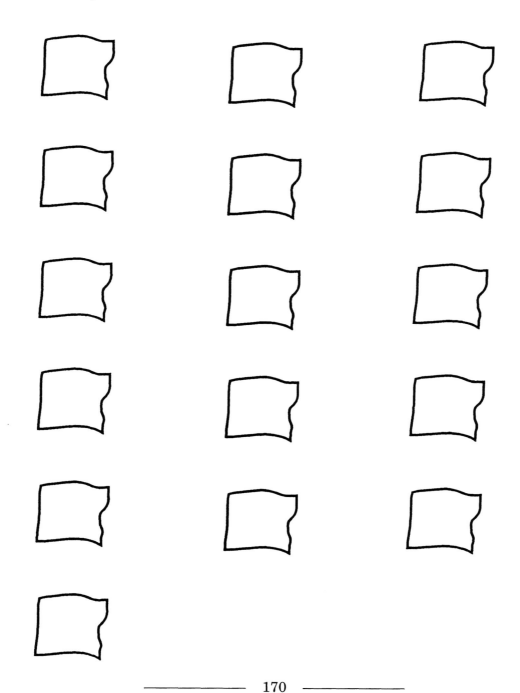

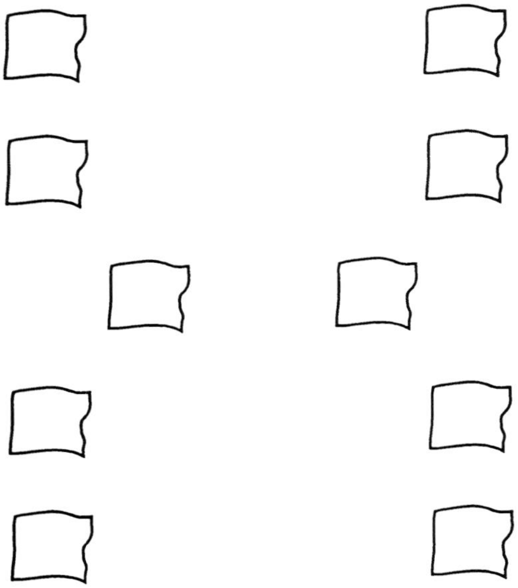

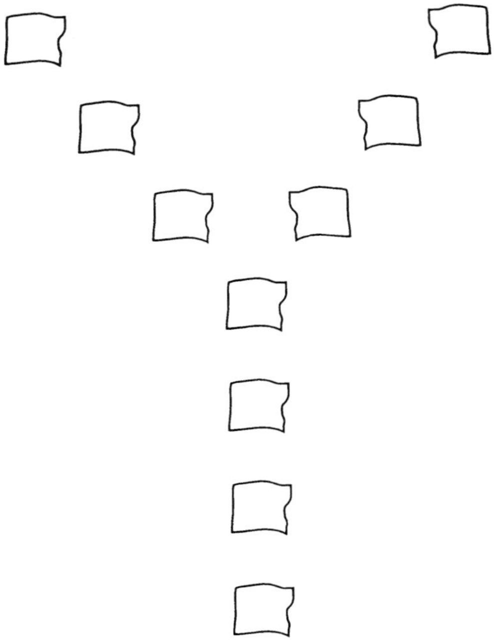

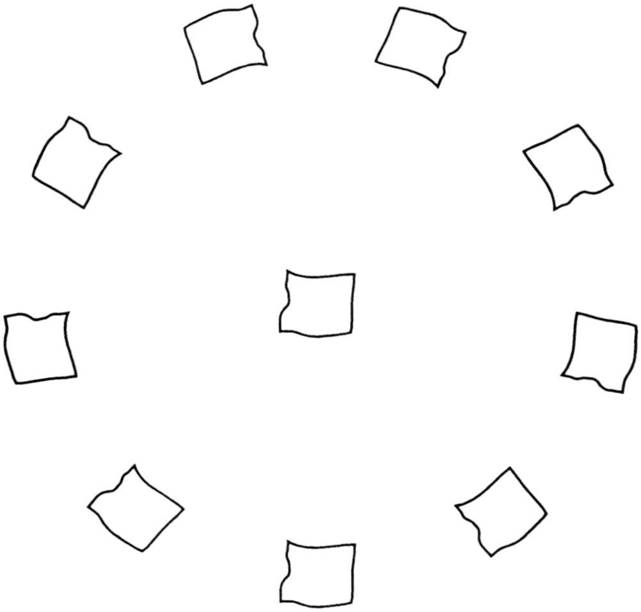

retrieve, but do not do it too often, just sufficiently to have him curious of the isolated and obvious. On occasions use a neutral cloth to draw your dog to the obvious before he goes on to discriminate for his article within the main group. However, if you are to use a decoy as the obvious, first place your scented cloth within six to twelve inches of it to minimize the risk of him returning with the decoy just because it is more obvious and scented.

There are two factors which will affect progression into Class 'C' and these should be given consideration during 'B' training.

1 Use of decoys – limit the number of different scents to be used in training and make a note of whose they are. You will wish to avoid using these decoy scents as a 'stranger's scent' during Class 'C' training.

2 Presentation of scent – although the cupped hands over the dog's nose are generally applied to induce him, you can put the scent on the cloth to be returned in Class 'A' and 'B'. It is required in Class 'C' that the dog is given the stranger's scent from a cloth. It can be helpful to make this change in presentation when competing in Class 'B' and give the dog your scent from a cloth. Your dog will then be accustomed to the process before introduction to Class 'C' scent work.

Class 'C' Routine

This is the ultimate in scent discrimination – to have your dog accept and memorize the scent of a stranger, then go out to a display of scent cloths and return with the matching scented article.

As all scenting to date has been accom-plished with cloths carrying the handler's scent this change, to that of a stranger, requires a great deal of consideration. It is not a single easy step from Class 'B' scent-ing but a series of small steps graduated to ensure a smooth changeover.

It must be remembered that your dog has been conditioned to ignore the scent of strangers. Now we wish to have him con-centrate on the scent of a particular stranger and at the same time to ignore the scents of other strangers during that particular discrimination session.

The manner in which the dog has been given scent to discriminate for the han-dler's scented cloth can now be developed further to ensure that he understands the scent on which he is expected to concen-trate. A cloth bearing the scent of the person in question can be placed over the dog's nose; this is the most common approach to giving the dog a particular scent and is probably the best method to use during the early period of tuition. Some handlers find that dangling the cloth in front of the dog's nose, or having it dropped on the ground so that he may pick it up, are quite acceptable methods for memorizing scent but I would suggest that these methods be ignored until the dog is reasonably experienced.

The new experience of giving a stranger's scent by means of a piece of cloth may well cause a certain amount of apprehension and this can create a men-tal block which could affect the dog's ability to memorize and, therefore, to dis-criminate. This apprehension can easily be overcome by introducing cloth scenting with the handler using his own scent as in Class 'A' and Class 'B' and developing to the other scents only when the dog is per-fectly happy to accept this procedure.

The introduction of other scents can

now be considered and one must appreciate the reaction of a dog to being given a different scent. Does he know what is expected of him? Will he connect the scented article with the scent he has been given? It is not a question of memorizing the scent, but a question of relating one scent to the other.

The process of discrimination should be made so easy that the dog has only a minimal chance of going wrong. The assistance of another member of your household, or a friend who is well known to your German Shepherd, will simplify the process. If you use a person who is well known to your dog he does not really require to memorize his scent; your dog knows it already. These friends or relatives will now become your scenting assistants. These assistants should not have been previously used for decoy scenting, nor should they be used for that purpose in the future, at least not until the dog is quite experienced and fully understands the requirements of the test. I am sure that many dogs become confused because they are expected to bring back an article bearing a particular scent at one training session, then they are expected to ignore the same scent used as a decoy during the next session.

A return to the dual scenting of cloths can help a dog to become accustomed to bringing back cloths with your assistant's scent as the subordinate scent and your dog's own scent as the real inducement to pick up the correct cloth. Every effort should be made to ensure that the handler's scent is not being transmitted to the dog instead of his assistant's.

Sighting should also play its part in assisting your dog to identify the correct cloth in the early stages. Have your assistant scent the cloths by rubbing them in

his hands. Having them in his pocket for a period or breathing on them will also help to leave a heavy scent. Your assistant will require additional cloths and these can be kept in his pocket until required. Take one of the scented cloths, handle it by the top corners only and place it over your dog's nose. At the same time your assistant should draw attention to himself as he drops the other scented cloth on the ground some ten paces away. He then steps back as you remove the cloth from your dog's nose and release him to retrieve the cloth. On his return take the retrieved cloth from your dog in a manner which will minimize the effect of your own scent and return it to your assistant for re-scenting.

The scenting cloth used to put over the dog's nose will now be contaminated with the scent from your own hands and should not be used again. A freshly scented cloth from your assistant will be required.

Have one to three cloths suitably placed on the ground by a third party, then your scenting assistant can place his dual-scented cloth beside the others whilst your dog is watching. If necessary have your assistant draw the dog's attention to his activities. Place the freshly scented cloth over your dog's nose for a few seconds and again release him to find your assistant's dual-scented cloth. Repeat the process with two freshly scented cloths to see if your dog can achieve success without the aid of his own scent.

Some dogs catch on very quickly and do not require the inducement of dual-scented cloths whilst others take some time before they fully understand your requirements. It is simply a case of adjusting your approach to suit your dog. Dual-scented cloths may be used two or three times between washes. The heavy contamination with saliva from a dog's mouth after a few retrieves may well mask your assistant's scent to the degree that it is meaningless to the dog. The additional cloths placed on the ground by the third party should be slightly decoy-scented. This gives a background of human scent to each cloth without being particularly distinctive and attractive to your dog. Success through practice can influence your decision on when to increase the strength of decoy scents.

Progress to the full exercise with ten cloths can be planned by building up to single-scented cloths from one assistant, then returning to the earliest stage with a fresh assistant and then repeating the full process with other assistants until your dog is fully competent with any four to six different assistants. The alternative is to carry out the full elementary stages with a variety of scenting assistants before progressing with each assistant in turn until the full exercise has been accomplished with single-scented cloths.

The work involved in continually washing and drying used cloths to remove all scent can be minimized by making use of kitchen towelling or paper handkerchiefs during practice sessions, especially beyond the stage of dual scenting.

Other Scenting Considerations

So far this chapter has been concerned with the build-up of a routine to ensure that a dog can be quite capable of interpreting his handler's scent-discrimination requirements and carrying out this function to his satisfaction. There are a number of unknowns which may well affect advanced scenting and competitions at the level of Class 'C'.

The atmosphere round the scenting cloths will contain an infinite variety of scents and odours in differing concentrations. Although these atmospheric conditions should not have any effect on Class 'A' and 'B' scents, where the handler's personal scent is known to the dog, the stranger's scent used in Class 'C' can change the nature of the exercise to the extent that the diversity of scents in the atmosphere can, on occasions, prove too great an obstacle for dogs and handlers less capable of coping with the complexities of such conditions.

A selection of such possible conditions follows:

1 The presence of other human beings in the general vicinity of the working area will create a mixture of body scents in the atmosphere. Their clothes and footwear will also add to the composition of the atmospheric ingredients.

2 Other dogs at the training class or show will also make their contribution and can have a distracting influence, especially if there is a bitch just coming into, or just out of, season.

3 Odours from the composition of a floor or its surface, be it polish, a sealant or a disinfectant cleaner, may possibly add to the general accumulation within the atmosphere. These odours will be at their strongest at ground level, where the cloths have been placed for the exercise.

4 Outdoor venues in a playing field can create a different set of conditions, with the effect of handlers, dogs, stewards and judge trampling over the grass causing extensive bruising and crushing of vegetation. If a dog

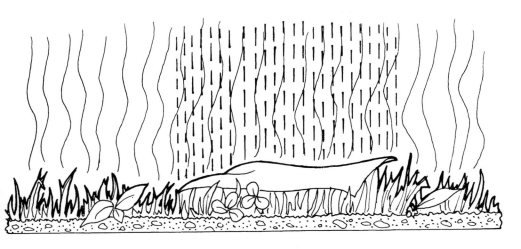

Effect of various odours from crushed vegetation.

can track a single set of footprints hours after a person has walked over such a piece of ground, I hate to think of the strength and variety of odours created within a typical obedience ring.

5 Identical scents from a decoy steward which may match with those of the judge may well cause confusion. The use of soaps, hand creams or even facial cosmetics of the same brand may have a misleading effect.

Many of these scents or odours will be of little significance but others may well be much stronger than the prime scent on the cloth which is intended for discrimination. One or more of these subordinate scents may tend to mask or distort the prime scent, sufficiently to mislead the dog with a less sensitive olfactory system or one which lacks the concentration to match the scent given with the scented cloth.

All of these factors can give the ill-prepared a mountain of excuses for failure but they must also be recognized as possible contributing factors to the unexplained failure of a good, well-educated, scent-discriminating German Shepherd.

Another more decisive factor can be the similarity of scents between one individual and another. Although in theory each person carries a distinctive scent, how distinctive are all of these individual scents? There are over fifty million people in the U.K. and all with distinctive scents; more than two hundred million in the United States and about a thousand million Chinese with each person emitting a distinctive scent. Are there really so many individual scents that a dog can differentiate between each and every one?

I remember stewarding at a Championship Class 'C' event when two young ladies were recruited as scent-decoy stewards. Their function was to scent cloths by rubbing them in their hands. The discrimination cloths were in a straight line and decoy steward A would place her cloth first in the line so that each dog would have the opportunity of checking it out on his way down the line. The judge had her cloth placed halfway down the line and decoy steward B would place hers at the far end of the line. The scented cloths were changed for each dog to ensure that the decoys and the judge's cloths all carried scent of the same age. Approximately half of the dogs returned to their handler with the correct cloth whilst the other half returned with the decoy from steward B. No cloths bearing the scent of steward A were brought in by any dog.

A statistical significance test involving the entry of twenty-four dogs would show conclusively that there was a bit more than the laws of chance involved here and I believe that the failures, who were proven scent workers, honestly believed that the decoy scent B was the scent they were given from the judge's second cloth. We have heard tales of this kind before, from other shows where an abnormally high failure rate occurs. Sometimes it is just an excuse from the handler of an ill-prepared dog but top dogs in their prime are known to suffer the same fate.

I have discussed earlier in this chapter the probability of human scent groupings, as with fingerprint, blood and saliva groupings. Was it a case of decoy steward B and the judge coming from the same scent group, and closely related within this group? Were the scents so closely related that the pollution of other odours, especially from crushed vegetation immediately below the cloths, had masked that minor difference? Or perhaps the judge and steward had washed their hands with the same brand of soap, or they may have used the same type of hand cream. I do not know the answer but it does pose an interesting question.

I also recall watching a judge at an outdoor show have the scent cloths placed on the grass where the dogs had just carried out both the Sit and Down/Stay exercises. Only one dog returned with the correct cloth. Just consider the variety of strong scents on the ground at the time of the exercise, and his own scent was probably very prominent in that area as well.

Consider each group of scents as a colour in the spectrum. What an infinite variety of combinations and shades can be seen by the human eye! One shade can be very close to another and one dash of primary colour can make a distinctive difference to a shade. Can we relate those fifty million human scents in the U.K. to this infinite variety of colours and shades?

It should also be remembered that a dog is working from memory; he must memorize the scent he is given and match it with one from a selection of scents. Consider our own limitations with memorizing a visual identification. Each person looks different, but is there such a difference within like groups without their distinctive clothing or hairstyles, etc? How often do police identity parades fail because people of a certain likeness are brought together and all in similar clothing? How many of us choose to dial a strange telephone number without having it written down in front of us? To walk from one room to another with a memorized telephone number is often sufficient to have some of us doubt our powers of retaining numerical information. These considerations may not be of any consequence when decoy and judge's scents are distinctively different, but minor differences could be masked by one or more of the many subordinate scents and odours which hang around a scenting area. A dog's memory and his keenness to satisfy could well result in a case of mistaken identity.

Armed with these theories a judge and his ring steward can only set out to minimize the subordinate scents and give each dog a reasonable chance of success. Any planning decisions are likely to be a compromise; after all it is supposed to be a practical exercise and completely sterile conditions would be out of the question. I would, therefore, suggest that the following points be given some consideration:

1 Minimize the amount of traffic within the area to be used for the scent cloths, particularly for outdoor shows where crushed vegetation can give off the most prominent odour. Remember how sweet newly mown grass can smell to the human senses.
2 As there is quite a strong opinion that human male scent is always distinctively different from that of a female it may be advisable to choose decoy stewards of the opposite sex to that of the judge.
3 Check on the subordinate human scents: soap, hand cream, tobacco, etc.

American Scent Discrimination

The principal features of this exercise are very similar to those of Class 'B' scent already discussed. There is one important difference which can affect the general approach to the schooling of the exercise and the competitive application.

The articles in competition are provided by the handler, and the judge determines which article will be scented by the handler and retrieved by his dog. As the handler supplies all the bits and pieces it is very important that none of them carries his scent prior to their presentation to the judge.

During my visit to the American and Canadian scene it was apparent that scent failures are common. It was also noted that competitors attend two or three shows on consecutive days and use the one group of articles at each. As the judges choose the articles to be handled by the competitor, the situation during the second or third show is very likely to contain more than one handler-scented article on the ground.

Even with attempts to minimize the handler scents between shows this seems to me to be the most likely cause of failures. However, the preparation for this exercise does necessitate a good, sound, happy retrieve with the types of articles to be used. Remember that the articles are the handler's own choice, so long as the one type is of metal base and the other of leather.

Dual scenting can again be the basis for schooling in the routine and the three-phased application described in the Class 'B' section can also be followed.

Although the metal and leather objects are mixed in the competition set-up it may be preferable to concentrate on perfection with both types of article in parallel, then to mix the objects for both metal and leather discrimination.

Problems

Scenting problems are many and varied, although they may manifest themselves in limited diversity. Some dogs seem to forget the reason for going out to the scenting area and meander around without a care in the world. Others will dash out and pick up anything in sight, whilst a number seem to be so confused and worried that they are quite incapable of acknowledging the scent they have been given. It is also notable that some dogs are severely chastised for bringing the wrong cloth back and they are finally left in a sea of confusion.

A number of devious devices are used by some handlers and trainers to try and overcome these problems without giving due consideration to the root cause. Cloths can be weighted or pinned to the ground so that the dog cannot bring back the wrong one, and on occasions these methods do work, but do they get to the source of the problems?

The answer to any of these problems should be reached through an analysis of the cause. Is it basically a retrieving fault? Perhaps there is a hang-up due to a hasty or ill-prepared change from the handler's scent to that of a stranger? Whatever the cause, a return to basic schooling should be considered with the motto of 'Success breeds success and failure encourages confusion.'

To continue attending shows where the opportunities for failure are great can only compound a fault. It is not uncommon to find handlers struggling with a particular problem for a year or more after the fault has initially become evident. This is mainly because the handler will not give up a few weeks of competing so that the problem can be cleared up without the pressure of the following week's show.

For the Domestic Pet

The owner of the domestic pet dog, who has no interest in attaining a competitive standard, will find innumerable party tricks where success is guaranteed if discrimination is limited to his own scent. Schooling should be based on the Class 'A'

and 'B' routines with the enthusiasm of a good retriever. The precision required for competitive work can be ignored with scenting being carried out in a more care-free and relaxed atmosphere.

1 A dog who likes to retrieve your car keys will soon find them if they are placed amongst those of your friends when all keys have been distributed over the floor.
2 Your handkerchief displayed on the floor with a number of others should not create any difficulties. Your dog's patriotism can be demonstrated by having him return to you with a handkerchief-sized Union Jack, which you have handled and laid out with the flags of other nations.
3 To take a playing card from a pack, scent it well and then have it placed on the floor with others well spread out will ensure a hearty round of applause when your dog returns to you with the chosen card.
4 A favourite game for a number of training clubs when they are giving a demonstration is to have each participant with a piece of white cloth marked distinctively with a letter to make up the name of the club or location of the demonstration. A demonstration for a gala day at Kirkcaldy could have a team of nine members, each with a cloth lettered in the correct order, so that each dog would return with his handler's scented cloth to be displayed until the full name of 'Kirkcaldy' was evident to the audience.

As these exercises are intended principally for the domestic pet owner and the use of scenting in party tricks, there is no harm in taking advantage of dual scenting, when the audience does not realize that you have removed some saliva from the dog's mouth with your finger tips whilst you were fondling him. Holding the article or cloth in the hand will then ensure dual scenting and a more positive identification of your article.

Dogs enjoy showing off just as much as their owners and this helps to develop a happy companionship.

CHAPTER 10

Article Searching

General

Searching for articles which have been lost or dropped in the undergrowth is one of the most pleasurable pastimes a dog can enjoy. It is another application which involves the use of his olfactory system where he can cast around with his nose near to the ground to seek out any article bearing a human scent. It is a pastime to be enjoyed by the domestic pet, an exercise to be worked at more seriously in the working trials schedule or a practical task in the pursuit of crime detection.

Although this chapter is written around the requirements of the competitive exercise for the U.K. Kennel Club Working Trials schedule, the approach to the schooling of a domestic pet is the same, where a dog can be taught to search around for lost keys, a glove or a piece of jewellery which has been dropped by accident. The schooling of a service dog is based on the very same principles.

Object of the Exercise

To have your dog search an area with sufficient undergrowth and twenty-five yards square for four articles which have been placed by a stranger to the dog. The area to be marked with a post at each corner and the articles to be of such a size that they will not be clearly evident on the terrain being used.

Kennel Club regulations for the principal stakes require that at least two articles be retrieved within the allotted five minutes.

The basic elements. Dog to:

1 Go out and search the designated area to locate an article;
2 Pick up the article and retrieve to hand;
3 Immediately return to the designated area and continue to search for and retrieve further articles;
4 Maintain a dedicated searching attitude until all articles have been retrieved or for a period of up to five minutes.

It should be noted that during a competitive search the handler is not permitted to enter the search area but may move around the perimeter to control his dog to the greatest advantage. He is also permitted to talk to, instruct or encourage his dog without penalty.

These conditions are relevant to the full exercise required for the qualifying stakes through Utility Dog (U.D.) to the top Police Dog (P.D.) or Tracker Dog (T.D.) titles. The preliminary stake for the Companion Dog (C.D.) title involves searching for three articles in a marked area of fifteen yards square. A maximum time limit of four minutes is set and a minimum of two articles must be found.

Schooling should be based on the

requirements for the full exercise unless the handler has no intention of progressing beyond the C.D. stake. The details which follow are based on requirements for the major exercise. Competitors who wish to concentrate on the C.D. stake, can restrict their working area, also limit the searching time and number of articles to suit the exercise.

Developing the Correct Attitudes

The search exercise can be the downfall of many a dog in working trials. A busy dog working all the time but failing to achieve the success his efforts deserve will find the five-minute time limit to be rather short, but to the disinterested dog who is forced to spend the full period in the search area it will seem like eternity.

Many handlers stumble from trial to trial breathing a sigh of relief if the dog manages to bring out two articles and considering the third one to be a bonus. Unfortunately, some poor searchers qualify because a good track mark can on occasions subsidize a poor search, and there can be little incentive for some handlers to reconsider their attitude towards the exercise. At the same time, I think it is a pity to waste a good tracking performance because of a poor search.

To become a good, enthusiastic, competitive searcher a dog must be a determined retriever, one who is reluctant to give up when he knows there is something to be found, one who will pick up any reasonable material in most shapes or forms. Any attempt to develop the full routine with a dog who is not a proficient retriever can, at the very best, detract from a competent performance and, at the

worst, can result in many more failures than successes.

The groundwork is, therefore, built on keenness to retrieve. With a number of dogs this can be considered as a project in itself, not necessarily for the requirements of a controlled obedience-style retrieve but a free and easy application where the dog is prepared to return immediately and deliver to hand. In fact, a competitive, obedience-style retrieve is more likely to inhibit a dog and can easily result in a mediocre searching performance. However, the basis for good, sound retrieving has already been given in Chapter 5.

The keenness to search can be developed at any time; specific training sessions are not necessary in the early stages and they may in fact inhibit your own approach. Anytime you are out for a walk throw a suitably weighted article into the undergrowth or into grass which is long enough to ensure that your German Shepherd is more likely to pick up the scent rather than the sight of it. Let him pinpoint the dropping zone with his eyes and watch how his nose takes over when he gets within scenting distance.

If you throw an article into the wind he should locate the scent before he reaches that article, but if you throw with a following wind he must cast beyond the article to determine its location. Schooling for the search exercise can begin when the groundwork has been achieved with a reasonable measure of persistence in finding a thrown article.

A dog can only search for the required period, up to five minutes in competition, if he is allowed to develop at his own rate. To ask a dog to continue searching after he has lost the desire can only encourage boredom and resentment, with performances deteriorating to predictably low levels. It is, therefore, very important that consideration be given to terminate on success, before the dog reaches his limit of persistence.

The handler's attitude whilst a dog is searching is also important. He must learn to keep quiet whilst the dog is working well, he should be prepared to give a little encouragement when the dog seems to 'wind' an article, he should also show pleasure when the dog has picked up the article and then genuine pleasure when the article is delivered to hand.

To try and apply strict control or to nag at the dog for any reason whatsoever can only distract him from the job in hand. If his mind has already been distracted, nagging or pressurizing will not meet with the desired long-term result and is likely to ensure that distractions become an excuse for, rather than the cause, of failures.

Developing the Routine

The process to date has been based on scent retrieving where visual acknowledgement of the thrown article has been followed by the dog scenting to pinpoint its exact location. To develop a routine which will ensure that the dog understands what is wanted of him, and to maintain his enthusiasm for lengthy periods, a visual approach should be continued until the full exercise has been successfully accomplished. The excitement of searching and the knowledge that articles have been placed in a specific area are the primary inducements. The finding of articles is essentially the supreme inducement which will become the vehicle of enthusiasm throughout your German Shepherd's working life.

To develop the full exercise, schooling must be based on the following considerations:

1 Ensure that the dog is quite happy to work at a distance. As the search area is twenty-five yards square, the dog should become accustomed to working at the extreme distance. A dog who insists on working round a handler's feet is quite useless.

2 The dog should have the enthusiasm to return to the search area to find more articles as soon as he has brought one to hand. Working distances and a widening of the search area should be given the first consideration.

When a dog watches an article being thrown or placed and is then released for a scent retrieve he will make directly for the dropping zone. Some German Shepherds can visually locate the area to within a couple of feet whilst some others seem to have a less accurate sense of visual location. The area of search should be gradually broadened and the first step can be achieved by breaking the dog's continuity of vision after throwing or placing the article. This can be done by turning him round in a circle or walking in front of him immediately before he is released to search for his article. It is amazing how this little ploy can break the accuracy of visual contact and, although your German Shepherd will go out in the general direction, he will need to make greater use of his nose to identify the actual location of the article.

At the same time the creation of distance between handler and the working area should be developed. Every search should be based on a distance of fifteen to thirty yards from the handler and where

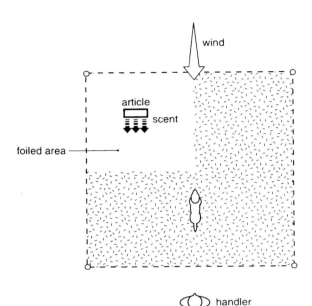

wind

article

scent

foiled area

handler

Conditioning to work at a distance.

possible the dog should be worked into the wind. However, if your dog has difficulty in finding an article, your positioning in relation to the wind and distance become secondary considerations. Rather than direct the dog towards an article it is preferable to be positioned so that your German Shepherd can be drawn towards you and across the scent of the article.

Drawing a dog onto an article brings out a very important point. To send or direct a dog into an area requires a certain amount of enthusiasm and each send-out or re-direct can be draining enthusiasm from a dog's searching desire, whereas drawing a dog towards you and across an article will not have any adverse effect unless it is carried out in a demanding manner.

Whilst repositioning yourself it is important that you do not draw your dog's attention to your movements. The advan-

tage is lost if your dog comes back to you every time you move and we often see handlers running round the search area with their dog following to heel. This only encourages a dog to watch his handler's every movement and to respond to these movements by returning to him and needing to be sent out again. As already stated, every send-out eventually drains enthusiasm.

Care should also be taken not to inhibit your dog in a search, even a most elementary search. When you throw or place an article give your dog freedom at the end of the lead, either by holding the lead or hooking it onto a post, and encourage eager anticipation for the exercise. At this stage a variety of decent-sized articles can be used; they will be dual scented but this is quite acceptable until the full routine has been established.

Multiple searching can now be developed by applying the principles of both scent retrieving and searching. Take two articles and throw them out together so that they land reasonably close to each other. The dog will visually focus on one and will carry out a scenting retrieve. Encourage him to go out for the second and if need be help him. It is this second article which helps to develop the dog's approach to searching. It is the knowledge that another article is somewhere in the region which induces him to return to the area.

Some dogs catch on very quickly whilst others take some time before they fully appreciate the significance of the second article. It is very important not to develop to a third or fourth article until the two-article routine is well established.

Developing a keenness for the second article ensures a quick return with the first and the desire to get back out there to search. A continuation of this procedure with three articles, then with four and possibly five articles, and with the dog working at a good distance, will establish the basic pattern required for a good search.

The issuing of commands should be avoided at all times and gentle encouragement should be the order of the day. I find it helpful to talk my dog into a state of mind where he expects a search and this approach sets the pattern for the dog when he has not witnessed the placing of search articles. When I release my dog to search it is with an encouraging question, 'Are you going to find it, son?' As there can be no penalties for extra commands, there is never any need to shorten the phrase although the shortened 'Find it, son' can be used as required for encouragement during the period of searching.

Developing the Search

In developing the routine the area for searching has not been purposely foiled. (The process of foiling a piece of ground is simply to walk back and forth to cause additional odours and scents.) This has made it easier to locate the articles and witnessing them being thrown has been sufficient to take the dog into the correct area.

As the dog has always been released to go straight out in front of the handler, he anticipates and responds by going out in the general direction required. The area for searching should now be foiled so that the dog can associate the odours of crushed vegetation, the scent of humans and possibly a dog with the searching area and can eventually restrict his own movements to within the invisible perimeter of the scented area.

If the articles are always to be found within a foiled area, or at least an area bounded by the human scent left behind by the search steward when he placed the four corner marker posts, the dog will eventually learn to spend his time working within the area of scent. Remember that wind will carry the scent beyond the boundary markers and a dog should not be discouraged from using that scent to locate an article.

The use of the four corner posts to mark the search area is intended to be for the benefit of the handler, the steward and the judge in competition and should not be considered as a guide to the dog. Without the corner posts or the use of some natural markers it would be difficult to remember precisely where the articles were located.

At each working session set out the full twenty-five yard search area and foil one quarter only. As you will always be working into the wind the area to be foiled will be the left- or right-handed quarter furthest from you.

It is essential to keep working from a distance. Your dog can be tied to a fence or held by somebody and the articles can also be dropped whilst the area is being foiled. If necessary draw your dog's attention to the fact that the articles are dropped for his benefit. Return straight back to your dog; the single scent path caused by your return will probably help to ensure that your dog makes straight for the foiled area when released. During the period of searching do not enter the marked area unless you have decided to terminate by helping to finish on an article.

At each session alternate between the left- and right-handed quarter until you feel your dog is ready to tackle the full back-half of the marked area. Do not be in any hurry to develop into the full area; it can take quite some time to develop the keenness to maintain working distance. Even when the full working area has been developed, I have generally found it beneficial to foil the back-half of the marked area on two out of three searches until the dog is well experienced, and periods of re-education may necessitate a return to this technique.

The time taken to develop the pattern of searching is spread over quite a period and this allows the starting routine to become firmly established whilst the dog is watching the articles being placed into the search area.

Bringing a dog to a marked-out search area with a post in each corner may now be sufficient to stimulate the desire to search even without seeing the articles being placed. Although some German Shepherds may not respond quite so

readily, it can be helpful to break in to the blind search gradually. Let the dog see the articles being placed in the area, then take him for a short walk to allow a few minutes to elapse before releasing him to search. When your German Shepherd is prepared to accept a ten-minute delay without losing his enthusiasm he is probably ready for a completely blind search.

Articles and Scents

Success in schooling depends to a great extent on the articles which are used, the amount of scent on them and the nature of that scent.

As the principle of progress is again based on 'success breeds success and failure encourages confusion', the size and scenting of articles contributes to the end result.

Initially, good sized articles which are easily picked up must help to give a dog confidence. The type of article used for tracking can also be used for searching.

Dual scenting can be the basis for building up a keenness to search and can also be used intermittently to help maintain a vigorous approach to searching.

The introduction of other people's scents can be helped by having fun retrieves with articles thrown by friends to encourage a dog to accept the presence of their scent on articles in the search. This introduction of other people's scented articles to the search area should again be carried out in full view of your German Shepherd, with the assistant taking your dog's attention. Progress to blind searches should only be made when your dog responds accordingly.

Although these searches may be blind

Indicating an article during a free search.

To let him ignore the article and continue the search is likely to introduce an undesirable attitude towards certain articles or scents. To make him pick it up, especially from a distance, is likely to inhibit future searches, but to make a retrieving game of it will certainly ensure that the article or scent is more acceptable in the future.

A continuation of single and dual scenting can be used along with a variation in size or type of article in the search area. One or two articles bearing the dog's scent as well as the assistant's, and the rest with the assistant's scent only, can help to give a dog an encouraging start to a search. As most dogs become discouraged through failure or a long time between the finding of each article, a few searches for three or four poorly scented articles can do more harm than good.

It is not necessary to make every search an easy one, but too many frustrating searches will soon demoralize a dog. Where possible finish each search on success, even if your assistant has to drop another article surreptitiously to ensure a find.

CONTROL

A German Shepherd should require the minimum of control whilst he is searching. He may need to be drawn into a section of the search area which has not been fully investigated, or he may spend unwarranted effort searching outside the marked area and may need to be drawn back again into the correct area for searching. It must be remembered that articles may have been deposited at the base of a marker post or right on the perimeter of the search area, and that markers show

to the dog the handler should know precisely where the articles have been placed until he has full confidence in his dog. A dog who indicates an article, then fails to pick it up, is likely to develop the habit of ignoring the articles he would prefer not to know. If the handler does not know where the articles were placed he will not know whether his dog is investigating one or not.

Acknowledging an article's presence but failing to bring it back must be countered immediately by the handler moving up to the article and giving his dog encouragement and close moral support so that he will pick up the article. It is possible that even with moral support a dog may refuse to pick up an article. This is the time to terminate the search and concentrate on fun retrieves with the article in question.

Delivering an article to hand.

only the boundary for articles, not necessarily the absolute limit of the area to be worked.

A handler should be prepared to reposition himself at any time before venturing to draw his dog into a selected area. Talking to a dog whilst he is working can be an irritating distraction and nagging plays no part in maintaining or regenerating an enthusiastic performance.

A handler needs to be absolutely vigilant whilst his dog is working and any indication of article recognition may require that little word of encouragement to convince the dog that he should stop and investigate. Many an important article is lost because that slight indication from the dog has gone unnoticed by his handler.

During a search the dog is expected to give his full concentration – he is also entitled to expect the same consideration from his partner.

CHAPTER 11

Quartering for a Hidden Person

General

To have a dog quarter a piece of ground or a building is to have him searching for someone, either a missing person or a criminal in hiding. The person may be hidden in a wood, in a ditch, behind a rock or in some obscure and unexpected location in a building. A properly trained dog is expected to cover the ground to the left, to the right and ahead of his handler until he finds some indication of that person's presence. One or all of his three senses can become operative to acknowledge the presence of the person in question and in practice any of these senses can determine the true location. These senses are SIGHT, SOUND and SCENT.

Although sight and sound will be fully utilized during the initial period of schooling, scenting is the principal sense which will locate the majority of hidden persons and the objective is to bring the principle of wind scenting to the fore, where the body scent of the hidden person is borne by currents of air so that it can be detected by the dog's olfactory system.

Quartering is a practical application of wind scenting used extensively by the police, security services and the armed forces. Used professionally a dog should be able to detect, locate and give voice when he finds a missing person. This person may be lying asleep or injured, or he could be a hardened criminal who would be prepared to go to any length to make his escape. Quartering is also an exercise which is applied within the P.D. stake schedule in working trials and the protection work section of Schutzhund or F.C.I. It is also worked within the requirements of practical police, security and service dogs.

As already stated, the objectives can be to find an innocent missing person or a hardened criminal and a fully trained dog must react in a manner to suit the circumstances. In the case of an innocent person the dog should give voice and let his handler know of the location, but he should show no sign of aggression which could cause alarm to an innocent party who may already be in a distressed condition. On the other hand there could be a suspected criminal to be located and the dog would have to be extremely watchful and be prepared to defend himself or prevent the suspect from escaping until his handler was available to take control of the situation.

To prepare a dog for the latter he would be introduced to the fundamental principles of attack training and an introduction to that field of study will be given in the following chapter.

Schooling to quarter and react on finding an innocent person may not be as dramatic or exciting as developing the process through aggression and some dogs can lack the real incentive to go out and find without having some form of attack training, but the principle being put forward is very effective in training this exercise. This approach will allow a greater number of handlers to achieve the full development of quartering, locating and giving voice without the worry of attack training. The final element for aggression can be developed at a subsequent stage with experienced assistants if it becomes a desirable feature of the complete exercise. The quartering exercise is only one part of protection or police work, where attack and defence training is essential.

Although all who wish to teach their dogs to quarter and search do not wish to carry out protection training many a household pet German Shepherd can enjoy the less formal approach and thus can add a new dimension to his life.

Object of the Exercise
To have your German Shepherd go out in various directions, principally to the left, right and ahead of you to seek out a hidden person, give voice and maintain contact with that person until the arrival of the handler.

The basic elements. Dog to:

1 Go out to the left and then right (or vice versa) and investigate any cover or suitable hiding place, also to go ahead with left or right directional investigations for the same purpose.
2 Make contact with a hidden person and to stay with the person and bark to draw the handler's attention.

NOTE: Although the object of the exercise is based on quartering open ground the same principles are applied for the quartering of buildings.

Inducement to Speak

An approach to teaching your dog to speak (bark) when you require it has already been dealt with in a previous chapter, so we now wish to make use of this function and adapt the teaching to ensure that your German Shepherd will speak when he finds a missing person. If food has been used as an inducement to speak, consideration must be given before continuing with this form of inducement if protection work is part of your overall objective. The change from food to some other inducement must be made by the handler and not a third party, as will be evident to those interested in protection or guarding.

I find that the combination of a check chain and a ball is very useful. The chain in a closed hand can make the amount of noise required for the occasion to attract and maintain attention, and the ball can be thrown as a reward. The chain can be discarded and an empty but clenched fist may be sufficient to create an adequate signal for some German Shepherds to speak. On the other hand the chain may need to be replaced by the ball.

The whole process is based on exaggerated signals being gradually replaced by diminishing indications until the dog responds to the situation rather than a signal. If your dog can be taught to respond to a hand movement with a ball in view, especially with the hand held high and with a vigorous movement, the arm can eventually be dropped with a slight twist of the wrist to show the ball.

The quick, but minor, movements can help a dog to give voice when he finds a hidden person during training and the association of finding and speaking, which is immediately followed by a fun retrieve, can keep a dog very attentive to the presence of the hidden person until the handler arrives on the scene.

As friends or members of the family can be used as hidden persons they can all help with the initial speak training if this suits the dog, or they can be introduced with the inducive article when you have perfected this element of the exercise yourself.

The second stage, that of going out to find the hidden person, should not be considered until at least one assistant can be depended on to have the dog giving voice at will. The development of an instant speak on finding the assistant, without minor movements as an inducement, can become part of the follow-up training for the quarter and seek out.

Inducement to Seek Out

The initial purpose which should now be instilled into the dog's mind is to go out to a known hiding place, find the assistant who is acting as the missing person and speak so that he can get his ball.

With your dog on the lead, have the assistant tease him with the ball just sufficiently to get him excited and to want it. The assistant can then run off with the ball and hide behind a tree, in a ditch or round the corner of a building – a distance of some twenty to thirty yards should be sufficient. Your German Shepherd should be encouraged to watch and should be desperate to follow. As soon as the assistant is out of sight let your dog take you to the

hiding place or release him so that you can follow at your own pace.

You should not be required to play any further part in the procedure, as the assistant is now in full control and he will create any inducement necessary to have your dog give voice. If the previous training has been correctly carried out the inducement should result in an immediate response; three to five seconds of giving voice should be sufficient; then the dog should be fully rewarded by fun and games with his ball.

One to three similar seek outs in one session are probably quite sufficient and it is important that your dog is full of enthusiasm on each occasion. With some dogs one seek out is quite sufficient whilst others can enjoy more frequent trials in each session.

The dog is not taught by command, but each time he is released a phrase should be used which will eventually trigger off the seek out. I usually use the trigger phrase 'Where is he?' to focus the dog's attention on the proceedings. Initially, of course, he is watching the assistant go out of sight and the expression is just fixing it in his mind for the day he does not see the assistant disappear from view. 'Where is he?' is usually followed by 'Go and get him' as the dog is released

If your inducement is strong enough, your dog will soon respond by giving voice as soon as he finds the assistant or when the assistant gives a very minor movement of the hand to indicate the presence of the ball.

A variety of hiding places can be used and with each one your dog should initially see the assistant going out of sight. A trial can then be made by having the assistant going out of sight before your dog is brought to the scene. Wind scenting now becomes an important feature of the exercise and your dog should be brought to the area in a direction which will give him the opportunity of picking up the body scent of the assistant as it drifts through the air. It may be advisable to have your dog indicate the presence of the assistant via the body scent in the air before releasing him for the first few trials. Thereafter, canine confidence through success can dictate the working distance.

As the assistant is still the main controlling influence he should be watching the release of your dog and any indecision should immediately be countered by the assistant drawing attention to himself, either by noise or coming into sight, or both, but for just sufficient time to achieve his objective.

As your German Shepherd gains experience and confidence the period for giving voice can be extended until your dog's attention automatically remains with the assistant until the handler arrives on the scene.

The initial inducement should never be forgotten and the dog must be given the reward which will induce him to go out with confidence and keenness the next time he is asked.

This stage of training can be considered satisfactory when the dog is prepared to go to an obvious hiding place which has not been used before and immediately give voice on finding the hidden person.

To Quarter in the Open

The dog knows from his earlier experience that a landmark, be it a tree, a bush, a telegraph pole, a wall or a building, may well conceal a person in hiding, but the person could also be lying on the ground or in a ditch. The pattern for quartering should be developed to cover the unseen as well as the obvious hiding place.

Quartering is very much an activity of having your dog visually focus in the direction you wish to send him, but on moving out he should be prepared to deviate if an airborne scent indicates the presence of a person out of his direct line of movement. His olfactory system will then act as a homing device which will lead your dog directly to his objective.

Select a field or suitable area with points of cover; most cover should be suitable for an assistant to stand or crouch behind, others can be at ground level where a person can remain out of sight until your dog is right on top of him.

The starting point and the handler's base line should be right up the centre of the area from one end to the other. This can be seen as line X – Y in the illustration on Page 192. Two hiding places will initially be required, one to the right and the other to the left, shown as hides A and B in the illustration. Whilst you are at the end of the field with your dog have the assistant walk round the edge and disappear behind A; you do not wish to have a scent path between yourself and the hide. The dog has been watching and he knows what is coming; this is a simple seek out from a sighting. Now release your dog to find the assistant and then to give voice. As soon as he starts speaking go and join your dog to finish the element with a fun retrieve.

Walk back round the field with your dog and the assistant, then take the dog out of sight as the assistant returns round the field and conceals himself again behind hide A. When you have returned and taken up your stance as before, release your dog with the trigger phrase 'Where is

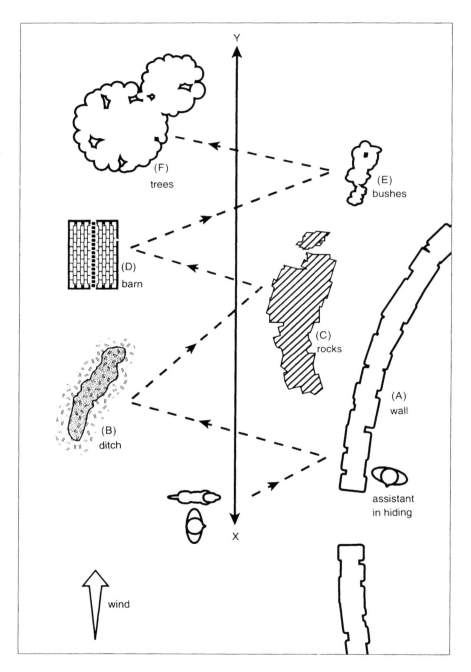

Quartering on open ground.

he?' Any indecision should bring an immediate reaction from the assistant to draw attention to himself, but I doubt if this will be necessary.

On completion of this element and if you are satisfied with your dog's response, have the assistant move round the edge of the field to hide B, but with this new hide make sure your dog is well out of sight as you want him to believe that hide A is still occupied. Return to point X with your dog and release him in the direction of hide A with the usual encouragement. His quartering to the right will be fruitless and, as soon as he has discovered the hide to be empty, have the assistant come into view and shout to draw attention to himself. Immediately your dog reacts, the assistant should hide again so that the element can be completed in the normal manner. This should be sufficient for one training session.

During the next training session repeat this procedure, but this time start with hide B and finish with hide A. The training sessions should be repeated until your dog is prepared to work the two hides in any order without knowing which will be occupied.

Line X – Y in the illustration should be maintained as the handler's base line during this and the more advanced stages and he should not leave this line until the dog has located the assistant and given voice. Remember the assistant is in full control after you release your dog and your role is now passive until the hidden assistant has been located.

Hide C can now be added to the active hides with your dog quartering to hide A and hide B, then the assistant draws your dog's attention to the new hide. The fourth hide, D, should not be attempted until your dog is prepared to work each active hide without knowing which one will be occupied. On some occasions it will be hide A, on others hide B will be in use and sometimes hide C will be occupied. Keep your German Shepherd guessing, but enthusiastic.

This procedure should be developed until your dog can work his way through half a dozen hides. A change of venue will probably require a return to hides A and B until your dog becomes familiar with his new surroundings. Each change of venue will give added experience until the routine is firmly planted in his mind.

Wind direction can be important and it is your German Shepherd's ability to wind scent which results in him making a find. To train in a direction which results in a head or crosswind can have your dog pick up the scent of an assistant earlier than intended and any attempt to make him quarter the hides in the opposite direction may only result in confusion; his mind is tuned to locating and highlighting the position of the assistant. The illustration opposite shows the direction of working in relation to the wind when training with three or more hides.

It is also preferable that the assistant moves round the perimeter of the field when going from one hide to another to avoid leaving a scent path behind him, but on the other hand you could have the area for quartering so contaminated with human scent that the assistant walking across the area would make little, if any, difference.

Natural hides are generally advisable but occasional portable, canvas hides can have their value although Schutzhund and F.C.I quartering involves a stipulated number of six hides which are artificial in nature.

To Search a Building

Assuming that the element of giving voice has been perfected and your German Shepherd responds to an assistant with a ball, the search of a building can be started in a similar manner to that of quartering in the open. Although your dog responds to an assistant in the open he may not be so ready to give voice whilst in a building, so make sure he will give voice where and when required before beginning indoor work.

Farm buildings are an ideal site; derelict warehouses, factories or such like where there are plenty of places to hide are also suitable for searching.

Have an assistant go and hide at a pre-arranged spot behind a door, a piece of machinery, in a cupboard or some such place. As you bring your dog to the vicinity of the hiding place have your assistant make his presence known, by sight, by sound or both. Again remember that the assistant is in control of the situation and the reward of a thrown ball or some such article can still be the initial inducement to find the assistant.

Your dog now knows the hiding place and will remember it for the second trial. Take him out of sight again, then release him with the trigger phrase 'Where is he?' It is now more difficult for the assistant to assess the dog's reaction: in the open he could watch your dog's movements from his hiding place but now he must judge your dog's reaction and help when necessary with a cough, a scuffle of feet or the movement of a door to help draw his attention.

Scenting the assistant in a building can be much more difficult than wind scenting in the open, as the scent in a building tends to become trapped; a room may well be filled with human scent but the hiding place may go undetected until the dog becomes experienced.

I remember an assistant who hid in a wooden trunk and the relatively inexperienced dog who was being trained kept passing the trunk. It was only the sound of movement inside which finally drew his attention to this hiding place.

Two hiding places can now be used in different areas of the building or even two rooms of a derelict house. Follow your dog to the one which was already in use and when he finds it vacant indicate the direction to the second hide. Your directing will be heard by the assistant and he can draw attention to his new hiding place.

Success can bring in a third hide and the build-up should be generated in the same manner as outdoor quartering. A new venue means starting again until experience and enthusiasm ensure success when breaking fresh ground.

The full value of experience is shown by your dog's ability to cope with more difficult or unusual situations. Have him use his eyes and ears as well as his nose, as the slightest sound or movement can help to locate a hidden person. A man hiding in the rafters will be missed by a novice, but not by a properly trained dog.

One police dog handler, who was acting as a wanted person, sat quite openly on a window-sill in a derelict farm house. He was sitting reading a newspaper when the dog came in, nosed round the likely places and, ignoring the obvious, went out to declare the room as clear. There was a lesson to be learned and one dog handler certainly taught the other.

Control

Quartering to seek out a hidden person is another exercise where the element of control is most evident when it is lacking and the handler has to keep shouting commands to try and direct his dog to the hide in question, or his dog just ignores him and goes his own way.

The handler's function should be a simple one, that of directing his dog from one hide to another. He will then take charge of events when that person has been found.

The assistant who is acting as the missing person is the key to a well-trained dog and the handler is but a junior partner.

CHAPTER 12

Protection Work

General

The aptitude for protection work or guarding duties is an inherited ability which has been bred into the German Shepherd and unless there is a character or temperamental weakness in a particular dog he can show all the resilience required to uphold this reputation.

However, whatever inherited abilities the German Shepherd has, protection or guarding instincts MUST be controlled, even if they are not being extended beyond the scope of a normal domestic environment. If training is carried out to extend his abilities into the field of advanced protection work or guarding, then absolute control and obedience are essential conditions.

The German Shepherd has the physique and stature, along with the reputation, to act as a warning to any transgressor and this can be a major deterrent which is sufficient for most domestic purposes. Although this is also of great value to the operational dog, extensive training is required to achieve the requirements of protection, guarding or police work.

It is the purpose of this chapter to describe some of the outlets and opportunities for this type of training. The training routines are not detailed, being an extremely specialized subject where great care must be taken for each development of the training routines. It is recommended that my book *All About Guard Dogs and their Training** be considered as a suitable training publication for guidance in the field of protection work.

General protection activities can be split into three principal activities, i.e. Domestic, Competitive, Operational. The domestic field encompasses the majority of German Shepherds, even though many of these can be listed as operational dogs who live at home. More owners of domestic German Shepherds, and this includes breed show dogs in various countries, are showing an interest in competitive activities which include protection work.

Operational dogs are trained for various purposes but protection work, guarding and police work all entail training which is based on aggression and defence.

The competitive activities which are open to civilians are covered by various national and international regulations. Our own Working Trials Regulations cover a Patrol Dog stake with one section allotted to the Patrol (Protection) group of exercises. This stake is also included in the South African schedule and those of the bordering countries.

Schutzhund and F.C.I. trials are very similar with Schutzhund originating in Germany and F.C.I. with its headquarters

* Published by Pelham Books in 1986 but now out of print .

in Belgium. The influence of these trials is now very far reaching and world wide; they are also becoming important to show dog owners.

Although each form of competition has its own approach and appeal the exercises have the same basic requirements. They are as follows:

Quartering the Ground

The missing person or criminal should be protected to the minimum extent consistent with safety. He should remain motionless out of sight of the handler but should be accessible to a dog which has winded him.

When the dog has found the person he should give warning spontaneously and emphatically without being directed by the handler. After detection and giving voice the dog may be offered meat or other food which he should refuse. A dog which bites the person must be severely penalized.

Test of Courage

This is a test of courage rather than control. Dogs will not be heavily penalized in this test for lack of control. Handlers must be prepared to have the dog tested when on the lead by an unprotected judge or steward and/or when off the lead by a protected steward. Method of testing at the discretion of the judge.

Search and Escort

The criminal will be searched by the handler with the dog off the lead at the sit, stand or down. The judge will assess whether the dog is well placed tactically and ready to defend if called to do so.

The handler will then be told to escort the prisoner(s) at least thirty yards in a certain direction; he will give at least one turn on the direction of the judge. During the exercise the criminal will turn and attempt to overcome the handler. The dog may defend spontaneously or on command and must release the criminal at once either when he stands still or when the handler calls him off. The handler should be questioned as to his tactics in positioning the dog in both search and escort.

Recall from Criminal

The criminal, protected to the minimum extent consistent with safety, will be introduced to the handler, whose dog will be free at heel. After an unheated conversation the criminal will run away. At a reasonable distance the handler will be ordered to send his dog. When the dog is approximately halfway between the handler and the criminal he will be ordered to be recalled. The recall may be by whistle or voice. The criminal should continue running until the dog returns or closes. If the dog continues to run alongside the criminal, the criminal should run a further ten or dozen paces to indicate this.

Pursuit and Detention of Criminal

The criminal (a different one for choice) and handler should be introduced as above, and the dog sent forward as per 'Recall from Criminal'. The criminal must continue to attempt to escape and, if possible, should do so through some exit or in some vehicle once the dog has had a chance to catch up with him. The dog must be regarded as having succeeded if it clearly prevents the criminal from continuing his line of flight, either by holding him by the arm, knocking him over or close circling him till he becomes giddy.

Training for these activities is very specialized and requires the assistance of a suitably experienced person. This person is known as the agitator or training criminal. He is all-important and can make or break your German Shepherd.

A wrong choice of agitator can create a liability out of a good-natured German Shepherd.

CHAPTER 13

Competitive Events

Working Trials

Judging

The judge is the person the centre of all the activity, the person to whom the competitors look for a fair chance to qualify and the person the organisers hope will work to their timetable and all the other arrangements.

The judge's responsibility starts with his planning of each exercise. Conditions on the day may change – this is outside his control – but he can plan to give each dog an equal chance. The stiffness of the exercises and his marking should be such that each performance will receive its just reward. It is quite easy to plan within the regulations and yet create situations where it would be unreasonably difficult for a dog to qualify.

The planning of tracks and searches, and the articles to be used on these, can depend a great deal on the type of ground available. A judge may be given a description of the ground prior to the trials and can select his articles accordingly, but there can be occasions when the type of ground is not quite as anticipated. A wise judge will take spare articles in case he finds that his selection is not really suited to the conditions.

On the day of the trials, or the evening before, the judge will get together with his chief tracklayer or steward and present the details of his track and articles, etc. Although he has full authority over, and responsibility for, his arrangements, he will be wise to listen to any comments on local conditions and then carefully consider the suitability of his plans. The tracklayers and stewards will, of course, work to the judge's instructions.

A judge is only considered as good as his last appointment, and a good reputation built up over a period can soon be destroyed by a thoughtless, inconsiderate or inconsistent performance. Past experience has shown that, on average, three quarters of competitors fail to qualify and will go home with some measure of disappointment. A pleasant and constructive attitude from the judge can make a competitor feel that his entry was worth while and not a waste of time and money. Lastly, the judge's duties are not over until he has written his report for the *Working Trials Monthly*.

Competing

The system of Open and Championship Trials has been built up over many years and changing conditions result in modifications from time to time in the Kennel Club Working Trials Regulations I. (1). It is, therefore, essential that competitors obtain an up-to-date copy of the regulations to ensure that they fully understand and appreciate the conditions under which they expect to be working. Copies of the Kennel Club Working Trials Regulations can be obtained from the Kennel Club, 1 Clarges Street, Piccadilly, London W1Y 8AB.

Very briefly, the conditions are that dogs are required to qualify through each Open Stage of U.D., W.D., T.D., and P.D. to enter the appropriate stake at Championship Trials. Full qualifications can only be gained at Championship level. To control the number of entries at trials, the number of times in an individual stake may be modified by the Kennel Club at any time. The C.D. Stake is the beginner's stake and, although it is not at this time a compulsory qualification to progress, it has been found to be a very useful introduction to the trials scene.

The training routines for the various exercises in Working Trials have already been given in this publication and the schedule of exercises and points for the various stakes is as follows.

COMPANION DOG (C.D.) STAKE

	Marks	Group Total	Minimum Group Qualifying Mark
GROUP 1 CONTROL			
1 Heel on Leash	5		
2 Heel Free	10		
3 Recall to Handler	5		
4 Sending the Dog Away	10	30	21
GROUP 2 STAYS			
5 Sit (2 minutes)	10		
6 Down (10 minutes)	10	20	14
GROUP 3 AGILITY			
7 Scale (3) Stay (2) Recall (5)	10		
8 Clear Jump	5		
9 Long Jump	5	20	14
GROUP 4 RETRIEVING AND NOSEWORK			
10 Retrieve a Dumb-Bell	10		
11 Elementary Search	20	30	21
TOTALS	100	100	70

UTILITY DOG (U.D.) STAKE

	Marks	Group Total	Minimum Group Qualifying Mark
GROUP 1 CONTROL			
1 Heel Free	5		
2 Sending the Dog Away	10		
3 Retrieve a Dumb-Bell	5		
4 Down (10 minutes)	10		
5 Steadiness to Gunshot	5	35	25
GROUP 2 AGILITY			
6 Scale (3) Stay (2) Recall (5)	10		
7 Clear Jump	5		
8 Long Jump	5	20	14
GROUP 3 NOSEWORK			
9 Search	35		
10 Track (90) Articles (10+10=20)	110	145	102
TOTALS	200	200	141

WORKING DOG (W.D.) STAKE

	Marks	Group Total	Minimum Group Qualifying Mark
GROUP 1 CONTROL			
1 Heel Free	5		
2 Sending the Dog Away	10		
3 Retrieve a Dumb-Bell	5		
4 Down (10 minutes)	10		
5 Steadiness to Gunshot	5	35	25
GROUP 2 AGILITY			
6 Scale (3) Stay (2) Recall (5)	10		
7 Clear Jump	5		
8 Long Jump	5	20	14
GROUP 3 NOSEWORK			
9 Search	35		
10 Track (90) Articles (10+10=20)	110	145	102
TOTALS	200	200	141

TRACKING DOG (T.D.) STAKE

	Mark	Group Total	Minimum Group Qualifying Mark
GROUP 1 CONTROL			
1 Heel Free	5		
2 Send Away and Directional Control	10		
3 Speak on Command	5		
4 Down (10 minutes)	10		
5 Steadiness to Gunshot	5	35	25
GROUP 2 AGILITY			
6 Scale (3) Stay (2) Recall (5)	10		
7 Clear Jump	5		
8 Long Jump	5	20	14
GROUP 3 NOSEWORK			
9 Search	35		
10 Track (100) Articles (10+10+10=30)	130	165	116
TOTALS	220	220	155

PATROL DOG (P.D.) STAKE

	Marks	Group Total	Minimum Group Qualifying Mark
GROUP 1 CONTROL			
1 Heel Free	5		
2 Send Away and Direction Control	10		
3 Speak on Command	5		
4 Down (10 minutes)	10		
5 Steadiness to Gunshot	5	35	25
GROUP 2 AGILITY			
6 Scale (3) Stay (2) Recall (5)	10		
7 Clear Jump	5		
8 Long Jump	5	20	14
GROUP 3 NOSEWORK			
9 Search	35		
10 Track (60) Articles (10+10=20)	80	115	80
GROUP 4 PATROL			
11 Quartering the Ground	45		
12 Test of Courage	20		
13 Search and Escort	25		
14a Recall from Criminal	30		
14b Pursuit and Detention of Criminal	30	150	105
TOTALS	320	320	224

NOTE: The minimum qualifying mark given against the total for each stake is only applicable for the basic qualification at Championship Trials. The added 'EXCELLENT' at Championship Trials or for a Certificate of Merit at Open Trials requires eighty per cent of the total marks available.

Obedience Shows

Judging

An obedience judge does not require quite as much forward planning as a trials judge, but he is certainly under more sustained pressure during his judging stint. A good steward will ease the burden, but judging forty to sixty dogs in one day requires continued concentration over a lengthy period. A judge will make mistakes or misjudgments. He will also be accused by 'knowledgeable' ringsiders of various failings. As long as he has the courage of his convictions and is genuinely fair, he will not be condemned for being human. It is said that the only person who never makes mistakes is the person who never makes a decision.

Many judges bring their own stewards with them, and this is where good teamwork can be very evident, with both organisers and the competitors reaping the benefit. Courteous judges and stewards can help to make obedience competitions a real pleasure.

Show reports from judges are most welcome and I feel it is the duty of every judge to submit a report to the dog press, *Dog Training Weekly* and the *Obedience Competitor* being the most widely read magazines for obedience enthusiasts.

Competing

The system of Open and Championship Shows is one where each class, with the exception of Class 'C', is of identical importance. Competitors can enter two classes for which they are eligible. As the Kennel Club regulations covering tests for Obedience Classes G.(1) are liable to change from time to time, it is essential that competitors obtain an up-to-date copy to ensure that they fully understand and appreciate the conditions under which they expect to be competing. Copies can be obtained from the Kennel Club, 1 Clarges Street, Piccadilly, London W1Y 8AB.

The training routines for the various tests in Obedience have already been given in this publication and the schedule of tests with the respective points available and basic difference from one class to another is as follows.

COMPETITIVE EVENTS

PRE-BEGINNERS

1	Heel on Lead	15 points
2	Heel Free	20 points
3	Recall from Sit or Down Position at Handler's Choice	10 points
4	Sit (1 minute), Handler in Sight	10 points
5	Down (2 minutes), Handler in Sight	20 points
	TOTAL	75 points

BEGINNERS

1	Heel on Lead	15 points
2	Heel Free	20 points
3	Recall from Sit or Down Position at Handler's Choice	10 points
4	Retrieve any Article, Handler's Choice	25 points
5	Sit (1 minute), Handler in Sight	10 points
6	Down (2 minutes), Handler in Sight	20 points
	TOTAL	100 points

NOVICE

1	Temperament Test	10 points
2	Heel on Lead	15 points
3	Heel Free	20 points
4	Recall from Sit or Down Position at Handler's Choice	10 points
5	Retrieve a Dumb-Bell	15 points
6	Sit (1 minute), Handler in Sight	10 points
7	Down (2 minutes), Handler in Sight	20 points
	TOTAL	100 points

CLASS 'A'

1	Heel on Lead	15 points
2	Heel Free	25 points
3	Recall from Sit or Down Position at Handler's Choice	15 points
4	Retrieve a Dumb-Bell	25 points
5	Sit (2 minutes), Handler in Sight	10 points
6	Down (5 minutes), Handler out of Sight	30 points
7	Scent Discrimination, Handler's Scent	30 points
	TOTAL	150 points

CLASS 'B'

1	Heel Free	40 points
2	Send Away, Drop and Recall	40 points
3	Retrieve any Article Provided by Judge	30 points
4	Stand (1 minute), Handler in Sight	10 points
5	Sit (2 minutes), Handler out of Sight	20 points
6	Down (5 minutes), Handler out of Sight	30 points
7	Scent Discrimination, Handler's Scent	30 points
	TOTAL	200 points

CLASS 'C'

1	Heel Work	60 points
2	Send Away, Drop and Recall	40 points
3	Retrieve any Article Provided by Judge	30 points
4	Distance Control	50 points
5	Sit (2 minutes), Handler out of Sight	20 points
6	Down (2 minutes), Handler out of Sight	50 points
7	Scent Discrimination, Judge's Scent	50 points
	TOTAL	300 points

Index

INDEX